Totally Tasteless Photoshop® Elements®

Wally Wang

McGraw-Hill/Osborne

New York   Chicago   San Francisco   Lisbon
London   Madrid   Mexico City   Milan   New Delhi
San Juan   Seoul   Singapore   Sydney   Toronto

McGraw-Hill/Osborne
2100 Powell Street, 10th Floor
Emeryville, California 94608
U.S.A.

To arrange bulk purchase discounts for sales promotions, premiums, or fund-raisers, please contact **McGraw-Hill/**Osborne at the above address. For information on translations or book distributors outside the U.S.A., please see the International Contact Information page immediately following the index of this book.

Totally Tasteless Photoshop® Elements®

1234567890 DOC DOC 019876543

ISBN 0-07-222884-9

Publisher	**Technical Editor**	**Indexer**
Brandon A. Nordin	Tom Babcock	Karin Arrigoni
Vice President & Associate Publisher	**Peer Reviewers**	**Graphic Artist**
Scott Rogers	David Palmer	Frank Zurbano
	Karen Palmer	
Acquisitions Editor	Dwight Cochran	**Computer Designer**
Chris Johnson		Happenstance Type-O-Rama
	Copy Editor	
Senior Project Editor	Bart Reed	**Series Design**
LeeAnn Pickrell		Happenstance Type-O-Rama
	Proofreader	
Acquisitions Coordinator	Claire Splan	**Cover Design**
Athena Honore		Jeff Weeks

This book was composed with QuarkXPress 4.11 on a Macintosh.

Some of the images in this book are © 2003 Hemera Technologies Inc. and its licensors. All rights reserved.

The views and opinions expressed herein by the author do not necessarily represent the policies or positions of the McGraw-Hill Companies, Inc.

This book is dedicated to everyone who loves the idea that they can use their computer to alter their digital photographs—but who hates the idea of having to learn the so-called user-friendly commands of a program like Photoshop Elements, which was supposedly designed for novices but feels more like it was designed for rocket scientists. Have patience. Photoshop Elements isn't as easy or as hard to use as you might think, and with a little bit of instruction from this book, you'll be capable of doing a wide variety of modifications to your digital photographs in no time.

About the Author

Wally Wang

The author of this book is a completely anonymous figure from the viewpoint of practically everybody in Hollywood. From the viewpoint of the rest of the country, the author still isn't very well known except as a name on many different computer books that have mostly gone out of print by now.

Some of the author's past accomplishments include getting offered a job to work for the CIA, appearing as an extra in a soft core porno movie for the Playboy Channel, appearing as an extra in the much bigger budgeted movie called *The Hanoi Hilton* (which fewer people have probably seen than the Playboy Channel), living and working in Zimbabwe, and appearing on the nationally syndicated show A&E's *Evening at the Improv*.

Perhaps the author's most unusual accomplishment involves talking to intelligent people on National Public Radio on the same day he appeared on *The Extreme Gong Show* on the Game Show Network, performing stand-up comedy in front of an obnoxious studio audience with a collective IQ of 1.

For the future, the author plans to continue pursuing the seemingly illogical dual goals of writing books and performing stand-up comedy. If you see the author performing at a comedy club, stop by and say hi. He probably won't have the slightest idea who you are or why you're talking to him, but at least it can help him keep track of an unofficial survey to see how many people will actually do anything that they're told to do whether they receive instructions from another person, their television or radio, or from a series of words they happened to read in print somewhere in a book much like this one.

Acknowledgements

A big round of thanks goes to Chris Johnson who put the entire concept of this book together and weathered the bureaucratic storms in order to get it actually published. If I had the power to give you a raise at McGraw-Hill/Osborne, I would, but since I don't, you'll just have to settle for this paragraph of acknowledgement instead.

Thanks to LeeAnn Pickrell, who not only managed the fine details of the project right down to the very frantic end, but also made sure that this book is suitable for children and their uptight parents.

To Frank Zurbano, who assisted with many of the photographs, goes my appreciation. You really can manipulate a photo!

Matt Wagner and Bill Gladstone at Waterside Productions deserve acknowledgement for their contributions to this book, too. They didn't really do anything; they're just nice guys to have around whenever you have to deal with legal issues like contracts, copyrights, and the all-important royalty payments.

Thanks also go to Greg Sato at Data Recovery Service, who managed to recover Lesson 2 from the remnants of my crashed hard drive. If anyone thinks that hard drives are reliable, visit the friendly folks at Data Recovery Services to see a shelf full of crashed hard drives that committed suicide and tried to take most of their data down with them.

More thanks go to all the friendly people who I've met performing stand-up comedy around the country:

Steve Schirripa (who appears on HBO's hit show *The Sopranos*) for giving me my break performing in Las Vegas at the Riviera Hotel & Casino (www.theriviera.com). The next time you're in Las Vegas, stop by the Riviera and see a comedy show to take your mind off the fact that you're probably losing at the slot machines and gaming tables.

Don Learned for helping me get into the Riviera at Las Vegas and also for running the best comedy club in Houston, the Laff Spot (www.laffspot.com).

Mark Ridley for running the best comedy club in Detroit, the Comedy Castle (www.comedycastle.com).

Russ Rivas for running the best place to see comedy on a regular basis in Albuquerque, Laffs Comedy Club (www.laffscomedy.com).

Connie Ettinger for booking me at the delightfully strange Holly Hotel Comedy Club (www.hollyhotel.com), located in a haunted hotel in the middle of nowhere in Holly, Michigan, the only place where it's possible to see stand-up comedy and a spirit from another dimension at the same time.

Joe Jarred for running his Comedy Corral comedy shows in the Bingo room at the Saddle West Hotel and Casino (www.saddlewest.com) in Pahrump, Nevada, a town better known for its legalized brothels than for its gambling. The Saddle West is the only place where the hotel registration desk and the convenience store cash register are run by the same person.

Conrad at the Rascals Comedy Club (www.rascalscomedyclub.com) in Phoenix for giving me a chance to become the comedy standard that he uses to measure how funny other comedians' videotapes may or may not be.

Doug James for his strange one-night comedy shows in various locations around Southern California.

Thanks also go to all the wonderful comedians I've met on the road: Bob Zany, Bruce Clark, Dante, Darrell Joyce, Patrick DeGuire, Larry Omaha, Leo "The Man, the Myth, the Legend" Fontaine, Gerry Bednob, Dobie "Mr. Lucky" Maxwell, and Chris Clobber. Until these guys get their own comedy clubs, they won't get an entire paragraph dedicated to them on this Acknowledgements page.

Finally, thanks go to my wife Cassandra, my son Jordan, and my four cats Bo, Scraps, Tasha, and Nuit. These cats regularly squirt various colored fluids out of every orifice of their body, forcing me to take a break from my computer once in a while just to clean up their latest semi-liquid offerings.

Contents at a Glance

Contents

Introduction

Most books about Photoshop Elements are written by professional photographers who provide simple examples on how to turn flawed pictures into great works of art in a few simple steps. Of course, when you try to follow their simple step-by-step instructions on your own photographs, nothing seems to work right, your pictures look worse than ever, and you wind up feeling like an incompetent idiot.

The problem is simple. Professional photographers take dozens of pictures just to find that one great picture that they can use as an example in their books, and they also know which Photoshop Elements tool to use in which order and with the correct settings to achieve the effects they want to demonstrate in their instructions. In reality, most people capture less than ideal photographs that no amount of digital editing can revive, and most people have no idea what the different Photoshop Elements tools can do for them, let alone which order to use them in or which setting to use for each particular tool.

The truth is that digital editing is an arduous trial-and-error process that involves a lot of experimenting with different tools and techniques until the final result looks acceptable. So is digital editing with Photoshop Elements difficult to learn? Not really. Will digital editing with Photoshop Elements be fast and easy? Sometimes yes, but most often, probably not, and any book that gives you that impression is just lying to you. Just because you have a program like Photoshop Elements doesn't mean you can effortlessly alter your digital pictures like an expert, any more than learning how to use a word processor can magically make you write plays like William Shakespeare.

Of course, that doesn't mean that digital editing can't be fun. Anyone can learn how to improve their pictures with Photoshop Elements and anyone can learn the basics of digital editing. What makes this book different is that instead of providing step-by-step instructions that only seem to work on one specific photograph, this book uses whimsical examples to keep you amused while teaching you not only what the different tools in Photoshop Elements do but also when and why you might want to use them. That way when you're faced with altering your own digital images, you'll know which tools to consider and how each tool can modify your own photographs to achieve the effect you want.

So grab your digital camera, fire up your scanner, and get ready to start having fun with Photoshop Elements. While not all of us can take breathtaking photographs or capture spontaneous moments like a professional photographer, all of us can strive to improve the quality of our own photographs while having fun at the same time. As long as you're having fun and learning, you may surprise yourself one day and create that one special image that you can be proud to display, thanks to your growing digital-editing skill and the wonderful tools in Photoshop Elements that you are about to discover.

Part

ONE

Getting Pictures into Photoshop Elements

LESSON 1

What You'll Learn in This Lesson

- The three basic ways to edit a picture

- How to decipher the cryptic menus and screens of Photoshop Elements

- The differences between the Windows and Macintosh versions of Photoshop Elements

What You Can Do with Photoshop Elements

(or How to Mess with Your Head by Toying with Reality)

IF YOU LOOK AT THE PHOTOSHOP ELEMENTS BOX, you'll see that Photoshop Elements is a "powerful yet easy-to-use image-editing software for print, e-mail, and the Web." If that simple statement, loaded with more adjectives than nouns, still doesn't tell you what Photoshop Elements can do, don't worry, that's why you have this book.

Put simply, Photoshop Elements can change the appearance of any picture stored on your computer, whether you captured that picture using the latest digital camera, a scanner, or an old-fashion camera that still uses film. At the simplest level, Photoshop Elements can make a lousy picture look better. On a more advanced level, Photoshop Elements can alter a picture to create something that never existed in the first place—such as a balanced government budget or a true democratic society in the Middle East.

No matter what kind of picture you've captured, basically there are three ways to modify an image:

- Alter the appearance
- Add new details to the picture
- Delete existing details from the picture

Alter the Appearance

Nothing's more frustrating than capturing a picture that could almost be perfect—if the lighting wasn't too dim, the colors washed out, or the subjects in your picture too blurry. In the old days, you'd have to toss that picture in the trash and forget about it, but in today's world that offers us the marvels of both microwave ovens and radiation sickness, nothing is impossible.

With the digital wizardry of Photoshop Elements (remember, it's "powerful yet easy-to-use"), you can take any picture and apply all sorts of corrections that can salvage even the most flawed image and turn it into a picture worth keeping after all. When you alter a picture, you keep the details of the image intact while changing the way it looks. Two common ways to modify a picture include

- Making it lighter or darker
- Applying a filter or special effect

REMEMBER *When you alter a picture, you can either improve its "natural" appearance or create an interesting visual image to evoke a certain mood or idea.*

Lighten or Darken an Image

If you didn't use a flash or the sun suddenly ducked behind a cloud just as you took a picture, your perfect picture may look too dark, as you can see in Figure 1.1. Similarly, you could have used a flash inside a room brimming with lights and suddenly your perfect picture looks too bright. Either way, you can use Photoshop Elements to lighten or darken any image so the lighting looks perfect in every picture you take, as shown in Figures 1.1 and 1.2.

Lightening or darkening an image isn't just something that photography hobbyists might find useful—it's a technique used by professionals as well. Even the venerable *Time Magazine* used this technique for the front cover of their June 27, 1994 issue when they depicted a photograph of O.J. Simpson, who was then accused of killing Nicole Simpson and Ron Goldman.

Time Magazine simply took an ordinary mug shot of O.J. Simpson, taken by the Los Angeles police department, and darkened it to make him look more sinister. This modification might have gone unnoticed if *Newsweek* hadn't coincidentally used that exact same mug shot for the cover of their magazine for that very same week. Unlike *Time Magazine*, *Newsweek* printed the unaltered version of Simpson's mug shot.

So if *Time Magazine* has no qualms passing fiction off as reality in the name of honest journalism, then you should feel equally free to experiment with darkening and lightening your photographs to create the proper mood, whether it's to make an innocent man look guilty or a guilty man look innocent.

FIGURE 1.1

Although the focus of the picture centers on the panda bear Halloween mask, the image appears too dark to see clearly.

FIGURE 1.2

Lighting up the center focuses the viewer's attention on the mask, because nothing says "Happy Halloween" better than a plastic toy depicting the decapitated head of a panda bear.

Apply a Filter or Special Effect

To create special effects, many photographers attach special filters or lenses onto their cameras so that every picture they capture gets altered by that filter or lens. If you take a picture and suddenly decide that it would look better if you captured it through a filter or lens, you would have to retake that same picture after attaching that lens or filter onto your camera. Of course, after fiddling around with a lens or filter, the chances that you'll capture that exact same picture again is about zero.

So rather than force you to attempt the impossible, Photoshop Elements lets you apply a filter to any picture as an afterthough,t as shown in Figures 1.3 and 1.4. With so many filters to choose from, you can freely experiment with different types until you find the one you like best.

FIGURE 1.3

A nuclear bomb explodes some-where in the Nevada deserts, creating the distinct mushroom cloud that terrified thousands of people in the '50s.

(Photo courtesy of the U.S. Department of Energy.)

USDOE

Filters are most often used to create art from ordinary images. After applying a filter to an image, it's unlikely that anyone but a complete moron will be fooled into thinking that you captured a filtered image exactly as it appears.

Like filters, special effects can turn an ordinary image into an unusual one, or they can add realistic details to an image while maintaining that image's natural appearance, such as adding clouds or snow to a background (see Figure 1.5), or blurring an object to make it appear as if it were moving at high speeds.

Using special effects to distort reality is nothing new, especially in the cherished field of objective journalism. In 1994, Peter Jennings, the ABC News anchor, introduced ABC journalist Cokie Roberts as reporting live from in front of Capitol Hill. Unknown to Peter Jennings and the entire network audience, Cokie Roberts was actually inside the ABC News Washington bureau, wearing a coat and standing in front of a photograph of Capitol Hill, where she proceeded to give her report as if she were really outside.

FIGURE 1.4

That same horrifying mushroom cloud now appears through the calming filter of a stained glass window.

(Photo courtesy of the U.S. Department of Energy.)

Add New Details

Adding new details to an image can be as simple as pasting someone else in a picture, or as subtle as changing the color of someone's eyes or the size of their nose. When you add new details, you're creating something new that wasn't originally in the picture before.

Combine Multiple Images

The most common way to add new details to a picture is by creating a photomontage, which combines images from two or more pictures and smashes them together to create one single image as shown in Figures 1.6, 1.7, and 1.8.

When you combine multiple images, the final result can either be an obvious collection of multiple images or a cleverly disguised fake. Cheap supermarket tabloids

FIGURE 1.5

A special effect can make it appear that the camera captured a nuclear bomb exploding in the Nevada desert during the middle of a blizzard.

(Photo courtesy of the U.S. Department of Energy.)

favor the obvious distortion of multiple images, such as a photograph purporting to show the President of the United States in the Oval Office meeting with bug-eyed space aliens. For more subtle distortions with the intention to deceive, you have to turn to the more reputable news services, such as the CBS Evening News.

FIGURE 1.6

This picture shows two people floating serenely down a river in canoes. Little do they know that the river they're traveling on is the same river used in the book and movie *Deliverance*, where hillbillies attack and sexually assault any visiting city slickers.

FIGURE 1.7

Many religious groups are against Halloween because they believe it represents a devil-worshipping ritual. As this picture clearly shows, this group of cult members have decided to worship the devil dressed as a surgeon, a princess, and a fish head.

FIGURE 1.8

The result of combining two images can make it appear as if the fish head mask now appears on every person in the water. By disguising themselves as fish, these city slickers hope to avoid the fate of their fellow city dwellers when they encounter shotgun-toting hillbillies with overly aggressive sexual desires.

During a live broadcast of the *CBS Evening News* from Times Square on New Year's Eve, CBS technicians digitally placed a billboard advertising the CBS News in the background behind broadcaster Dan Rather. However, if you had actually been in Times Square at that moment and looked in the same direction, you would have seen an ad for Budweiser beer along with the NBC logo, which the CBS billboard, as seen on TV, "coincidentally" covered up.

Modify an Existing Item

Another way to add a new detail to an image is to modify an existing item by selectively changing the color or size of that item as shown in Figures 1.9 and 1.10, such as changing a red sweater to green or enlarging the size of a someone's lips.

With enough patience, you can modify colors and even an object's shape in a picture, much like *Newsweek* did back in 1997 when they featured Bobbi and Kenny

McCaughey on their cover, the proud parents of septuplets. But while *Time Magazine* ran an unaltered photograph of Bobbi McCaughey on their cover, *Newsweek* digitally straightened and fixed Bobbi McCaughey's teeth to make her look more attractive, presumably to help sell more issues.

FIGURE 1.9

A pair of ordinary, plain-looking goldfish enjoying a swim in a backyard pool, just days before they die and get flushed down the toilet.

FIGURE 1.10

The same pair of goldfish after getting an expensive color makeover, courtesy of Photoshop Elements.

Delete Details

Rather than modify an existing detail or adding something to a picture, sometimes you may want to take something away from a picture, such as a telephone wire stretched across a gorgeous sunset, acne scars on someone's face, or Communist Party members who have lately fallen out of favor with the current dictatorial government, as shown in Figures 1.11 and 1.12.

FIGURE 1.11

In this 1950 government film titled *In Our Hands, Part 3: How To Lose What We Have*, government officials debate on whether to accept a Communist-style Master Plan for America.

(Archival footage supplied by Archive.org.)

FIGURE 1.12

Uh oh! The Party official to the speaker's left has fallen out of favor, so he must unofficially "disappear" and all photographs of him must be confiscated and burned. Anyone caught possessing photographs of this disgraced Party member will be executed. Have a nice day.

(Archival footage supplied by Archive.org.)

When you delete details from a picture, you must carefully blend in the surrounding image to hide the missing object. If you don't touch up an image carefully, traces of the missing detail might still emerge, such as the missing man's legs still visible under the table.

Before You Get Started

Now that you know the three basics to digital editing (alter, add, and delete), you may be anxious to rush to your computer, start up Photoshop Elements, and start editing your pictures right away. Wait! If you try to use Photoshop Elements without knowing what you're doing, you're likely to get overwhelmed, frustrated, and totally discouraged because few people can figure out how Photoshop Elements works without a little bit of training beforehand.

Choose Commands

Like most programs, Photoshop Elements gives you several ways to choose the exact same command as shown in Figure 1.13. Even more confusing is that you can often achieve the same results in modifying a picture using entirely different commands. So to keep you from losing your mind when using Photoshop Elements, you need to understand how to navigate your way around the less-than-intuitive screens, menus, and windows that Photoshop Elements throws in your way.

The menu bar displays every possible command available, organized into menu categories such as File and Image. The problem with the menu bar is finding the right command you want and knowing which command to use. Once you get more familiar with Photoshop Elements, you can often skip the menus completely and press certain keystrokes to choose the more common commands, such as pressing CTRL-S (the CTRL key followed by the S key) to choose the Save command.

To give you another alternative to using menus, Photoshop Elements also displays groups of icons in a shortcut bar. By clicking an icon, you can choose a common command. The trick to using the shortcut bar is knowing which command each icon represents.

REMEMBER *If you move the mouse pointer over an icon, a brief description of which command that icon represents will appear underneath the mouse pointer.*

Edit Your Picture

When you edit a picture in Photoshop Elements, that picture appears in a window that you can move around the screen. If you want to edit several pictures at once, each picture appears in its own window.

As you edit your pictures, Photoshop Elements displays information in *palettes*, which look and act like miniature windows. Each palette contains different data about your picture, such as the specific colors in an image or a list of the previous commands you recently used.

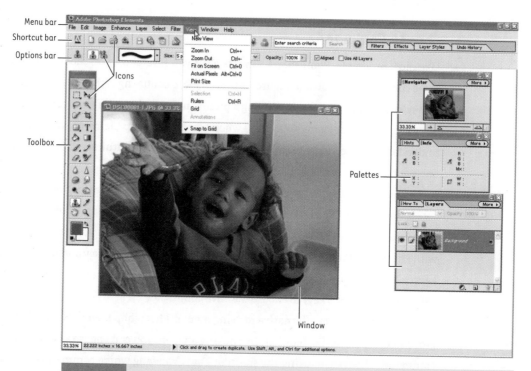

FIGURE 1.13

The different ways Photoshop Elements displays commands for you to choose.

To make any changes to your picture, you need to use the Toolbox, which contains icons that represent different tools you can use to edit your pictures, such as a Brush or an Eraser tool. The window containing your picture lets you visually see your changes, whereas the palettes let you see specific values and settings that define how your picture appears.

Each time you choose a different tool from the Toolbox, the options bar changes to display all the options available for customizing that particular tool. For example, if you choose the Brush tool, the options bar displays options for changing the brush size or type. If you choose another tool from the Toolbox, such as the Text tool, the options bar displays options for choosing different fonts and font sizes.

Where to Go from Here

Now that you have a preliminary introduction to Photoshop Elements and digital editing, you're ready to start editing your own digital images. To help you learn how to use Photoshop Elements one step at a time, each lesson in this book focuses on one or two important features for editing your digital images. Although you could jump from one lesson to another, you may want to follow the lessons in chronological order because some of the later lessons rely on your knowledge of earlier lessons.

Depending on whether you're using the Windows or Macintosh version of Photoshop Elements, your screen may look slightly different from the examples shown in this book. Some examples use the Windows version of Photoshop Elements, and others use the Macintosh version as shown in Figure 1.14. Both versions of Photoshop Elements look nearly identical, but you will find slight differences between the two versions.

Under Windows, the close box of a window appears in the upper-right corner. Under the Macintosh, the close box of a window appears in the upper-left corner. The most common key to press to give a command under Windows is the CTRL key (for example, CTRL-S). With the Macintosh, the most common key to press to give a command is the COMMAND key, which is the key with the apple and cloverleaf icon on it (for example, CMD-S). Table 1.1 shows a list of Windows and Macintosh equivalent keys.

TABLE 1.1: Equivalent Windows and Macintosh Keys	
Windows Key	**Macintosh Key**
ENTER	RETURN
CTRL	CMD
ALT	OPTION

No matter what version of Photoshop Elements you may be using or what your background in photography and computers may be, remember the whole point is to have fun. With a digital camera, you can freely experiment with different shots and just erase the ones you don't like. Then you can goof around with Photoshop Elements to modify your pictures in a thousand different ways until you can turn your favorite ones into the best images possible.

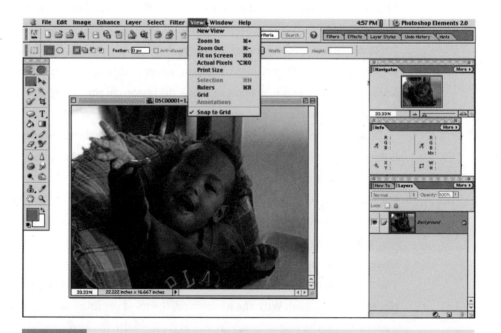

FIGURE 1.14

What the Macintosh version of Photoshop Elements looks like—just like the Windows version, except it's running on an operating system that most people don't hate.

So have fun and don't be afraid to experiment. The worst that can happen is that you'll just make a mistake that you can always erase later so that nobody will ever know you did it—unless, of course, your mistake happens to make it onto the front cover of a major magazine or into a live broadcast from a major television news network.

LESSON 2

What You'll Learn in This Chapter

- How to get a picture into Photoshop Elements

- How to magnify an image

- How to fix a crooked image

- How to save a picture

Load, Align, and Save Images

(or How to Get Pictures from Cameras to Your Computer Without Losing Your Mind in the Process)

IN MANY PRIMITIVE CULTURES, PEOPLE BELIEVED that they could lose their souls to the camera if someone took their picture. Fortunately, that isn't true because now we know that people just lose their souls whenever they put greed and selfishness ahead of principles and ethics, whether a camera is involved or not.

Although primitive people never really lost their souls until foreigners from other lands came along to exploit them, capturing souls or just really cool landscapes with a camera doesn't explain how to overcome the biggest problem with digital photography: How the heck do you get pictures from your digital camera or scanner into Photoshop Elements so you can start editing them?

Get Pictures on to Your Computer

Before you can edit any digital image, you must first store that image on your computer. Of course, before you can store any image on your computer, you must capture that image first. Two popular ways to capture digital images include the use of digital cameras and scanners.

Digital Cameras

Digital cameras are great for capturing new images that you can save on a variety of inexpensive, easy-to-carry, and easy-to-lose devices, dubbed "digital film." Digital film is simply any portable storage device that can save images from your camera. Some digital cameras can store images directly onto a floppy disk or CD, but most digital cameras save images on smaller storage devices with odd names such as Compact Flash, Memory Sticks, and SmartMedia cards.

With the exception of floppy disks and CDs, most computers can't access anything stored on digital film. So once you've captured an image, you need to figure out how to get that image off your digital camera and on to your computer.

Most digital cameras come with cables that connect to your computer. Theoretically, you can just copy the images from your digital camera to your computer through this cable—provided, of course, your computer recognizes the digital camera attached to the cable and your camera doesn't run out of power while you're trying to copy the pictures to your computer. Most of the time when you connect a digital camera to a computer, the computer simply stares at it with a dumbfounded blank look of incomprehension, and your images remain forever trapped on your digital camera.

To overcome the unreliability of transferring images directly from your digital camera to your computer through a cable, many people simply buy special media-reader devices that let you take digital film (Compact Flash, Memory Stick, and so on) out of your digital camera and plug it directly into the media reader, which then plugs into the computer. Now your computer treats the media reader like another disk drive, so you can copy files directly off your digital film (Compact Flash, Memory Stick, and so on) on to your computer. Of all the methods for transferring images from a digital camera to your computer, media readers are the most reliable.

Some companies that sell media readers for digital film include Atech Flash Technology (http://www.atechflash.com), Belkin (http://www.belkin.com), Kanguru (http://www.kanguru.com), Lexar Media (http://www.digitalfilm.com), SanDisk (http://www.sandisk.com), and SmartDisk (http://www.smartdisk.com).

If you loaded the driver for your digital camera on to your computer, Photoshop Elements *may* (note the emphasis on the word "may") be able to recognize your camera through the Import command, as shown in Figure 2.1.

REMEMBER *A driver is a special program designed to tell your computer how to work with any equipment connected to it, such as a printer, a scanner, or a digital camera. The driver usually comes on a CD when you buy a scanner or digital camera, although you can also download drivers from the manufacturer's web site.*

To load images through the Import command, make sure you have installed the driver for your camera and then plug your camera into your computer. Click the File menu and then click the Import command (or click the Connect to Camera or Scanner button on the Photoshop Elements opening screen and then click the Import list box). A list appears.

FIGURE 2.1

The Import command, located under the File menu, lets you directly load images from a digital camera into Photoshop Elements. Here, we see a web cam connected to Photoshop Elements, showing a cameo appearance by the Linux penguin.

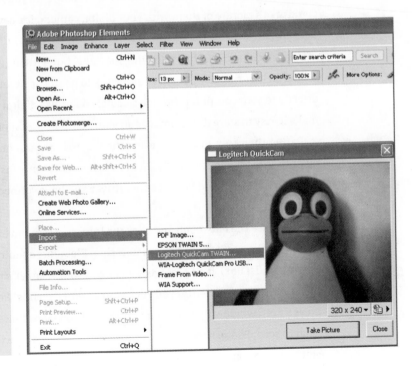

If you're lucky, you'll see the name of your digital camera listed on this menu. If you don't see your camera's name listed, either you didn't install the camera's driver correctly or Photoshop Elements can't recognize the camera driver no matter how many times you install it. In this case, you'll have to try to copy your images from your digital camera to your computer through the cable or through a media reader that you'll have to buy.

If you're one of the lucky ones who actually see your digital camera name in the menu after choosing the Import command, click this name. Photoshop Elements displays a window showing you all the images currently stored on your digital camera. At this point you can choose the picture you want to load into Photoshop Elements.

Scanners

Digital cameras are great for capturing new images, but sometimes you might want to store old photographs, magazine covers, or drawings in your computer. Although you could take a picture of them with your digital camera, it's easier just to use a scanner instead.

A scanner looks just like a copying machine, but without the bored office workers sitting on it during their lunch hour, trying to photocopy their butts. Scanners connect directly to your computer through a cable, and unlike digital cameras, they actually make it easy to store digital images on your computer most of the time.

Rather than scan in an image and then store it on your hard disk, you might just want to scan an image directly into Photoshop Elements instead. To do this, make sure you have installed your scanner driver and have connected your scanner to your computer.

Next, click the File menu and click the Import command (or click the Connect to Camera or Scanner button on the Photoshop Elements opening screen and then click the Import list box). If all goes well, you'll see your scanner's name in the list next to the Import command. After you click your scanner's name, Photoshop Elements displays a Scan window that lets you define what you want to scan. When you choose what to scan, Photoshop Elements displays that image in a window, ready for you to edit and save it as shown in Figure 2.2.

Find and Open a File

Once you've stored pictures on your hard disk, you have to find them again so you can load them into Photoshop Elements. As always, Photoshop Elements provides several ways to load a picture, so you can either choose the way you like best or just get confused by all the choices and still not know what to do.

REMEMBER *To make life simple for yourself, create one folder to store all your digital images and then remember where that folder is on your hard disk.*

Browse Visually

The easiest way to load a picture into Photoshop Elements is through the Browse command, which shows you both the file name and its image. To choose the Browse command, click the File menu and then click Browse (or just click the Browse icon on the shortcut bar or the Browse for File button on the Photoshop Elements opening screen). The File Browser window appears as shown in Figure 2.3.

FIGURE 2.2

The Import command can store a picture into your computer through your scanner, such as this monkey eating from a bag of potato chips processed with the fat-free substitute Olestra. Note the monkey's surprised look on his face as he begins to experience the first signs of Olestra-induced cramps, intestinal gas, and anal leakage.

(Photo courtesy of Gracie Vincenza.)

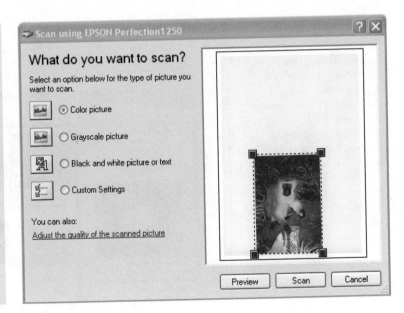

The File Browser window consists of four separate panes. The upper-left pane displays the folders and drives on your computer. By clicking a different folder or drive, you can search for pictures stored in a different location.

The right pane shows all the pictures stored in the folder currently selected in the upper-left pane. When you click a picture, the middle-left pane displays a slightly more detailed version of your image so you can examine it more closely.

The bottom-left pane displays information about your selected picture, such as the file name, the date it was created and last modified, the color mode, the file format, the width and height, and the file size.

When you see a picture that you want to load into Photoshop Elements, just double-click that picture.

Open a Recent File

If you want to load a file that you opened in the past few days, it's faster to use the Open Recent command. To use this command, click the File menu and then click Open Recent. A menu appears that lists your recently opened files as shown in Figure 2.4. Click the file name you want to open.

Browse icon

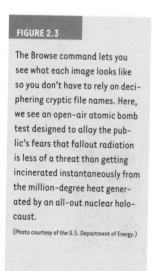

FIGURE 2.3

The Browse command lets you see what each image looks like so you don't have to rely on deciphering cryptic file names. Here, we see an open-air atomic bomb test designed to allay the public's fears that fallout radiation is less of a threat than getting incinerated instantaneously from the million-degree heat generated by an all-out nuclear holocaust.

(Photo courtesy of the U.S. Department of Energy.)

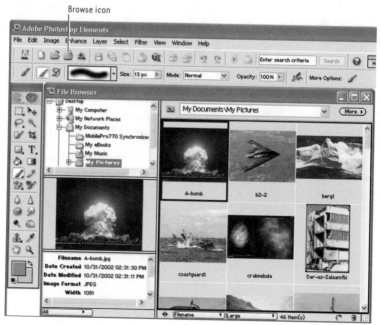

Normally, the Open Recent command only displays the last ten files you previously used. In case you want to increase or decrease this number, click the Edit menu, click Preferences, and then click Saving Files.

A Preferences dialog box appears as shown in Figure 2.5. Click the Recent File List Contains text box and type the number of files you want the Open Recent command to remember. Then click OK.

Open a File

The ordinary Open command works just like the Browse command except that it won't display the images stored in each file. If you just want to open a picture, it's easier to use the Browse command instead.

The one time you may want to use the Open command is when you want to search for files stored in specific file formats as shown in Figure 2.6. For example, you may only want to look for images stored in the GIF (Graphic Interchange Format) file format,

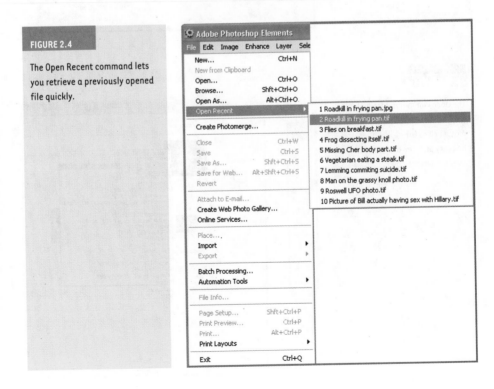

FIGURE 2.4

The Open Recent command lets you retrieve a previously opened file quickly.

a common file format used for displaying graphics on web pages. So rather than overwhelm you with files of all types, the Open command can just display GIF files. That way, you can quickly browse through your different drives and folders to look for files of that specific file format.

The Preferences dialog box lets you define how many files the Open Recent command will remember.

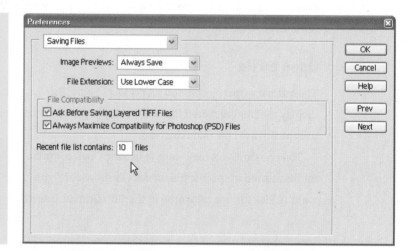

The Open command lets you look for files stored in a certain format, such as GIF or JPEG files of naughty pictures downloaded over the Internet.

Open icon

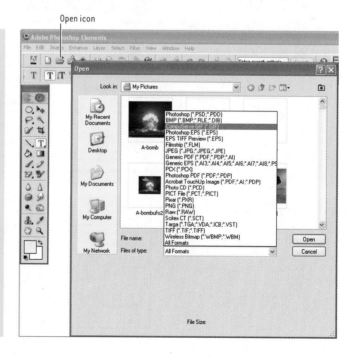

To use the Open command, click the File menu and then click Open, click the Open icon in the shortcut bar, or press CTRL-O (Windows) or CMD-O (Macintosh).

The Open dialog box appears. Click in the Files of Type list box, and a list appears showing you all the different file formats Photoshop Elements recognizes. Click a file format type, such as JPEG or TIFF. Now as you browse through your drives and directories, Photoshop Elements only shows you files of your chosen file type.

Magnify a Picture

Sometimes a picture may appear too small to let you see any details. To help you see the details of an image, you can zoom in (expand) and zoom out (shrink) the view of your picture. That way, you can zoom in to focus on the details of your picture and then zoom back out to see how the entire picture looks after you've made any changes to it.

Photoshop Elements gives you several ways to increase or decrease the magnification of an image, depending on whether you want to use the mouse, the keyboard, or the pull-down menus.

Magnify with the Mouse

To change the magnification of a picture with the mouse, you need to use the Zoom tool as shown in Figure 2.7. When you click the Zoom tool, the mouse pointer turns into a magnifying glass icon.

To zoom in, click the Zoom tool, move the Zoom tool over a part of the picture that you want to magnify, and then click the mouse. You can also choose this command if you click the View menu and then click Zoom In.

If there's a specific part that you want to magnify, click the Zoom tool in the Tool-box and then drag the Zoom tool to select the part of the picture you want to magnify. When you let go of the mouse button, Photoshop Elements shows a zoomed-in view of the area you selected.

To zoom out, hold down the ALT key (Windows) or the OPTION key (Macintosh) and click the mouse. You can also choose this command if you click the View menu and then click Zoom Out.

Magnify with the Keyboard

The fastest way to change the magnification of a picture is with keyboard commands. Press the CTRL key followed by the plus sign (CTRL-+) (Windows) or the Command key followed by the plus sign (CMD-+) (Macintosh) to zoom in. To zoom out, press the CTRL key followed by the minus sign (CTRL--) (Windows) or the Command key followed by the minus sign (CMD--) (Macintosh).

If you find these keyboard commands clumsy or hard to remember, just click on the View menu and then click Zoom In or Zoom Out.

You can also use the keyboard to specify an exact percentage to magnify your picture. Just click in the Zoom text box, type a value from 1 to 100, and press ENTER (Windows) or RETURN (Macintosh). Photoshop Elements magnifies your picture by the percentage you typed into the Zoom text box.

Fix Crooked Images

Sometimes you may have the perfect picture but find that you held the camera at a weird angle, so everything looks crooked. Other times you may scan in an image and find that you didn't get it perfectly straight.

Zoom tool

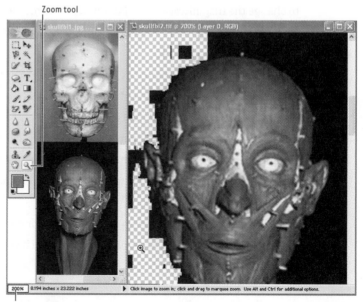

FIGURE 2.7

The Zoom tool increases the detail of an image so you can see what you've selected or deleted. This picture models a person in shock after receiving a really bad acupuncture treatment that accidentally removed the seven outer layers of the skin.

(Photo courtesy of the Federal Bureau of Investigation.)

Zoom text box

Although it's easy to go back and rescan a crooked image with a scanner, it's nearly impossible to go back and reshoot a crooked picture with a digital camera. In either case, Photoshop Elements may be able to straighten out any crooked picture and make it look perfect.

Straighten a Crooked Scan

When you capture an image through a scanner, it's easy for the image to appear slightly crooked as shown in Figure 2.8. Rather than constantly trying to straighten out the image by scanning it again, you can let Photoshop Elements try to straighten it out for you.

Because scanning in an image crooked is so common, Photoshop Elements offers two ways to automatically straighten out most crooked images: the Straighten Image command and the Straighten and Crop Image command.

The Straighten Image command simply rotates your picture until the image appears straight as shown in Figure 2.9. Unfortunately, if your crooked scan shows part of the scanner cover, that part of your image now appears crooked. After you use the Straighten Image command, you'll have to trim away the excess part of your image.

To use the Straighten Image command, click the Image menu, click Rotate, and then click Straighten Image.

FIGURE 2.8

Photoshop Elements can fix a crooked scanned image as seen in the left picture. The right picture shows the same picture straightened out and touched up to accurately reflect the laughable nature of President Nixon's attempts to lie about the Watergate scandal, which would only be topped years later in sheer audacity by Bill Clinton's infamous statement, "I did not have sexual relations with that woman."

(Photos courtesy of the White House.)

The Straighten Image and Crop command does two things at once. First, it rotates your picture until the image appears straight. Then it trims away all the excess part of the image for you so it looks like you actually scanned it in correctly in the first place.

To use the Straighten and Crop Image command, click the Image menu, click Rotate, and then click Straighten and Crop Image.

Rotate

The simplest way to correct a crooked image is to rotate it until it looks straight. If you turned your camera sideways to capture a picture, that picture will likely appear sideways when you load it into Photoshop Elements.

To rotate a picture, just click the Image menu, click Rotate, and click one of the following options:

- 90° Left
- 90° Right
- 180°
- Flip Horizontal
- Flip Vertical

By using a combination of these rotate commands, you can rotate an image left or right until it appears oriented correctly on the screen. Unfortunately, images don't

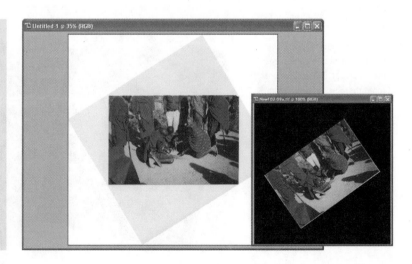

FIGURE 2.9

The Straighten Image command straightens the image but includes the scanned area around the picture. Here, we see a group of African tribesmen rubbing two sticks together to start a fire in a belated attempt to burn down parts of Africa as their contribution to the 1992 Rodney King beating riots in Los Angeles.

(Photo courtesy of Gracie Vincenza.)

always appear crooked at 90° angles. So, to correct images that only appear slightly crooked, you can rotate an image by specifying the exact number of degrees of rotation, or you can use the mouse to rotate the image until it looks straight.

To specify the exact number of degrees to rotate an image, click the Image menu, click Rotate, and click Custom. A Rotate Canvas dialog box appears, as shown in Figure 2.10.

Click in the Angle text box and type an angle, such as 45. Click the °Left or °Right radio button to specify which way you want to rotate your picture and then click OK.

How do you know exactly how many degrees to rotate a slightly crooked image? You won't. So as a visual alternative, you can simply rotate an image using the mouse. To do this, click the Image menu, click Rotate, and click Free Rotate Layer. Photoshop Elements displays handles around your image.

Move the mouse over a handle in the corner or the middle of the top, bottom, left, or right side of your image. When you move the mouse pointer near a handle, the mouse pointer turns into a curved, double-pointing arrow. Drag the mouse in any direction and Photoshop Elements rotates your picture in that direction. Double-click when you're happy with the position of your image.

FIGURE 2.10

The Rotate Canvas dialog box lets you type in the exact number of degrees to rotate an image. The left picture was scanned in crooked, and the subsequent right picture not only shows a straight image, but also the results of what happens if you get too aggressive shaving with a really sharp razor while still hung-over from the night before.

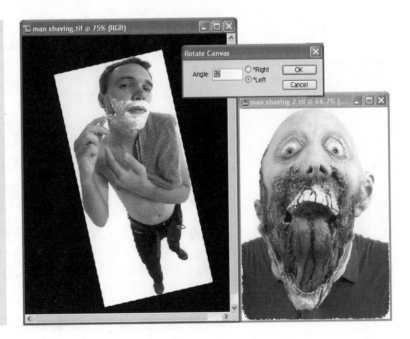

Change the Perspective

Sometimes your picture won't be crooked, but the image in your picture may appear distorted, as shown in Figure 2.11. In this case, rotating your picture won't help because the image will still appear at an angle. Rather than rotate the image, you can change its perspective.

To change the perspective, click the Image menu, click Transform, and click Perspective. A dialog box may appear and ask whether you want to transform the background into a layer. Click OK. (Don't worry. You'll learn more about layers in Lesson 7.)

A New Layer dialog box appears. Click OK. Photoshop Elements displays handles around the edges and corners of your picture. Move the mouse over a handle and drag the mouse to change the perspective of the picture until the sides appear straight, as shown in Figure 2.12.

Double-click the mouse when you're happy with the way you've changed the perspective of your picture. You may need to trim away the skewed background of your image so that the picture looks perfect, which you'll learn about (along with the Crop tool) in Lesson 8.

FIGURE 2.11

From this angle, the picture looks skewed.

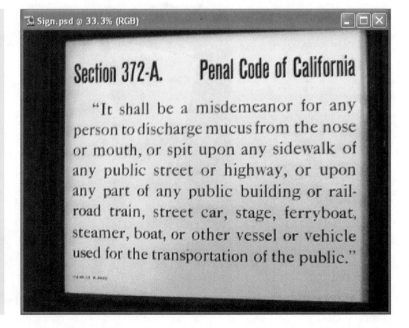

Sign.psd @ 33.3% (RGB)

Section 372-A.　Penal Code of California

"It shall be a misdemeanor for any person to discharge mucus from the nose or mouth, or spit upon any sidewalk of any public street or highway, or upon any part of any public building or railroad train, street car, stage, ferryboat, steamer, boat, or other vessel or vehicle used for the transportation of the public."

Handles

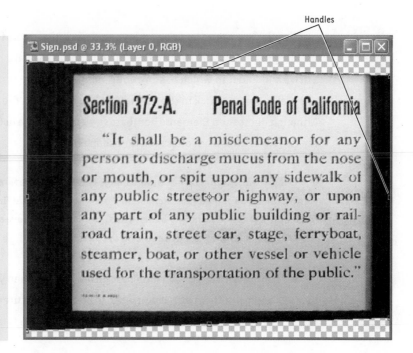

FIGURE 2.12

A fixed version of the distorted image looks nice and straight just by the perspective being changed.

Save a Picture

After you load a picture into Photoshop Elements, you need to save your work. To save a picture, click the File menu and then click Save, click the Save icon in the shortcut bar, or press CTRL-S (Windows) or CMD-S (Macintosh).

CAUTION *If you connect a digital camera to your computer, it's possible to open a picture that's only stored on your digital camera. To avoid modifying pictures directly on your camera, use the Save As command (described next) to save your pictures to your hard disk. If you try to save an edited picture directly on your digital camera, you could delete or wreck that picture.*

If you want the option of renaming your file, storing it in a different location, or saving it in a different file type, you have to use the Save As command, which you can choose if you click the File menu and then click Save As. A Save As dialog box appears, as shown in Figure 2.13.

Click the File Name text box and type a descriptive name for your picture, such as "Snail dying of salt" or "Hair on fire." If you click in the Save In list box, you can define a drive and folder in which to store your picture.

Finally, you can click in the Format list box to define a file format for your picture. Although Photoshop Elements bombards you with a huge list of possible file formats, the two most important ones are Photoshop and JPEG.

REMEMBER *Most digital cameras store images in the JPEG file format. If you want to modify your pictures, you should save them in the Photoshop file format first because the Photoshop format preserves image quality better. Then, you can always save a copy of that picture in the JPEG file format after you're done editing the picture.*

The Photoshop file format is the best format to use when you just want to edit your pictures and print them out. If you want to post your pictures on a web page or send them to friends through e-mail, save your file in the JPEG format, because this format

FIGURE 2.13

The Save As dialog box asks you to define a name, location, and file type when saving your picture.

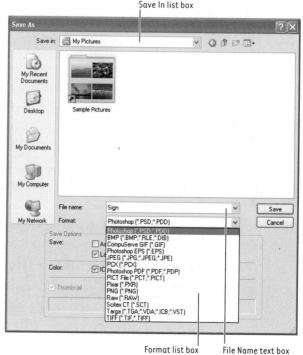

Save In list box

File name: Sign

Format: Photoshop (*.PSD;*.PDD)

- Photoshop (*.PSD;*.PDD)
- BMP (*.BMP;*.RLE;*.DIB)
- CompuServe GIF (*.GIF)
- Photoshop EPS (*.EPS)
- JPEG (*.JPG;*.JPEG;*.JPE)
- PCX (*.PCX)
- Photoshop PDF (*.PDF;*.PDP)
- PICT File (*.PCT;*.PICT)
- Pixar (*.PXR)
- PNG (*.PNG)
- Raw (*.RAW)
- Scitex CT (*.SCT)
- Targa (*.TGA;*.VDA;*.ICB;*.VST)
- TIFF (*.TIF;*.TIFF)

Format list box   File Name text box

reduces the size of your pictures without too much loss of detail. The other file formats listed in the Format list box are useful only if you need to transfer your pictures to another program that won't recognize the Photoshop file format.

 REMEMBER *If you repeatedly save a file in the JPEG format, the image quality may degrade with each save.*

After you choose a name, a location to store your picture, and a file format, click Save.

Where to Go from Here

Now that you know how to get pictures into Photoshop Elements, how to save pictures, and how to load them back into Photoshop Elements again, you're ready to take your first steps into the wonderful world of digital photography, where the distinction between fantasy and reality blurs and nothing you see may actually be the truth. So in other words, it's a lot like watching television but without any commercials.

LESSON 3

What You'll Learn in This Lesson

- How to grab a still image from a movie

- How to pull pictures off a web page

- How to save a page from a PDF file

Getting a Picture from the Movies and Other Sources

(or How to Turn a $500 Video Camera into a $12.95 Disposable Camera)

BEGINNING IN 1916, GENERAL MOTORS RESEARCH LABS tried to develop a fuel blend that would stop engine "knock," which prevented the development of more efficient, higher compression engines. Naturally, the oil industry took a dim view of ethyl alcohol as a fuel since it threatened their business, so GM continued researching alternate fuels until 1921 when their scientist, Thomas A. Midgley, discovered that tetraethyl lead stopped engine knock.

In 1924, General Motors joined with Standard Oil to form a partnership called the Ethyl Corporation. DuPont owned a third of General Motors at the time, so together these three major corporations helped develop and market leaded gasoline. Gulf Oil soon joined in the marketing of leaded gasoline. This was especially curious given the fact that Andrew Mellon, then Secretary of Treasury and in charge of the Public Health Service, which was investigating the possible health hazards of leaded gasoline, also owned part of Gulf Oil.

The public first became aware of the health hazards of leaded gasoline when five workers at a Standard Oil refinery became violently insane due to exposure to leaded gasoline. Yendell Henderson of Yale called the use of leaded gasoline "the single most important question in the field of public health that has ever faced the American public." Alice Hamilton of Harvard went so far as to call GM's vice-president, Charles Kettering, "nothing but a murderer" for distributing leaded gasoline to the public.

Throughout these debates on the safety of leaded gasoline, GM insisted that there were no known alternatives to leaded gasoline, despite Thomas A. Midgley's own belief that that ethyl alcohol was "the fuel of the future" because it could be made from plants and would be available indefinitely even in the event that the world's oil supply ran out.

After inventing leaded gasoline, Thomas A. Midgley withdrew from the health debates of leaded gasoline and in 1928, he invented Freon, which would later be blamed for eating a hole in the ozone layer. Despite the financial and technological success of leaded gasoline and Freon, both of Thomas A. Midgley's inventions have caused enormous ecological problems, which goes to show that if you always look for alternatives, you may find a better solution with a little more patience.

In the world of Photoshop Elements, most people will likely enhance pictures taken with a digital camera or captured through a scanner. Unfortunately, trying to capture the perfect image through still photography can be frustrating because you can miss a great shot by a fraction of a second if you don't shoot the image right away.

So when lining up a potentially great shot, do what professional photographers do. To increase their odds of capturing the right moment, professionals simply shoot several pictures in rapid succession, knowing there's a good chance that one out of a hundred pictures they take may actually be worth saving. For every breathtaking picture you see in *National Geographic*, the photographer took many similar shots that wound up in the trash.

Of course, there's still a chance you'll miss a great shot in between the time you capture one picture and the time your digital camera is ready to take another one. So as an alternative, use a video camera to capture several minutes of a particular scene. Then you can use Photoshop Elements to scroll through your video, frame by frame, until you find the best image to keep and enhance.

Whether you're editing a picture captured from a video, a scanner, or a digital camera, you may need some additional images to add into a picture. For example, you may want to doctor up a photograph of your backyard to make it look like a UFO is in the background, or you may want to include a landmine in a picture of your boss strolling across the executive parking lot after he has laid off thousands of workers and gave himself a multimillion-dollar bonus as a reward.

Whenever you need additional images, you can capture them from a web page, a compact disc loaded with stock photography images, or even an Adobe Acrobat PDF (Portable Document Format) file. With so many diverse sources for images of practically anything, from jet fighter planes and Halloween pumpkins to landmark tourist sites such as the Eiffel Tower and the Statue of Liberty, you should have no trouble finding the perfect picture to use for any project. Now you just have to worry about the harder task of figuring out what you want to do with all those images and Photoshop Elements in the first place.

Freeze Frame

Capturing a video with a digital or analog video camera is easy. However, getting that video into your computer usually isn't as easy because it involves connecting a cable between your computer and your camera in the hopes that you'll be able to transfer the image from one to the other. Of course, if you're even slightly familiar with computers, you already know how successful computers are at doing anything that appears so simple and trivial at first glance—it usually winds up turning into a major headache every time.

From Your Video Camera to Your Computer

If you have a digital video camera, your biggest problem will be finding the right cable to connect your camera to your computer. If you're using one of the newer Macintosh computers, such as an iMac, it will likely have the right port, dubbed a *FireWire* port, for connecting to a digital camera. If you're using Windows, your computer probably won't have a FireWire port, which means you need to buy a FireWire card to plug into your computer and then pray that it actually works with your digital video camera, computer, and Microsoft Windows.

If you have an older analog video camera, you won't be able to connect it directly to your computer. Instead, you need to buy a video converter device that's either a card that you plug into your computer (and probably won't work) or an external box that plugs into a FireWire or USB (Universal Serial Bus) port in the back of your computer (and probably won't work).

Some companies that sell video converter devices include ADS Technologies (http://www.adstech.com), Adaptec (http://www.adaptec.com), Dazzle (http://www .dazzle.com), and Pinnacle Systems (http://www.pinnaclesys.com). To use these converter devices, just plug your analog video camera into the converter device, which transfers your video to your computer so you can save it in digital format.

If you actually manage to get your video image transferred to your computer, the final step involves saving your video in a file format that Photoshop Elements knows how to use.

The current standard for video files is called MPEG (Motion Pictures Experts Group). Not content to let someone else define a standard, both Microsoft and Apple have created competing standards. If you're using Windows, you may see video files stored in the AVI (Audio Video Interleave) format or Microsoft's other "standard," called WMV (Windows Media Video).

Microsoft also defined yet another standard, called ASF (Advanced Streaming Format), for streaming video. Unlike ordinary video, streaming video allows you to view video as it arrives on your computer from a web site, rather than waiting for the entire video file to arrive before you can view it. So if you can store your video in MPEG format or any of Microsoft's three video standards, you'll be able to load your video into Photoshop Elements.

If you're using a Macintosh, you have two choices: You can save your video in the MPEG video file format, or you can save your video in Apple's video file format, dubbed QuickTime.

No matter what video file format standard you decide to use, once you've managed to save your video in one of these "alphabet soup" acronyms of competing video standards, you'll be ready to (finally) capture a still image from your video.

REMEMBER *If you have a video stored in a file format that Photoshop Elements can't recognize, you can always convert that video into a file format that Photoshop Elements does recognize, using a special video-editing program such as Windows Movie Maker or iMovie.*

Grab a Still Image from a Video

After you've stored a video in one of the acceptable video file formats that Photoshop Elements can recognize, you can load a movie into Photoshop Elements and capture still images. To do this, click the File menu, click Import, and then click Frame From Video. A Frame From Video dialog box appears.

Click Browse. An Open dialog box appears. Click the video file you want to load and click Open. Photoshop Elements loads your movie in the Frame From Video dialog box, as shown in Figure 3.1.

Click the Play button to start viewing your movie from the beginning. If you want to capture a still image buried somewhere in the middle or end of your movie, you can either move the slider or click the Play, Rewind, or Fast Forward button. When you see an image that you want to capture, click the Grab Frame button, and Photoshop Elements saves the currently displayed image in a separate window. When you're done, click the Done button. Now you can start editing any of the images you captured from your movie.

FIGURE 3.1

The Frame From Video dialog box lets you capture a frame from a movie. Here, we see a 1940 film from the Soviet Film Academy that purports to show how Soviet scientists can keep the decapitated head of a dog alive.

(Archival footage supplied by Archive.org.)

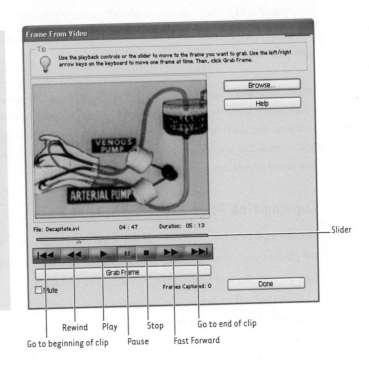

If you don't have any video images of your own or if you want access to a rich variety of films containing images that you may never be able to capture on your own (such as nuclear bomb explosions), visit the Prelinger Archives stored on the Internet Archives site (http://www.archive.org). The Prelinger Archives contain videos of government films that explain everything from how to behave on prom night to how to protect yourself from the blast of a nuclear explosion by covering your head with a newspaper. Other videos include old black-and-white television commercials from the 1950s, industrial films that explain how gasoline gets made and the importance of the pesticide industry to the average American, and historical footage of important events such as the aftermath of the 1906 San Francisco earthquake.

Picking Pictures off a Web Page

As you browse the Internet from your desk instead of doing any real work like you're being paid to do, you may run across an interesting web site with pictures that may be just perfect for your next Photoshop Elements project. Rather than try to capture a similar picture on your own, take the easy way out and just copy that picture off the web page and onto your computer.

REMEMBER *Web pages may contain copyrighted images, so you can't just copy a picture off a web page and use it commercially without getting permission first. If you copy a picture off a web page and use it for a birthday invitation, technically you're breaking copyright laws, but just pretend that you're a multimillionaire who has donated generously to various politicians and you can break the law with impunity, just like they do.*

Copying Web Page Graphics in Windows

To copy a picture from a web page using Windows, right-click the mouse pointer over the picture you want to save. A pop-up menu appears, as shown in Figure 3.2. Click Save Picture As, and a Save Picture dialog box appears.

Click the Look In list box to change the drive or folder in which to store your picture. Then click the File Name text box and type a name for your picture. You may also want to click the Save As list box to choose a file format to save your picture in. Then click Save.

Copying Web Page Graphics with the Macintosh

To copy a picture from a web page using the Macintosh, move the mouse pointer over the picture you want to save, hold down the CTRL key, and then click the mouse. A pop-up menu appears, as shown in Figure 3.3. Click Download Image to Disk.

A Save dialog box appears. Click the folder where you want to save your picture, click the Name text box and type a name for your picture, and then click Save.

REMEMBER *If you're running OS X and have a multibutton mouse, you can right-click an image rather than hold down the CTRL key and click the left button of your mouse, although that method will work under OS X just fine, too.*

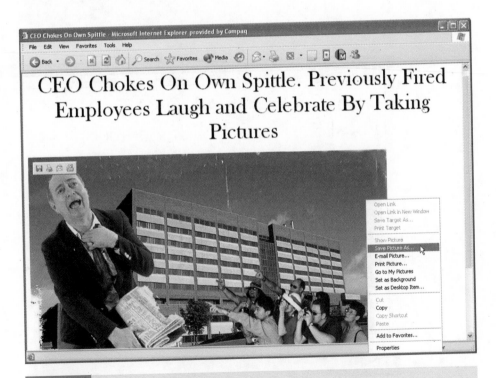

FIGURE 3.2

When you right-click an image, you can save it onto your own computer, such as this image showing a mob of employees mocking their former CEO after he started choking moments after telling them, "You're fired!"

Using Stock Photography

If you need a picture of the Leaning Tower of Pisa, a panda bear, a carved Halloween pumpkin, or a B-2 bomber, you probably won't be able to capture that image yourself. When you need a specific image right away, take the easy way out and use stock photography images instead.

Stock photography simply consists of photographs someone else took and sells to other people for personal or commercial use. Some stock photography images come on CDs, whereas others are sold through web sites where you can search and download the images you want (after paying for them, of course).

FIGURE 3.3

When you hold down the CTRL key and click an image, you can save it on your Macintosh. Here, we see a Macintosh user capturing an image of a giant cockroach terrorizing New York City. To most residents, giant cockroaches are the fourth most dangerous element of New York City right after muggers, purse snatchers, and taxi cab drivers.

To see the wide variety of stock photography available, visit Access Stock (http://www.accessstock.com), ClipArt.com (http://www.clipart.com), Comstock Images (http://www.comstock.com), Corbis (http://www.corbis.com), Getty Images (http://creative.gettyimages.com), Hemera (http://www.hemera.com), Index Stock Photography (http://www.indexstock.com), and Weststock (http://www.weststock.com). With so many stock images available, it might actually be cheaper to buy pictures rather than try to take decent shots yourself.

Grabbing Pictures from PDF Files

Perhaps the oddest way to find interesting pictures is by copying them out of an Adobe Acrobat PDF file. In case you've never seen or used a PDF file before, a PDF file is the digital equivalent of paper, but instead of printing text and graphics on paper (and sacrificing the lives of many trees in the process), a PDF file displays text and graphics on the screen nearly identical to what you might see if you printed them out.

REMEMBER *For more information about Adobe Acrobat, visit Adobe on the Web (http://www .adobe.com), the same friendly company that happens to make Photoshop Elements.*

Government agencies and corporations use PDF files all the time to store manuals, brochures, advertisement propaganda, and regulations. Because anyone can make, copy, and distribute PDF files all over the world, using them can be a great way to publish information without the cost of printing, postage, storage, or possible police prosecution if you wrote something particularly critical of an oppressive government.

Given the large number of PDF files floating around the Internet at any given time, there's a small chance one of them might contain an image you'd like to use. So when you see a particularly interesting picture in a PDF file, you can copy it using Photoshop Elements.

REMEMBER *An Adobe Acrobat PDF file may contain copyrighted images, so get permission before using any pictures stored in a PDF file that someone else created. If you violate someone else's copyright, you're breaking the law—which is probably one of the few laws NFL football players have yet to break on a regular basis.*

To copy an image from a PDF file, click the File menu, click Import, and then click PDF Image. A Select PDF Image for Import dialog box appears.

Click the Look In list box to switch drivers or folders, click the folder that contains the PDF file you want to load, and then click Open. If there is only one graphic image stored in your chosen PDF file, Photoshop Elements displays that graphic image in a separate window. If there are two or more graphic images in your chosen PDF file, Photoshop Elements displays a PDF Image Import dialog box, as shown in Figure 3.4, that lets you choose which images you want to copy out of the PDF file. Just scroll through the various images, and when you find the one you want, click OK. If you want to copy all the images out of a PDF file, click Import All.

Where to Go from Here

Now that you know some different ways to capture a picture from other sources besides your digital camera or scanner, you may want to start collecting a library of images that might come in handy sometime in the future.

That way, when you need the head of a penguin and a car wreck on the highway (so you can create a picture that makes it look like the head of a penguin is sticking out of a car in a wreck along a highway), you can grab that image right away instead of wasting time hoping to find it later.

FIGURE 3.4

The PDF Image Import dialog box can copy multiple images out of a PDF file, such as this 1950s government picture that explains how it's possible to survive a nuclear war and still continue the American way of life—or in the words of Thomas K. Jones, former U.S. Deputy Undersecretary of Defense, on the chances of surviving a nuclear war, "If there are enough shovels to go around, everybody's going to make it."

(Archival footage supplied by Archive.org.)

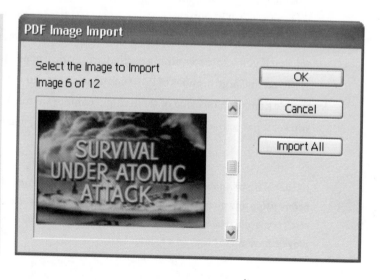

The key to having the most fun with Photoshop Elements is to get as many images as possible so you can mix and match them in bizarre, amusing, and ultimately entertaining ways. The more alternate sources you can choose from, the greater the chances that you'll be able to find exactly what you need, so you don't choose the photographic equivalent of leaded gasoline or Freon and cause headaches for yourself in the future. After you have a library of images to use, you're ready to start doctoring up your own pictures to make your boss or ex-spouse look like the morons they really are.

Part

TWO

The Basics

LESSON 4

What You'll Learn in This Lesson

- How to modify color

- How to fix the lighting in a picture

- How contrast and focus can improve a picture

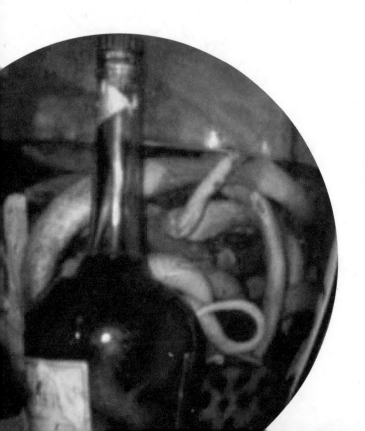

Quick Fixes for Improving a Picture

(or How to Widen the Hole in the Ozone Layer Without the Use of Fluorocarbons)

IN A PERFECT WORLD, you could load a picture into Photoshop Elements and magically fix any problems with no intervention on your part whatsoever. Of course, reality is a little less accommodating. After you load a picture into Photoshop Elements, your first question may be, "Okay, now what do I do next?"

Photoshop Elements may offer dozens of different commands for modifying your digital images, but none of them are any good if you can't figure out which one to use or what order to use them in. Right from the start, Photoshop Elements can overwhelm even the most battle-hardened computer veteran, who may know C++ and Java programming and how to build their own computer, but who may be completely baffled when it comes to the subject of digital editing.

Fortunately, Photoshop Elements offers a simple solution called *Quick Fix*. As the name implies, Quick Fix tries to make it easy for you to modify your pictures quickly and painlessly without wading through confusing menu commands or trying to decipher unfamiliar terms such as Auto Levels or Histogram. The idea behind Quick Fix is that you can load a picture into Photoshop Elements, make a few changes, and fix a picture with a minimal amount of fuss.

How Quick Fix Works

The Quick Fix feature simply organizes Photoshop Elements' most commonly used commands into a single dialog box, as shown in Figure 4.1. The four types of problems that the Quick Fix dialog box can solve involve lighting, colors, focus, and orientation.

REMEMBER *Anything you can do in the Quick Fix dialog box you can also do by choosing the right commands from pull-down menus. The main advantage of the Quick Fix dialog box is that you can experiment on an image with multiple commands, and if you don't like the way your picture looks, you can abandon all changes at once by clicking the Cancel or Reset Image button.*

FIGURE 4.1

The Quick Fix dialog box gives you easy access to commonly used commands, such as rotating an image of Saddam Hussein's portrait shown upright in the left picture and then toppling over on its face in the right picture.

(Photo courtesy of U.S. Marine Corps.)

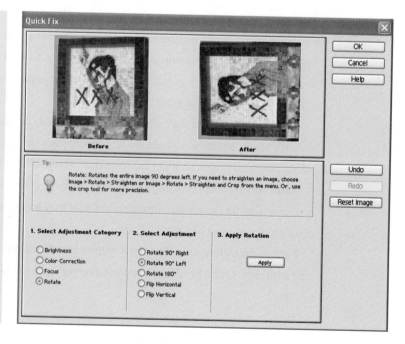

To display the Quick Fix dialog box, load a picture into Photoshop Elements, click the Enhance menu, and then click Quick Fix. The Quick Fix dialog box appears and displays two copies of your picture. The left picture displays your original image, and the right picture shows any changes you make.

Any time you make a change and don't like what you see, click the Undo button to reverse the last change you made. If you made lots of changes and suddenly don't like any of them, click the Reset Image button to return your image back to the way it originally looked so you can start over again. If you'd rather ignore all your changes and stop attempting any more changes, just click Cancel. When you're happy with the changes you've made, click OK.

Until you become more familiar with the different commands available in Photoshop Elements, you may want to let the Quick Fix dialog box modify every picture you take. After you use the Quick Fix dialog box, you may want to make any minor adjustments on your own. That way, you can spend more of your time taking pictures and let Photoshop Elements do most of the hard work making your pictures look better.

Correct Color

Colors in a picture may not always appear as bright or vivid as you might like, so feel free to alter nature like a genetic engineer. Like the edible layer of wax that appears on supermarket produce to make apples look shinier and more appetizing, Photoshop Elements can alter the colors in your pictures to make them look brighter, sharper, and more natural, despite being artificially enhanced.

REMEMBER   *In general, it's usually easier to fix the colors in your picture before you make any other changes. That way, when you start to add, modify, or delete items from a picture, you can work on an image that already looks good.*

Auto Color

If you aren't happy with the way the colors look in your picture, you should first try the Auto Color Correction command, which can fix the colors of an entire picture. To use the Auto Color Correction command, just load a picture into Photoshop Elements, click the Enhance menu, and then click Auto Color Correction.

You can also choose this command through the Quick Fix dialog box. First, load your picture into Photoshop Elements and open the Quick Fix dialog box. Click the Color Correction radio button in the Select Adjustment Category group. Then click the Auto Color radio button in the Select Adjustment group. Finally, click Apply. The Quick Fix dialog box shows you your original image and your new, improved image as shown in Figure 4.2. Click OK if you're happy with the way your image now looks, or you can click Cancel.

REMEMBER *Even if the Auto Color Correction command doesn't make your image look perfect, it can still fix many problems with your picture so that you only need to adjust a few colors yourself later. The Auto Color Correction command can be particularly useful to remove any tint of colors that sometimes appears when you capture an image through a scanner.*

FIGURE 4.2

The Auto Color Correction command can automatically fix the colors in a picture. This picture shows an ancient Chinese remedy that drowns live snakes and mice in alcohol to capture their chi (life energy) in wine, which people drink for medicinal purposes.

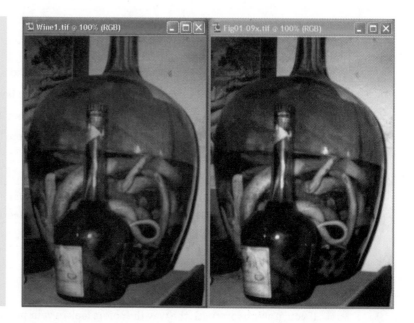

Hue/Saturation

Hue and saturation are two technical terms that mean absolutely nothing to most people. Put simply, *hue* defines the specific colors that appear. When you change the hue, you change the colors in your picture.

The amount you change the hue determines how the colors change based on the relationship of the six basic colors—red, orange, yellow, green, blue, and violet as shown in Figure 4.3. If you have a picture and decrease the hue, any blue in your image gradually turns green and then yellow. If you increase the hue, the blue gradually changes to violet, red, orange, and then yellow. When you change the hue of an entire picture, you change all the colors at once.

REMEMBER *If you don't want to change the colors of your entire picture, you can selectively change colors of just part of an image, which you'll learn about in Lesson 9.*

Saturation, on the other hand, defines the amount of gray that appears in the colors in a picture. Low saturation means more gray (and less color) appears, whereas high saturation means more color (and less gray) appears. Related to hue and saturation is the lightness level, which defines how dark or light the picture appears. By changing the hue, saturation, and lightness levels, you can modify the way the colors in your picture look.

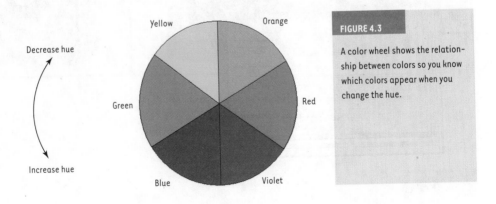

FIGURE 4.3

A color wheel shows the relationship between colors so you know which colors appear when you change the hue.

To change the hue, saturation, or lightness of an entire picture, load that picture into Photoshop Elements, click the Enhance menu, click Adjust Color, and then click Hue/Saturation to display the Hue/Saturation dialog box as shown in Figure 4.4. For a quicker way, just press CTRL-U (Windows) or CMD-U (Macintosh).

Move the Hue, Saturation, and Lightness sliders to change the way your picture looks. Then click OK.

If you opened the Quick Fix dialog box, click the Color Correction radio button in the Select Adjustment Category group. Then click the Hue/Saturation radio button in the Select Adjustment group to display the Hue, Saturation, and Lightness sliders as shown in Figure 4.5. Adjust these sliders and then click OK if you're happy with the way your image now looks, or you can click Cancel.

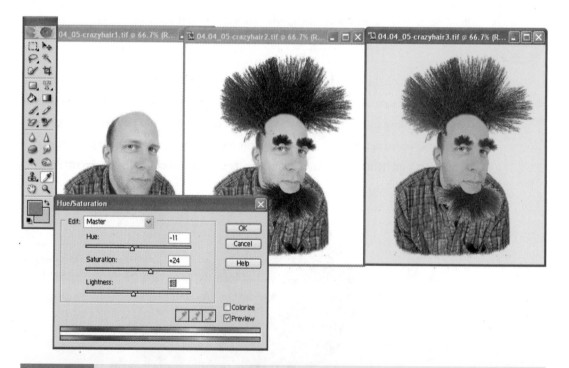

FIGURE 4.4

The Hue/Saturation dialog box displays sliders that you can move to increase or decrease the hue, saturation, and lightness levels of a picture. These pictures show a balding, middle-aged man's steady decline as he attempts to recapture his youth during a midlife crisis by trying to wear a punk hairdo.

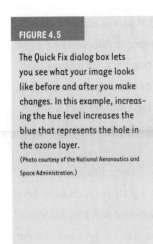

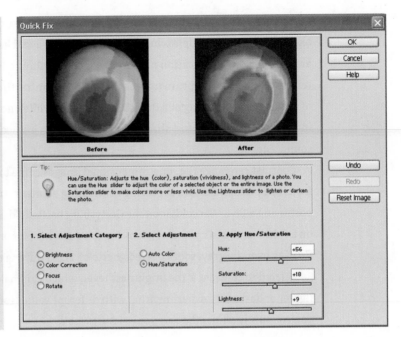

Adjust Brightness

A common problem with most pictures is that they look too dark or too light. Sometimes pictures can look too dark if you forgot to use a flash indoors, a cloud covered the sun just as you snapped the picture, or the image looked fine in real life but for some reason looks dull and lifeless when you captured it with your camera. On the other hand, sometimes a picture may appear too bright if you used a flash inside a well-lit building, the sun shone brighter than you thought, or the hole in the ozone layer burst open and flooded your picture with deadly ultraviolet rays that incinerated every living thing in your photograph.

When this occurs, let Photoshop Elements fix that image by artificially adding light or by subtly darkening portions of your image.

Brightness and Contrast

The simplest way to improve a picture is to adjust its contrast. In general, most people take boring pictures because the subjects of their pictures lack contrast.

Because you don't want to capture pictures that evoke stifled yawns and embarrassed excuses from other people who will do anything to avoid having to fake interest in yet another one of your vacation photos, try to do two things. First, capture images that tell a story. Second, capture images that include contrasting elements, such as a shot of a young crowd rioting at a British soccer game while one lone, older spectator sits in the middle of the chaos, slumped in his seat with his head leaning on his hand, sound asleep.

Contrast can make flat, one-dimensional images come to life by adding depth and focus to a picture. Besides capturing contrasting elements in a picture (such as an actor portraying a Civil War soldier on the Gettysburg battlefield, secretly checking his e-mail on a Palm handheld computer), look for contrasts in color (such as a bright red balloon floating over the gray, soot-covered ghetto of a coal mining town).

Related to contrast is the brightness level, which can make the overall image appear lighter or darker. By experimenting with different values for brightness and contrast, you can subtly adjust the way your pictures look.

Use the Auto Contrast Command

Although Photoshop Elements can't help you find contrast in the subjects you capture, it can help increase the visual contrast between the different images in your pictures by making dark areas darker and light areas lighter. When you want to increase contrast in a picture, use the Auto Contrast command.

To use the Auto Contrast command, load a picture into Photoshop Elements, click the Enhance menu, and then click Auto Contrast. Depending on your picture, you may see a subtle or dramatic change as Photoshop Elements increases the contrast of light and dark areas in your picture.

To give this same command through the Quick Fix dialog box, load a picture into Photoshop Elements, open the Quick Fix dialog box, and click the Brightness radio button in the Select Adjustment Category group. Then click the Auto Contrast radio button in the Select Adjustment group and click Apply. If you're happy with the way your picture looks, click OK. Otherwise, click Cancel.

Manually Adjust the Contrast and Brightness

In case you aren't happy with the way Photoshop Elements adjusts the contrast in your picture, or you want to fine-tune a picture after using the Auto Contrast command, you can manually adjust the contrast. Load your picture into Photoshop Elements, click the Enhance menu, click Adjust Brightness/Contrast, and then click Brightness/Contrast to display the Brightness/Contrast dialog box. Move the Contrast slider left or right to decrease or increase the contrast level and then click OK when you're done. See the results in Figure 4.6.

You can also manually adjust the contrast through the Quick Fix dialog box. Just load your picture into Photoshop Elements, open the Quick Fix dialog box, click the Brightness radio button in the Select Adjustment Category group, and then click the Brightness/Contrast radio button in the Select Adjustment group. Move the Brightness and Contrast sliders and when you're happy with the way your picture looks, click OK. Otherwise, click Cancel.

FIGURE 4.6

The Brightness/Contrast dialog box lets you manually adjust the brightness and contrast levels of an image, such as this picture of a parade passing by an adult bookstore, which despite being open 24 hours a day, has not raised the literacy level of the neighborhood one bit.

Levels

Levels is another one of those deceptively simple terms that tells you absolutely nothing. Basically, levels is short for *intensity levels*, which determines the intensity of an image's dark, light, and color areas. By changing an image's levels, you can increase or decrease the contrast while modifying the colors in your image at the same time.

Use Auto Levels

To make it easy for you to adjust the levels of a picture, Photoshop Elements offers the Auto Levels command. To choose this command, load a picture into Photoshop Elements, click the Enhance menu, and then click Auto Levels.

If you want to use the Quick Fix dialog box, load your picture into Photoshop Elements, open the Quick Fix dialog box, and click the Brightness radio button in the Select Adjustment Category group. Then click the Auto Levels radio button in the Select Adjustment group and click Apply. If you're happy with the way your picture looks, click OK. If you're not, click Cancel.

Manually Adjust the Levels

Generally, it's easier to let Photoshop Elements adjust the levels of your image, but in case you want to take the time to do it manually, you can. Just load a picture into Photoshop Elements, click the Enhance menu, click Adjust Brightness/Contrast, and click Levels to display the Levels dialog box as shown in Figure 4.7. As a faster alternative, just press CTRL-L (Windows) or CMD-L (Macintosh).

The Levels dialog box consists of an Input Levels slider and an Output Levels slider. The Input Levels slider contains black, white, and gray triangles along with a strange looking graph known as a *histogram*, which graphically shows you the amount of black, white, and color in an image. If an image is mostly dark, the histogram graph appears mostly to the left. If the image is mostly light, the histogram graph appears mostly to the right. If an image consists of multiple colors, the histogram graph appears mostly in the middle.

If you click the Channel list box, you can choose what colors to adjust, either RGB (all the colors) or just red, green, or blue. After you choose a color to adjust, the next step is to use the Input Levels slider.

If you move the black triangle on the Input Levels slider, you can lighten up the dark images of your picture. If you move the white triangle on the Input Levels slider, you can darken the light images of your picture. If you move the gray triangle, you can increase or decrease the intensity of the color you chose in the Channel list box.

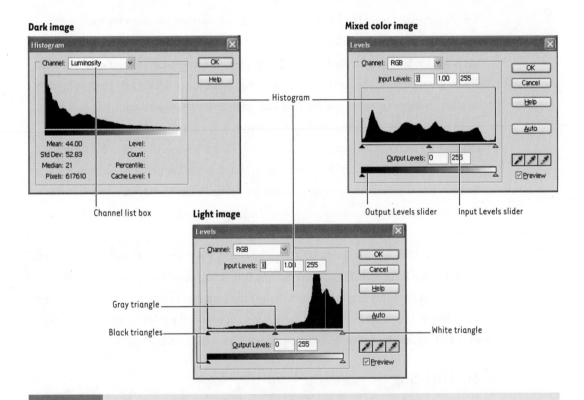

FIGURE 4.7

The Levels dialog box lets you adjust the intensity of black, white, and color in an image. This picture shows what the histograms of dark, colorful, and light pictures look like.

The Output Levels slider gives you another way to adjust the contrast of your image. If you move the black triangle to the right of the Output Levels slider, your image appears lighter. If you move the white triangle to the left of the Output Levels slider, your image appears darker.

Through the Input Levels slider, you can adjust the intensity of colors. Through the Output Levels slider, you can adjust the contrast. When you're done experimenting, click OK.

Fill Flash

Many potentially great indoor shots look awful because they came out too dark—either because the photographer didn't use a flash or actually did use a flash but the subject appeared too far away for the flash to do any good. So rather than toss out a dark but otherwise great picture, you can use Photoshop Elements to artificially add flash to lighten up a dark image or create a unique visual effect from an existing image.

To use the Fill Flash command, load a picture into Photoshop Elements, click the Enhance menu, click Adjust Lighting, and then click Fill Flash to display the Adjust Fill Flash dialog box. The Adjust Fill Flash dialog box displays Lighter and Saturation sliders that you can adjust to make the image appear lighter (using the Lighter slider) and to make the colors appear more vivid (using the Saturation slider). Adjust the sliders and click OK.

If you want to use the Quick Fix dialog box, load a picture into Photoshop Elements, open the Quick Fix dialog box, and click the Brightness radio button in the Select Adjustment Category group. Then click the Fill Flash radio button in the Select Adjustment group. Move the Lighter and Saturation sliders until you're happy with the way your picture looks, as shown in Figure 4.8, and then click OK or Cancel.

Backlighting

Backlighting defines how much light comes in from behind a subject toward the camera. By adjusting the backlighting, you can darken a picture, which can be handy to fix overexposed images that appear too bright and washed out, or just to give you yet another way to add contrast to an image.

The Fill Flash command can lighten up a picture, such as this image of a witch made from Lego building blocks, which fanatical religious fundamentalists believe can entice impressionable youngsters to turn away from religion and embrace witchcraft instead.

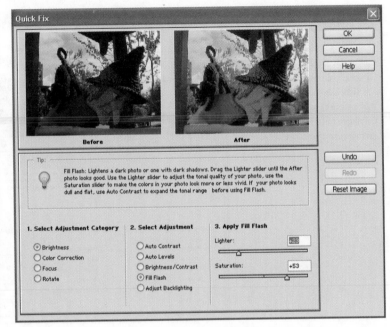

To use the Backlighting command, load a picture into Photoshop Elements, click the Enhance menu, click Adjust Lighting, and then click Adjust Backlighting to display the Adjust Backlighting dialog box, which displays a Darker slider. Adjust the Darker slider and click OK.

If you want to use the Quick Fix dialog box, load a picture into Photoshop Elements, open the Quick Fix dialog box, and click the Brightness radio button in the Select Adjustment Category group. Then click the Adjust Backlighting radio button in the Select Adjustment group as shown in Figure 4.9. Move the Darker slider until you're happy with the way your picture looks and then click OK or Cancel.

Just in case you're wondering, Photoshop Elements provides three different ways to change the lighting in a picture: Fill Flash, Backlighting, and Brightness/Contrast. Fill Flash is used exclusively to add light to a picture, whereas Backlighting is used exclusively to darken a picture. Brightness/Contrast gives you the choice of either lightening or darkening a picture.

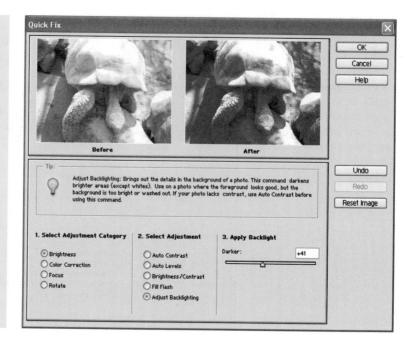

Backlighting can darken a picture, such as this photograph of a Galapagos tortoise trying to have sex. Little does the tortoise know that instead of screwing a female Galapagos tortoise, he's really just humping a rock.

Change the Focus

Another problem with many potentially great pictures is that they appear blurry, either because the photographer moved or the subject moved at the last second, thus creating a fuzzy image. Although blurry images are useless most of the time, sometimes they may come in handy, especially for close-ups of someone's face, which can reveal the harsh reality of acne scars, body hair, birthmarks, and larger-than-life sweat pores pocking the skin. In this case, blurring the image slightly can mask the vivid reminder that those oh-so-beautiful women you see in magazines are actually human beings who don't even look as good in real life as they do in their own photographs.

Auto Focus

The simplest way to sharpen the focus of an image is through the Auto Focus command, which tries to sharpen a picture by increasing contrast between its light and dark areas. Just load a picture into Photoshop Elements, open the Quick Fix dialog box, and click the

Focus radio button in the Select Adjustment Category group. Click the Auto Focus radio button in the Select Adjustment group and then click Apply. Each time you click the Apply button, Photoshop Elements sharpens the focus a little more, as shown in Figure 4.10, although if you go too far, your picture can start to look spotty, jagged, and completely unrealistic. When you're done sharpening the focus of your image, click OK or Cancel.

You can also sharpen the focus of an image through the Filter menu. Just load a picture into Photoshop elements, click the Filter menu, click Sharpen, and then click Sharpen again. To keep sharpening the appearance of your picture, press CTRL-F (Windows) or CMD-F (Macintosh) or click the Filter menu, click Sharpen, and then click Sharpen More until you're happy with the way your picture looks.

Blur

Blurring an image can make a picture look more appealing by hiding the unpleasant reality a photograph can capture. To blur an image, load a picture into Photoshop Elements, open the Quick Fix dialog box, and click the Focus radio button in the Select

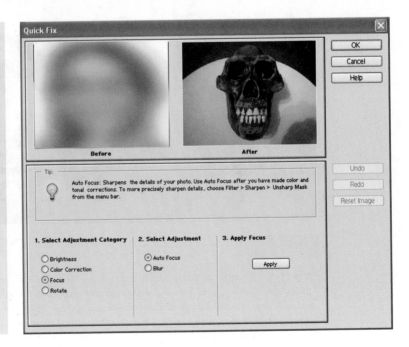

FIGURE 4.10

The Auto Focus command sharpens an image. The picture on the left looks like the blurred image of Cher; the picture on the right shows the sharpened image that reveals what Cher really looks like underneath all that makeup.

Adjustment Category group. Click the Blur radio button in the Select Adjustment group as shown in Figure 4.11, and then click Apply. Each time you click the Apply button, Photoshop Elements blurs the image a little more. When you're done blurring your image, click OK or Cancel.

You can also manually blur an image through the Filter menu. Just load a picture into Photoshop Elements, click the Filter menu, click Blur, and then click Blur again. To keep blurring the appearance of your picture, press CTRL-F (Windows) or CMD-F (Macintosh) or click the Filter menu, click Blur, and click Blur More until you're happy with the way your picture looks.

REMEMBER *If you experiment with sharpening and then blurring an image (or blurring an image and then sharpening it), you may be able to create some interesting visual effects. Either that, or you'll just create a mess.*

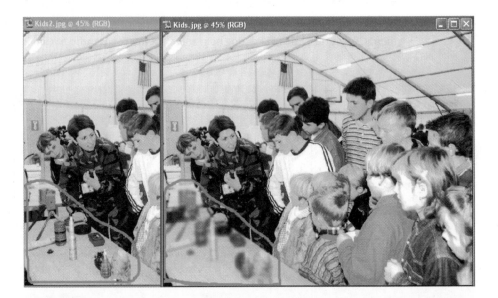

FIGURE 4.11

Blurring an image can soften the harsh realities of the truth. The original image shows children from Bosnia and Herzegovina listening to a translator explain the hazards of antipersonnel mines during Kids' Day. By blurring this image, the scene now looks less threatening to the general public so they can focus on the news that's really important to them, such as the latest sports scores or the hottest celebrity gossip.

(Photo courtesy of the U.S. Department of Defense.)

Rotate an Image

One of the most basic ways to correct an image is to straighten it up. Sometimes you may capture a picture that appears sideways. So before you start modifying it, you need to rotate it so that it appears correctly.

To rotate an image, load the picture into Photoshop Elements, open the Quick Fix dialog box, click the Rotate radio button in the Select Adjustment Category group, click on one of the radio buttons in the Select Adjustment group (such as Flip Horizontal), and then click Apply. When the picture appears oriented correctly, click OK or Cancel.

You can also rotate an image through the Image menu. Just click the Image menu, click Rotate, and then click a command such as Flip Vertical. Unlike the Quick Fix dialog box, the Image menu offers the Custom command, which lets you specify how many degrees to rotate an image.

 REMEMBER *If you captured an image at a crooked angle that makes something look distorted, you can fix this by changing the perspective, as explained in Lesson 2.*

Where to Go from Here

By using some of the more common and simple ways to fix a picture, you can salvage many pictures that you might otherwise have been forced to throw away. Once you understand the basic commands to fix a picture, you can experiment with those same commands to get creative when modifying your pictures.

Getting creative with Photoshop Elements means knowing what different commands do and how to combine them to achieve different visual effects. The more you play around with Photoshop Elements, the more you'll learn how the same command works on different images and colors. At that point, you'll be ready to move beyond basic image fixing and on to image manipulation—which is where the fun of digital editing really begins.

LESSON 5

What You'll Learn in This Lesson

- How to select parts of your picture

- What you can do after you select something

Selecting Stuff in a Picture
(or How to Point with the Mouse Instead of Giving Photoshop Elements the Finger)

ACCORDING TO CHARLES DARWIN'S THEORY OF EVOLUTION, life progresses through natural selection, where the strongest and smartest creatures survive to produce offspring while the weakest and dumbest creatures die off. Fortunately, technological advances have allowed the human race to reverse nature so even the dumbest human beings can survive and get elected to Congress while the smarter human beings die off through the incompetence of their HMOs.

Because the theory of natural selection can seem cruel and arbitrary, you may appreciate the greater control that Photoshop Elements gives over your small part of the world by letting you precisely select parts of a picture that you want to change. Normally when you choose a command to change colors or increase the brightness, Photoshop Elements assumes that you want to apply those changes over the entire picture.

But if you just want to change part of an image, you must first select that part you want to change. When you select part of an image, Photoshop Elements encloses your selection within a constantly moving dotted line, as shown in Figure 5.1. (Some people refer to this selection marquee as "marching ants," because it looks like a line of ants going nowhere, almost as if they were stuck in a dead-end job.) After you select something, any commands you choose will only affect that part of your picture that you selected.

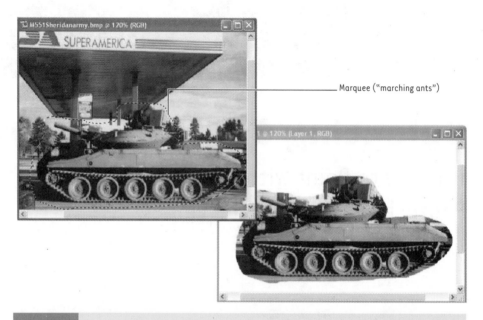

Marquee ("marching ants")

The moving dotted white line, called a marquee, selection marquee, or "marching ants," shows you what part of an image you have selected. Here we see an M551 Sheridan tank parked in front of a 24-hour service station. Despite the tank's 152mm canon and two machine guns, the service station got robbed that night again anyway.

(Photo courtesy of the U.S. Army.)

Because selecting part of a picture isn't as simple as selecting text in a word processor, where everything appears neatly aligned in rows and columns, Photoshop Elements provides several ways to select items in a picture based on shape, boundaries, and color. By using different selection tools, you can easily select anything in a picture—whether it's an irregularly shaped object, such as a tree branch, or an object of contrasting colors, such as a white tiger mauling its trainer against a black backdrop during a magic show in Las Vegas.

Use the Toolbox

The Toolbox, which appears on the left side of the screen in Figure 5.2, contains all the different digital editing tools you need to modify any digital image. To choose a tool from the Toolbox, just click that tool. When you choose a tool, the Toolbox highlights that tool's icon.

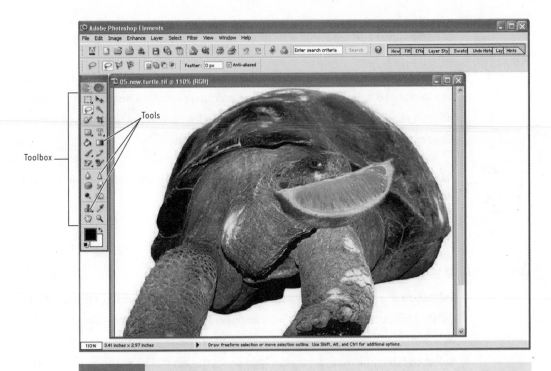

FIGURE 5.2

The Toolbox contains all the tools available for modifying your digital images. In this case, you see what happens when a lemon is placed in a tortoise's mouth. That's quite a pucker.

You can also choose a tool if you press that tool's shortcut key, which is always a single letter, such as M or V. To find out a tool's shortcut key, move the mouse pointer over that tool and wait a few seconds. Photoshop Elements displays a little window near the mouse pointer that identifies the name of the tool, along with that tool's shortcut key in parentheses, such as (T). Once you know a tool's shortcut key, you can press that shortcut key at any time to choose that particular tool.

Because the Toolbox can only display a limited number of icons, many related tools share the same location in the Toolbox. If you look at the different Toolbox icons, you'll notice that some display a black arrow in their bottom-right corner. This black arrow means that similar tools share this same space in the Toolbox, but you can't see those other tools right now.

REMEMBER *Tools that share the same location in the Toolbox also share the same shortcut key.*

If you right-click (Windows) or hold down the CTRL key and click (Macintosh) on any icon that displays that black arrow, a menu appears that displays additional tools you can choose, as shown in Figure 5.3. Just click a tool off the menu, and Photoshop Elements displays that tool in the Toolbox.

REMEMBER *You can also move the mouse pointer over an icon with a black arrow and hold down the mouse button. After a few seconds, a menu appears.*

Select by Shape

When you want to select a rectangular or elliptical part of an image, click the Rectangular or Elliptical Marquee tool, which appears in the upper-left corner of the Toolbox, as shown in Figure 5.4. Move the mouse over the area of your image that you want to select and drag the mouse—that is, hold down the left (Windows only) mouse button

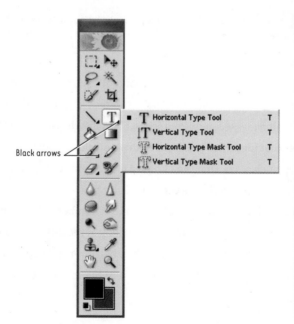

Black arrows

FIGURE 5.3

To change tools, right-click (Windows), hold down the CTRL key and then click (Macintosh), or just point and hold down the mouse button for a few seconds over an icon and choose a new tool from the menu that appears.

and move the mouse. As you drag the mouse, Photoshop Elements highlights your selection with the marquee or "marching ants." When you're done selecting an area, release the left mouse button.

 REMEMBER *If you hold down the SHIFT key as you drag the mouse, Photoshop Elements selects either a perfect square (if you chose the Rectangular Marquee tool) or circle (if you chose the Elliptical Marquee tool). If you click the mouse, hold down the ALT (Windows) or OPTION (Macintosh) key, and then drag the mouse, you can draw a rectangular or elliptical marquee in which the center appears where you first clicked.*

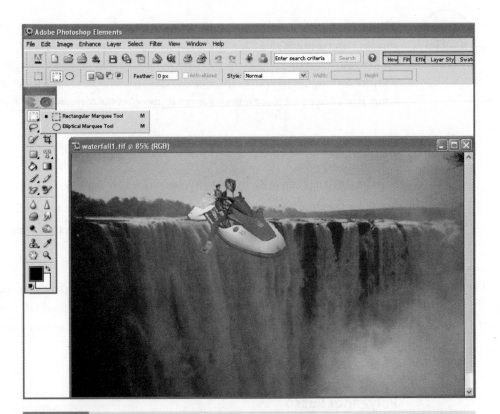

FIGURE 5.4

The Rectangular and Elliptical Marquee tools share the same spot in the Toolbox. The photo shown here is the result of selecting an elliptical object and placing it in another photo, thereby making what was a wonderful day at the beach into five seconds of thundering horror.

Select by Boundaries

Rather than select an arbitrary rectangular or elliptical part of an image, you may find it more useful to select the boundaries of an actual item in your image, such as a face in a crowd or a broken car parked in front of a mobile home. To help you select boundaries of objects, Photoshop Elements gives you the Lasso, Polygonal, and Magnetic Lasso tools. All three of these tools share the same spot in the Toolbox, as shown in Figure 5.5, so you may need to click and hold on the currently displayed Lasso tool icon to choose a different tool.

REMEMBER *To make it easier to see what you're selecting when you use any of the Lasso tools, click the View menu and click Zoom In. Alternatively, you can press CTRL-+ (Windows) or CMD-+ (Macintosh) to zoom in your picture. When you're done selecting an object, click the View menu and click Zoom Out, or press CTRL-- (Windows) or CMD-- (Macintosh) to zoom back out again. To return your picture back to 100% view, you can double-click the Zoom tool in the Toolbox.*

Lasso

The Lasso tool lets you draw around any object that you want to select, which makes it handy for selecting irregularly shaped objects, such as your boss's head. To use the Lasso tool, click the Lasso tool icon in the Toolbox and then drag the mouse to enclose your selection. When you're done, release the mouse button.

REMEMBER *If you hold down the ALT key (Windows) or the OPTION key (Macintosh) and release the mouse button, you can drag the mouse and temporarily make the Lasso tool act like the Polygonal Lasso tool (see the "Polygonal Lasso" section next). As soon as you release the ALT or OPTION key, the Lasso tool acts like itself again.*

Polygonal Lasso

The main advantage of the Lasso tool is its simplicity; you just draw freehand around the part of the image you want to select. Of course, the main drawback is that many people find it difficult to accurately select part of an image by dragging the mouse

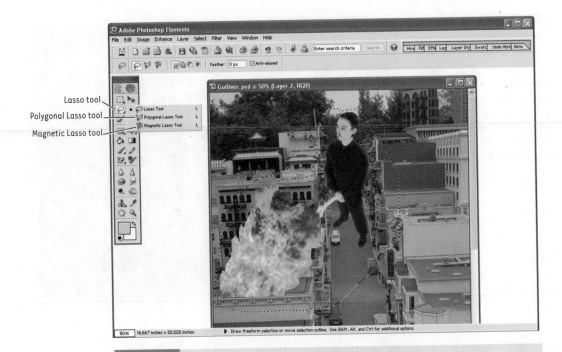

around. Because the ordinary Lasso tool can be hard to use, unless you have a steady hand that can select objects without selecting too much or too little, you may want to use the Polygonal Lasso tool instead.

Rather than force you to drag the mouse around everything you want to select like the ordinary Lasso tool, the Polygonal Lasso tool lets you click the mouse pointer around an object. As you click, Photoshop Elements automatically draws the marquee between each point, as shown in Figure 5.6.

To use this tool, click the Polygonal Lasso tool in the Toolbox and click around the object you want to select. When you're done, click near the first point where you started. If the marquee doesn't appear, double-click the mouse to tell Photoshop Elements that you're done selecting.

The Polygonal Lasso tool lets you select odd shapes with just a few mouse clicks. Here we see the results of what happens when a politician declares, "If I'm not telling the truth, may I be struck by lightning." (Photo courtesy of the National Oceanic and Atmospheric Administration and the White House.)

REMEMBER *If you hold down the ALT key (Windows) or the OPTION key (Macintosh) and release the mouse button, you can drag the mouse freehand around an object, temporarily making the Polygonal Lasso tool act like the ordinary Lasso tool. As soon as you release the ALT or OPTION key, the mouse starts acting like the Polygonal Lasso tool again.*

Magnetic Lasso

Using either the ordinary Lasso tool or the Polygonal Lasso tool can be cumbersome because you must try to maneuver the mouse as close to an object's edges as possible. Rather than force your eye-hand coordination to select objects in a picture, you can use the Magnetic Lasso tool instead.

When you use the Magnetic Lasso tool, you just need to move the mouse near an object, and Photoshop Elements automatically selects the edge of that object. The Magnetic Lasso tool works by detecting differences in contrast between one object in a picture and another. To make the Magnetic Lasso tool more or less sensitive, you can define the Width and Edge Contrast settings.

Width defines how many pixels, within a range of 1 and 40, you need to move the Magnetic Lasso tool before it recognizes the edge of an object. A high Width value means that you can move the mouse in the general direction of an object's edge, and the Magnetic Lasso tool will select it (or mistakenly select something else nearby). A low Width value means that you must move the Magnetic Lasso tool close to an object's edge before it will select it, as shown in Figure 5.7.

Edge Contrast defines how sensitive the Magnetic Lasso tool is to contrasts in a picture. This value can be from 1% to 100%, where a low value means that the Magnetic Lasso tool will likely select boundaries that may not be too distinct. A high value means that the Magnetic Lasso tool will only select edges that have a high contrast between them.

 FIGURE 5.7

The Magnetic Lasso tool lets you move the mouse near an object to select it. In this picture, we see a man losing two fingers and a pint of blood to a rabid red-eye tree frog.

To use the Magnetic Lasso tool, click the Magnetic Lasso tool icon. The Width and Edge Contrast text boxes appear in the options bar. Click the Width text box and type a value between 1 and 40. Remember, the lower the value, the closer you must move the mouse to an edge to select it.

Click the Edge Contrast text box and type a value between 1 and 100. Remember, the higher the value, the less likely the Magnetic Lasso tool will recognize an edge to select in an image.

Click the mouse near the object that you want to select. Photoshop Elements displays a fastening point where you click. As you move the mouse, Photoshop Elements draws the marquee and fastening points around your selection.

Sometimes the Magnetic Lasso tool won't recognize a boundary that you want to select, so you may need to click near that boundary to place a fastening point manually. When you're done, click near the first fastening point where you started. If the marquee of "marching ants" doesn't appear, double-click the mouse.

REMEMBER *If you hold down the* ALT *key (Windows) or the* OPTION *key (Macintosh) and click the mouse, you can drag the mouse and temporarily make the Magnetic Lasso tool act like the ordinary Lasso tool. If you hold down the* ALT *or* OPTION *key and just move the mouse without holding down the mouse button, you can make the Magnetic Lasso tool temporarily act like the Polygonal Lasso tool. As soon as you release the* ALT *or* OPTION *key, the mouse starts acting like the Magnetic Lasso tool again.*

Select by Color

When you use any of the Lasso tools, you must visually try to select the edges of an object. Because this can be tedious, Photoshop Elements offers an easier way—by using the Magic Wand, as shown in Figure 5.8.

The Magic Wand works by selecting similar colors in a picture. So if you want to select a UFO flying in the night sky, you don't have to manually trace the outline of the UFO with the mouse. You can just click on the UFO with the Magic Wand and Photoshop Elements automatically selects your chosen object.

Because the Magic Wand selects items in a picture based on color, you may want to adjust the Tolerance level of the Magic Wand, which can range in value from 0 to 255.

Tolerance text box

Magic Wand

The Magic Wand selects objects in a picture based on color. This picture shows two white tigers, selected by the Magic Wand, as they smile and congratulate one another after mauling two obnoxious Las Vegas magicians, their assistants, and most of the audience as well. (Photo courtesy of the U.S. Department of Defense.)

The lower the tolerance, the fewer colors the Magic Wand selects. The higher the tolerance, the more the Magic Wand selects, which may be more than you want.

To use the Magic Wand, click the Magic Wand icon in the Toolbox, click the Tolerance text box on the options bar, and type a tolerance value from 0 to 255. Now click anywhere on the object you want to select. Depending on the Tolerance level you defined, the Magic Wand either selects the entire object you want, selects too little of the object, or selects too much.

If the Magic Wand selects too much or too little, you can always correct this later, as explained in the section, "Add to or Subtract from a Selection."

After You Select Something

After you select part of an image, one of three situations might occur. The first possibility is that you selected everything you wanted exactly. If this happens, congratulate yourself on a rare occurrence and take a chance buying a lottery ticket today.

A second possibility is that the selection marquee contains too much or too little of what you really want, in which case you'll have to increase or decrease the size of the selection marquee or move the marquee to cover what you want. A third possibility might be that you selected the wrong part of your image, so you want to deselect what you've already selected and start over again.

Deselect and Reselect

In case you selected something and suddenly decide you want to start over again, you have three options:

- Press CTRL-D (Windows) or CMD-D (Macintosh).
- Click the Select menu and then click Deselect.
- Click anywhere on your picture.

If you deselected something and suddenly realize you made a mistake, you can tell Photoshop Elements to bring back and show the selection you just deleted. To reselect something after you just deselected it, choose one of the following:

- Press SHIFT-CTRL-D (Windows) or SHIFT-CMD-D (Macintosh).
- Click the Select menu and then click Reselect.
- Press CTRL-Z (Windows) or CMD-Z (Macintosh).

Move the Selection Marquee

After selecting something, you may notice that the selection marquee doesn't quite cover the part of the image you really wanted to select. Rather than try to select that part of the image all over again, you can just move the marquee instead.

To move the selection marquee, press the up/down or right/left arrow keys, which moves the marquee one pixel at a time. To move the marquee faster, hold down the SHIFT key and then press one of the arrow keys, which moves the marquee ten pixels at a time.

To move the selection marquee with the mouse, move the mouse pointer anywhere inside the marquee and then drag the mouse to move the marquee to a new position. If you drag the mouse and then hold down the SHIFT key, Photoshop Elements only allows the marquee to move at 45-degree angles.

Increase or Decrease the Size of a Selection

Sometimes you may have selected too much or too little of an image. If moving the selection marquee won't cover everything you want to select, you may need to increase or decrease the size of the selection marquee.

To increase the size of the selection marquee, select part of your image, click the Select menu, click Modify, and then click Expand. The Expand Selection dialog box appears. Type the number of pixels you want to expand your selection marquee by and then click OK. Photoshop Elements expands your entire selection marquee by the number of pixels you specified, as shown in Figure 5.9.

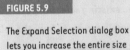
FIGURE 5.9

The Expand Selection dialog box lets you increase the entire size of your selection marquee by a fixed number of pixels, such as this scene, cut from the movie *The Planet of the Apes*, showing a topless orangutan dancing around a pole in a strip club.

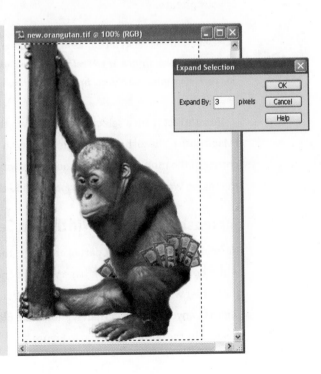

To decrease the size of the selection marquee, select part of your image, click the Select menu, click Modify, and then click Contract. The Contract Selection dialog box appears. Type the number of pixels you want to contract your selection marquee by and then click OK. Photoshop Elements contracts your entire selection marquee by the number of pixels you specified.

Add to or Subtract from a Selection

Sometimes when you select part of an image, you may find that you selected a little too much on one side, so you need to subtract that unwanted portion. Other times you may miss selecting everything you wanted, so you need to expand part of what you already selected.

To add to a selection, hold down the SHIFT key. Photoshop Elements displays a little plus sign near the bottom-right corner of the mouse pointer. Choose a selection tool (such as the Rectangular Marquee tool or the Lasso tool) and select another part of your picture.

REMEMBER *If you select an adjacent area next to the existing selection, you increase the size of the selection marquee. If you select an area completely separate from the selection marquee, you can select multiple objects in different areas of the picture.*

To subtract from a selection, hold down the ALT key (Windows) or the OPTION key (Macintosh). Photoshop Elements displays a little minus sign near the bottom-right corner of the mouse pointer. Choose a selection tool (such as the Magnetic Lasso or the Magic Wand) and select any part inside the selection marquee.

Increase the Border Width of a Selection

Normally, when you select part of an image, the marquee encloses your entire selection with a dotted line border that has a width of one (1). For a change of pace, you can change the border width of the marquee from 1 to 200 pixels. When you increase the border width to anything greater than 1, Photoshop Elements only selects the part of the image covered by the border as shown in Figure 5.10.

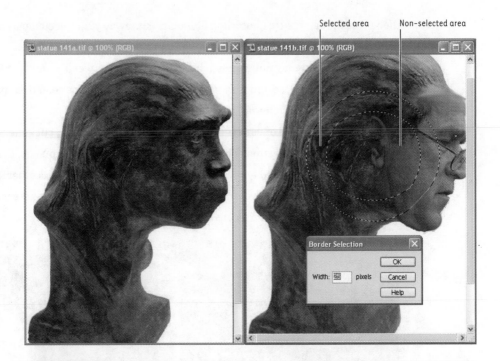

FIGURE 5.10

When you increase the border width, Photoshop Elements only selects the image framed within the border, such as the doughnut-shaped marquee on the side of the statue's face. The picture on the left shows a bust of a Neanderthal Man while the picture on the right shows a similar bust of a modern man, lending support to the theory that perhaps evolution really isn't progressing forward after all. (Photo courtesy of the White House.)

To increase the border width of a selected area, select part of the image, click the Select menu, click Modify, and click Border. The Border Selection dialog box appears. Click the Width text box and type a number from 1 to 200. Then click OK. Photoshop Elements expands your border by the specified number of pixels and only selects that part of your image covered by the border.

Soften the Edges of Your Selection

Normally, when you select something, the boundaries between your selection and the rest of the image appears very distinct. For example, if you select part of an image and then press the DELETE key, Photoshop Elements cuts away your selected part of the image as neatly as punching a hole through a piece of paper.

Sometimes you may not want such a distinct edge between your selection and the rest of the image, so you may want to blur the edges of the selection marquee—a process known as *feathering*, which is shown in Figure 5.11.

To feather the edges of your selection, select part of an image, click the Select menu, and then click Feather. The Feather Selection dialog box appears. Click the Feather Radius text box and type a value ranging from 0.2 to 250. The Feather Radius setting determines the width of the feathered edge. A small value means the feathered edge is thin, and a large value means the feathered edge is wide.

FIGURE 5.11

Without feathering, the edges between a selection and the surrounding area are distinct, as seen in the top-right image, which shows clean holes cut out of the eyes, giving the couple the appearance of what Little Orphan Annie might look like if she were drunk with her boyfriend. With feathering, the edges between a selection and the surrounding area are blurred, as seen in the bottom image of this same drunk couple.

REMEMBER *Feathering is most apparent after you move, cut, copy, or fill in the feathered selection.*

Inverse the Selection

If you need to select a large part of a picture, you have two choices. One, you can spend a good chunk of time selecting everything you want. Two, you can use the Inverse command.

Before you use the Inverse command, you select everything that you *don't* want. After you do this, click the Select menu and then choose the Inverse command, which tells Photoshop Elements, "See what I just selected? I really want to select everything but that part of the image that I just selected." So if you want to select a large part of a picture, it's easier to first select the small part of the picture that you don't want to select and then choose the Inverse command.

Save and Reuse a Selection

Selecting a particularly tiny or irregularly shaped object can be difficult. If you ever need to select this same part of the image again, you may not want to go through all the trouble to select it once more. So to save time, you can save your selection. That way, when you need that same selected part of the image, you can select it again quickly.

Save a Selection

Once you have selected part of an image, click the Select menu and click Save Selection. The Save Selection dialog box appears, as shown in Figure 5.12. Click the Name text box, type a descriptive name for your selected area, and click OK.

Retrieve a Selection

After you have saved a selected part of an image by name, you can reselect that same portion of the image again by clicking the Select menu and clicking Load Selection. The Load Selection dialog box appears, as shown in Figure 5.13.

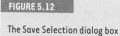
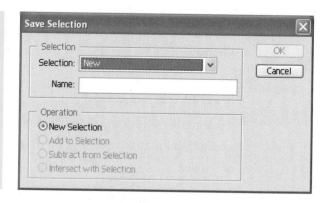

FIGURE 5.12

The Save Selection dialog box lets you save a selected part of your image by name. That way, you can reselect that part of your image without having to use one of the selection tools over again.

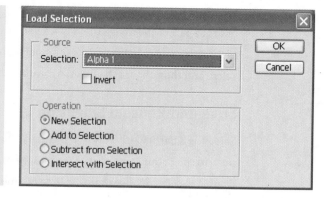

FIGURE 5.13

The Load Selection dialog box lets you retrieve a selected area of your image that you previously saved.

Click the Selection list box, click the name of the selected area you want to reselect, and click OK. Photoshop Elements reselects the area defined by your retrieved selection.

REMEMBER *If you already selected part of an image and then chose the Load Selection command, you can use the saved selection to add to, subtract from, or intersect (only select the area that both selections have in common) with the first selected area.*

Delete a Selection

In case you want to delete a previously saved selection, click the Select menu and click Delete Selection. The Delete Selection dialog box appears. Click the Selection list box, click the name of the selection you want to delete, and click OK.

Choose a Command

After you select part of an image, you can perform different actions on it, such as moving it, deleting it, or changing its brightness or color.

To move a selected area, hold down the CTRL key (Windows) or CMD key (Macintosh) and drag the selected area to a new part of your image, as shown in Figure 5.14. If you just want to move a selection marquee without moving the image enclosed inside, just move the mouse over the selected area and drag the mouse to a new location.

FIGURE 5.14

You can move a selected area by holding down the CTRL (Windows) or CMD key (Macintosh) and then dragging the mouse. If you use feathering (see the section "Soften the Edges of Your Selection"), moving a selected area can create a unique effect, such as shown in this picture of two scientists checking for radiation near containers full of toxic waste. Fortunately, the radiation level was low enough not to contaminate the toxic waste stored in the leaking metal drums nearby. (Photo courtesy of the Environmental Protection Agency.)

To copy a selected area, hold down the CTRL key and the ALT key (Windows) or the CMD key and the OPTION key (Macintosh) and drag the selected area to a new location.

To delete a selected area, press the DELETE key. To change the appearance of a selected area, choose any of the commands listed under the Enhance and Filter menus.

REMEMBER *After you select part of an image, any commands you choose will only affect whatever part of the image you selected.*

Where to Go from Here

Once you know how to select part of an image, you can apply different visual effects to it and start creating unusual images (or really messed up ones). After using all the different ways to select something in a picture, you can move on to the more interesting task of changing the way different parts of a picture look so you can really have fun playing with your digital images.

With your newfound knowledge about all the selection tools available in Photoshop Elements, you might be able to apply that information to create pictures that help support Charles Darwin's theory. While religious people argue for Creationism and scientists argue for evolution, you may be surprised to find that Charles Darwin didn't select either side of the argument. Instead, he clearly stated the following from his "The Origin of Species":

> *But as my conclusions have lately been much misrepresented, and it has been stated that I attribute the modification of species exclusively to natural selection, I may be permitted to remark that in the first edition of this work, and subsequently, I placed in a most conspicuous position—namely, at the close of the Introduction—the following words: "I am convinced that natural selection has been the main but not the exclusive means of modification." This has been of no avail. Great is the power of steady misrepresentation; but the history of science shows that fortunately this power does not long endure.*

Despite clearly stating that his theory of evolution doesn't rule out creationism, decades later people still misinterpret his words. So the next time you meet someone arguing purely for creationism or solely for evolution, you'll know that that person selectively chose the information they read and failed to select the entire text of Darwin's book to read, which lends support to the alternate theory that instead of evolution implying greater improvement in a species, the human race may just be getting dumber with each succeeding generation.

LESSON 6

What You'll Learn in This Lesson

- How to copy an image and paste it in another

- How to paste an image inside a selected area

- How to delete stuff

- How children's literature is actually bloodier than most R-rated movies

Copy and Paste
(or How to Make Fake Photographs Look Real)

PERHAPS NO OTHER FORM OF FICTION GETS CUT UP, rearranged, and "sanitized" as much as children's literature. In the original version of *The Wizard of Oz*, by L. Frank Baum, the Tin Man was once a woodchopper who fell in love with a Munchkin girl. Unfortunately, the old woman who lived with this Munchkin girl didn't want the Tin Man to marry her servant so she had the Wicked Witch of the East put a spell on him. Every time he swung his axe, he would chop off part of his own body. First he lost his legs, then his arms, then his head, and finally his torso. (Apparently the Tin Man wasn't smart enough to stop swinging his axe when it kept cutting him up, so maybe he really should have asked for a new brain like the Scarecrow.)

Each time the Tin Man cut off a part of his body, a helpful tinsmith replaced the missing part with a tin substitute, but the one item the tinsmith could not replace was the Tin Man's original heart. Without a heart, the Tin Man soon lost his love for the Munchkin girl. So the reason why the Tin Man wants a heart is so he can fall in love with the Munchkin girl once more.

Cartoon studios and children's book publishers understandably cut out the violent parts of children's stories, copy elements from other stories, and paste them back together to create a new version that often bears little resemblance to the original. Just as book publishers and cartoon animators can cut, copy, and paste images together to create something new based on something old, so can you with your copy of Photoshop Elements.

Unlike word processors and spreadsheets, which let you cut, copy, and paste text, Photoshop Elements lets you cut, copy, and paste pixels. You can cut or copy part of one picture and paste it in another, such as copying a picture of your boss and pasting it over the face of a porno star.

By letting you mix and match images, Photoshop Elements lets you create images that never existed. Even better, if you take a really lousy picture with your digital camera, don't erase it. Through the wonders of the Cut, Copy, and Paste commands, you just might be able to dissect a lousy picture and reuse its parts to spice up an almost-perfect picture that you really want to keep.

Copy and Paste: The Fast and Easy Way

Perhaps no single studio has warped more children's classics than Walt Disney. In the Disney version of *Peter Pan*, Tinker Bell appears as a sweet, smiling fairy. But in the original version, Tinker Bell is actually a jealous, vengeful fairy intent on getting rid of Wendy so she can have Peter Pan's attention all to herself.

Wendy was now almost overhead, and they could hear her plaintive cry. But more distinct came the shrill voice of Tinker Bell. The jealous fairy had now cast off all disguise of friendship, and was darting at her victim from every direction, pinching savagely each time she touched.

"Hullo, Tink," cried the wondering boys.

Tink's reply rang out: "Peter wants you to shoot the Wendy."

It was not in their nature to question when Peter ordered.

"Let us do what Peter wishes!" cried the simple boys. "Quick, bows and arrows!"

All but Tootles popped down their trees. He had a bow and arrow with him, and Tink noted it, and rubbed her little hands.

"Quick, Tootles, quick," she screamed. "Peter will be so pleased."

Tootles excitedly fitted the arrow to his bow. "Out of the way, Tink," he shouted, and then he fired, and Wendy fluttered to the ground with an arrow in her breast.

—Excerpt from the original version of *The Adventures of Peter Pan* by J.M. Barrie

Just as Walt Disney pasted a friendly fairy in place of the vengeful one in the original *Peter Pan*, so can you paste over a picture by copying an image from one picture to another. The simplest way to add images from one picture to another involves nothing more than the ordinary Copy and Paste commands. First, select all or part of a picture using one of the many selection tools, such as the Lasso tool or the Magic Wand. (See Lesson 5 for more information about how to select images in a picture.) Once you've selected part of a picture, press CTRL-C (Windows), CMD-C (Macintosh), or click the Edit menu and click Copy.

Now load a second picture into Photoshop Elements. Click anywhere inside this second picture and press CTRL-V (Windows), CMD-V (Macintosh), or click the Edit menu and click Paste. Photoshop Elements pastes your image onto this second picture.

REMEMBER *When you paste an image onto a picture, Photoshop Elements actually pastes that image on a separate, transparent layer on top of the original picture (see Lesson 7 for more information about layers). By pasting an image onto a layer, rather than directly on another picture, Photoshop Elements makes it easy for you to later move or resize the pasted image without affecting the original picture underneath.*

Once Photoshop Elements pastes an image onto a picture, chances are good that this pasted image won't be where you want it. So when you need to move a pasted image, use the Move tool, as shown in Figure 6.1.

Just click the Move tool in the Toolbox, move the mouse pointer over the pasted image, and drag the mouse to move the pasted image. If you move the mouse pointer

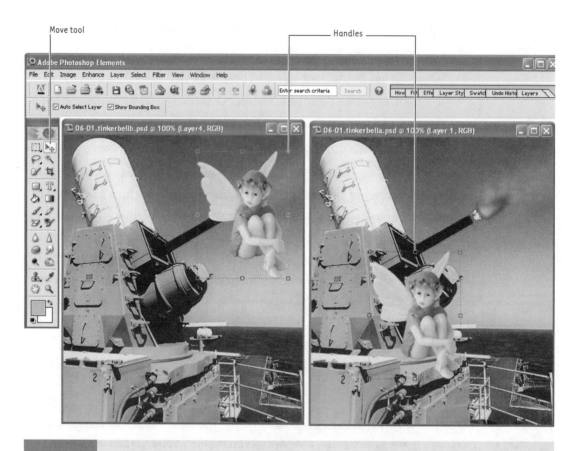

Move tool

Handles

FIGURE 6.1

The Move tool lets you move and resize images after you paste them. In this picture, Tinker Bell has given the Lost Boys a 20mm gatling gun, firing depleted uranium ammunition, to blast Wendy out of the sky the next time she flies overhead. (Photo courtesy of the United States Navy.)

directly over one of the handles of the pasted image, the mouse pointer turns into a double-pointing arrow, which means you can drag the mouse to resize the image.

If you move the mouse pointer around the outside edges of a handle, the mouse pointer turns into a curved double-pointing arrow, which means if you drag the mouse, you can rotate your pasted image.

Copy and Paste for Special Effects

"I know what you want," said the sea witch; "it is very stupid of you, but you shall have your way … Your tail will then disappear, and shrink up into what mankind calls legs, and you will feel great pain, as if a sword were passing through you. But all who see you will say that you are the prettiest little human being they ever saw. You will still have the same floating gracefulness of movement, and no dancer will ever tread so lightly; but at every step you take it will feel as if you were treading upon sharp knives, and that the blood must flow."

Every step she took was as the witch had said it would be, she felt as if treading upon the points of needles or sharp knives; but she bore it willingly, and stepped as lightly by the prince's side as a soap-bubble, so that he and all who saw her wondered at her graceful-swaying movements.

—Excerpt from the original version of *The Little Mermaid* by Hans Christian Andersen

In the story *The Little Mermaid*, a mermaid swallows a magic potion to exchange her fish tail for a pair of human legs so she can fall in love with a handsome prince. Naturally, the Disney version of the story omits the fact that every step the Little Mermaid takes puts her in excruciating pain—and that at the end of the story, the prince winds up marrying someone else.

If just a few changes can dramatically alter the tone of a story, think what a few changes can do to your pictures. To give you another way to use the Copy and Paste commands to create special effects, Photoshop Elements also offers the Paste Into command. Unlike the ordinary Paste command, which plops a copied image in exactly the same shape you selected it, the Paste Into command shoehorns an image into a shape defined by any of the selection tools.

To use the Paste Into command, first select the image you want to copy and paste onto another picture. Because the edges of your pasted image probably won't be visible after you paste it onto another picture, save yourself time and use one of the faster selection tools, such as the Rectangular Marquee tool or the Lasso tool. Now copy the image.

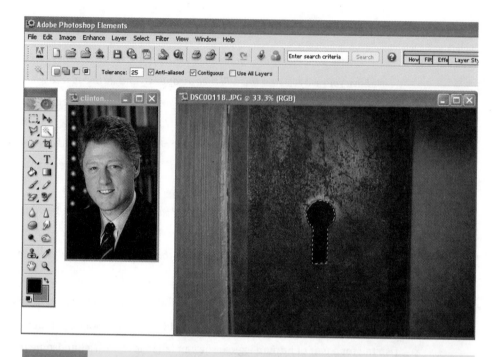

FIGURE 6.2

After the entire picture of Bill Clinton is copied, the Magic Wand is used in the second picture to define the keyhole.
(Photo courtesy of the White House.)

Load a second picture and use one of the selection tools to define an area on this second picture. Whatever you select on this second picture will act like a cookie cutter that defines the boundaries where any pasted image (from the first picture) will be visible, as shown in Figure 6.2.

Click the Edit menu and click Paste Into. Photoshop Elements pastes your image and displays the selection marquee around your pasted image, as shown in Figure 6.3.

After you paste an image into a selected area with the Paste Into command, you can use the Move tool to move and resize the pasted image. If you move or resize the pasted image past the boundaries of the area you defined (such as the keyhole in Figures 6.2 and 6.3), Photoshop Elements hides that part of your image.

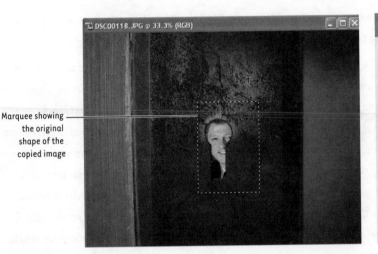

Marquee showing the original shape of the copied image

FIGURE 6.3

The Paste Into command pastes a copied image into a shape, such as Bill Clinton's face in the shape defined by a keyhole. Now it looks like Bill Clinton is peeking through a keyhole leading to the Little Mermaid's dressing room.

(Photo courtesy of the White House.)

CAUTION *Make any changes, such as moving or resizing your pasted image, right away. The moment you choose another command, you won't be able to move or resize your pasted image again.*

Copy and Paste for a Natural Look

When you copy and paste an image from one picture to another, the pasted image rarely blends in naturally with the background of the second picture. Sometimes this can be useful when you want to focus the viewer's eyes on the pasted image against the background image as an inset, as shown in Figure 6.4.

More often than not, though, you will want to paste an image onto another picture so that the pasted image blends naturally into the background to create a convincing fake photograph, such as a CIA agent or television broadcaster might do. To create such realistic composites, you need to spend time using additional tools besides the ordinary Copy and Paste commands. Depending on the shape of the image you want to copy, Photoshop Elements offers a variety of different ways to copy an image.

Method 1: Trim and Blur Your Selected Image

Another beloved Disney classic is *Aladdin*, taken from the original stories of *The Arabian Nights*. While Disney generally left the story of Aladdin intact, they trimmed away any mention of why the story of Aladdin was told in the first place. *The Arabian Nights* story begins with the topic of marital infidelity, as explained in the following excerpt:

> *Now the Sultan Schahriar had a wife whom he loved more than all the world, and his greatest happiness was to surround her with splendour, and to give her the finest dresses and the most beautiful jewels. It was therefore with the deepest shame and sorrow that he accidentally discovered, after several years, that she had deceived him completely, and her whole conduct turned out to have been so bad, that he felt himself obliged to carry out the law of the land, and order the grand-vizir to put her to death. The blow was so heavy that his mind almost gave way, and he declared that he was quite sure that at bottom all women were as wicked as the sultana, if you could only find them out, and that the fewer the world contained the better. So every evening he married a fresh wife and had her strangled the following morning before the grand-vizir, whose duty it was to provide these unhappy brides for the Sultan. The poor man fulfilled his task with reluctance, but there was no escape, and every day saw a girl married and a wife dead.*

> —Excerpt from the original version of *The Arabian Nights*, selected and edited by Andrew Lang

FIGURE 6.4

An inset consists of one image pasted onto another image, without any effort being made to make the inset look natural within the other image, thus calling attention to the inset. In this picture, a wicked witch offers a poisoned apple to lure unsuspecting children to her gingerbread house while a businessman representing the candy industry (inset) talks to his lawyers regarding the fact that the poisoned apple is still much healthier to eat than any of the candy used to make the gingerbread house.

To put a stop to the Sultan's nightly slaughter of fresh virgins, the grand-vizar's own daughter, named Scheherazade, volunteers to become the Sultan's next wife. Her only request is that her sister, Dinarzade, also be allowed to spend the last night with her, to which the Sultan agrees.

Now before the end of the night when the death sentence should be fulfilled, Dinarzade asks Scheherazade to entertain herself and the Sultan with a story, to which Scheherazade agrees. However, the end of the night occurs before the end of the story, so wishing to hear how the story ends, the Sultan agrees to keep Scheherazade alive one more day. Inevitably, Scheherazade finishes the first story but begins another one, which also fails to end before the next night. Because the Sultan wants to hear how each story ends, he keeps Scheherazade alive one more day until she has managed to stay alive for a thousand and one nights. One of the many stories that Scheherazade tells to keep herself alive within this timeframe is the story of Aladdin.

The friendly folks at Walt Disney studios simply trimmed away the bulk of *The Arabian Nights* and focused on telling just the part about Aladdin as a complete story in itself. As an example of a strained analogy, you too can trim away large chunks of something in a picture that you don't want to keep.

To trim away most of the background, use any of the selection tools to select the image as you can. If you have a steady hand, you can use the Lasso tool to trace the outline of the image you want to copy, but it might be easier to use the Magnetic Lasso tool or the Magic Wand instead (see Lesson 5).

REMEMBER *You may want to magnify your image so you can see exactly what you want to select or delete. See the "Magnify a Picture" section in Lesson 2 for more information about magnifying an image.*

After you select an image, click the Select menu, click Modify, and click Contract. The Contract Selection dialog box appears, as shown in Figure 6.5. Click the Contract By text box and type the number of pixels you want to shrink the selection marquee by, such as 5. Then click OK. By contracting the selection marquee, you can further cut away any unnecessary background surrounding your image.

FIGURE 6.5

The Contract Selection dialog box lets you tighten the selection marquee around an image to trim away the unwanted background, such as this image of an alien's head. Many UFO researchers believe that Captain Hook, in the story of Peter Pan, might actually have been a space alien as depicted in this figure.

CAUTION *If you contract the selection marquee too much, you may actually remove part of the image you want to keep.*

When you paste an image onto another picture, the borders of that pasted image may appear too distinct, destroying the natural illusion you may want. To fix this problem, Photoshop Elements gives you the chance to "feather" your selection, which blurs the edges of your selected image by a certain number of pixels. The greater the number of pixels used to feather the selected image, the softer and less obvious the borders of the pasted image appear.

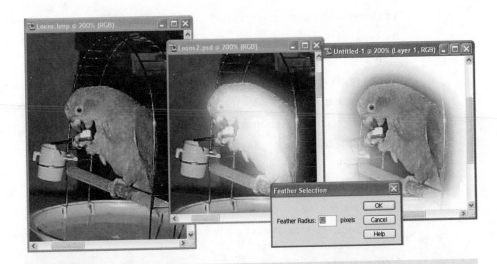

FIGURE 6.6

The Feather Selection dialog box lets you blur the edges of your selection so they won't appear too obvious when you paste it in another picture. This picture shows a parrot brushing its beak, thereby demonstrating more knowledge of dental hygiene than most people who live in trailer parks.

To feather a selected image, click the Select menu and click Feather. The Feather Selection dialog box appears, as shown in Figure 6.6. Click the Feather Radius text box and type the number of pixels to feather or blur the edges of your selection. Then click OK.

After contracting the selection marquee and feathering the edges, you may need to adjust the contrast, brightness, colors, and saturation to make the pasted image match the contrast, brightness, color, and saturation of the other picture. When you're happy with the way the selected image looks, you can copy and paste the image onto the other picture. After you paste the image, use the Move tool to resize and move the pasted image to its proper position.

Method 2: Select What You Don't Want

If you need to select an irregularly shaped object, such as a tree branch or a car wreck, tracing the outline of such an image can be tedious and cumbersome. As an alternative, you may find it easier to select what you don't want to keep, such as a blue sky or black background that may be surrounding the image you really want.

You can do this in one of two ways. First, select the background that you don't want using a selection tool such as the Magic Wand. When you have selected everything but the image that you want, click the Select menu and click Inverse. Photoshop Elements now deselects the background and selects the image that you want. At this point, you can copy the selected image and paste it on another picture.

For another way to remove the background from an image, use the Magic Eraser tool. The Magic Eraser tool works like the Magic Wand by selecting areas of similar colors. Instead of selecting an area like the Magic Wand, however, the Magic Eraser tool deletes that area and replaces it with a transparent background, as shown in Figure 6.7.

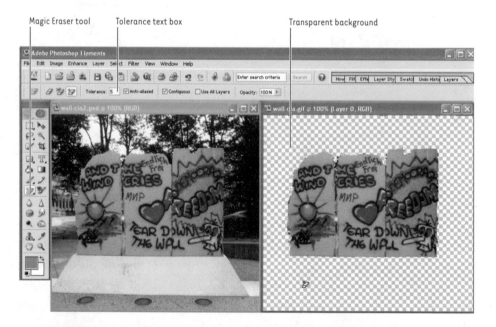

FIGURE 6.7

The Magic Eraser tool removes part of an image and replaces it with a transparent background, which can be perfect for isolating images from a cluttered background. These pictures show how the Magic Eraser tool has isolated a graffiti-covered part of the Berlin Wall, which West Germans created to show their East German counterparts that freedom means you can spray paint graffiti on public property just like they do. (Photo courtesy of the Central Intelligence Agency.)

Now click around the image that you want to copy. Each time you click, Photoshop Elements replaces that area with a checkerboard pattern that represents a transparent area. When you're done erasing every part of the image that you don't want, click the Select menu and click All, or you can press CTRL-A (Windows) or CMD-A (Macintosh). Photoshop Elements highlights the entire image. At this point, you can copy and paste it onto another picture.

Smudge the Edges

Whether you take the time to select an image using a selection tool, such as the Magnetic Lasso tool, or strip away the background with the Magic Eraser tool, a final problem occurs when you paste your image onto another picture. Despite any feathering you may have done, the boundary between your pasted image and the rest of the picture may appear too stark and distinct, making the pasted image stand out and look unnatural. To fix this problem, use the Smudge tool, which lets you blur or smudge the border between your pasted image and the background, as shown in Figure 6.8.

To use the Smudge tool, click the Smudge tool icon. Photoshop Elements displays the various options for the Smudge tool in the options bar. The Brush Preset list box lets you choose a brush size and type. The Size list box lets you define the size of your brush. The Mode list box defines the way the Smudge tool works. Some of the options include Normal, Darken, and Lighten.

The Strength list box displays a percentage from 1% to 100%. The lower the percentage, the less the Smudge tool blurs part of the image. The higher the percentage, the more the Smudge tool blurs part of the image.

To see more detail when you're smudging the edges of an image, you may want to magnify the image (see the "Magnify a Picture" section in Lesson 2 for more information). Once you've defined the settings for the Smudge tool, move the mouse over part of the image and then drag the mouse. The Smudge tool blurs the image based on the direction you drag the mouse and the color that the Smudge tool started on.

For example, if you move the Smudge tool over a black image and drag the mouse, the Smudge tool smears black in the direction you drag the mouse. If you move the Smudge tool over a white area and drag the mouse, the Smudge tool smears white in the direction you drag the mouse. By using the Smudge tool, you can blur the edges of a pasted image and make it blend in naturally, as shown in Figure 6.9.

FIGURE 6.8

The Smudge tool can smear the edges of a pasted image to make them seem less distinct so that the pasted image blends more naturally into the background. Here we see a woman bungee jumping off the top of the Eiffel Tower in an effort to find a natural way to cure her constipation.

The Smudge tool would have come in particularly handy in the original version of *The Story of Doctor Dolittle*. Unlike the 20th Century Fox movie version starring Eddie Murphy, the original story of Dr. Dolittle has the dubious distinction of being one of the few works of children's literature that has been banned for what some people perceive as its racist content.

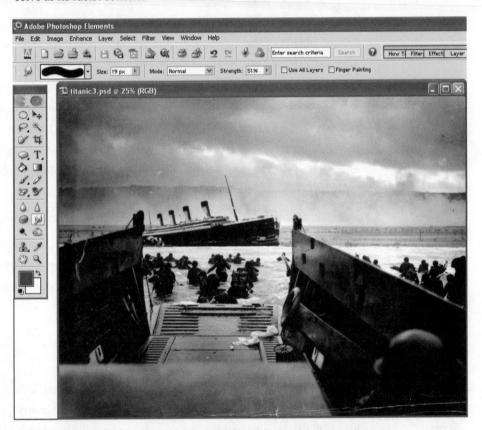

FIGURE 6.9

The Smudge tool can blur the edges of the Titanic so it appears in the D-Day invasion of Normandy. Now it looks like troops are wading toward the Titanic to rescue the first-class passengers from suffering the indignity of drowning in the same water as the third-class passengers. (Photo courtesy of the United States Coast Guard.)

In the original story, an angry African king imprisons Dr. Dolittle and his animals because a previous white man had destroyed his lands, so the king has vowed that no white man shall travel freely through his kingdom again. To escape, Dr. Dolittle discovers that the king's son, Prince Bumpo, has fallen in love with a white woman after reading the fairy tale "Sleeping Beauty."

"White Man, I am an unhappy prince. Years ago I went in search of The Sleeping Beauty, whom I had read of in a book. And having traveled through the world many days, I at last found her and kissed the lady very gently to awaken her—as the book said I should. 'Tis true indeed that she awoke. But when she saw my face she cried out, 'Oh, he's black!' And she ran away and wouldn't marry me—but went to sleep again somewhere else. So I came back, full of sadness, to my father's kingdom. Now I hear that you are a wonderful magician and have many powerful potions. So I come to you for help. If you will turn me white, so that I may go back to The Sleeping Beauty, I will give you half my kingdom and anything besides you ask."

—Excerpt from the original version of *The Story of Doctor Dolittle*, by Hugh Lofting

If Dr. Dolittle had the Smudge tool, he could have helped wipe out racism by smearing white across Prince Bumpo's face (or black across the white woman's face), and everyone would have lived happily ever after. (Everyone, that is, except for the politically correct censors.)

Where to Go from Here

Once you understand how to copy and paste images in Photoshop Elements, you'll know the basic commands needed to digitally edit any picture. Of course, once you know how to digitally edit a picture, chances are good you'll also make a mistake while experimenting with Photoshop Elements.

If you're not careful, a mistake could wreck a file beyond repair, so before you get too eager to edit your digital images, take some time to learn how to protect yourself from the inevitable mistakes you're likely to make as you learn how to use Photoshop Elements.

In the meantime, you may want to read the original versions of *The Wizard of Oz*, *The Adventures of Peter Pan*, *The Arabian Nights*, and *The Story of Doctor Dolittle*, just to find out what you've been missing. Perhaps sometime in the future, the movie studios will give us children's versions of other literature classics, such as *A Clockwork Orange*, *Brave New World*, or *Johnny Got His Gun*. But until then, you can spend your time practicing your copying and pasting skills with Photoshop Elements.

LESSON 7

What You'll Learn in This Lesson

- How to use the Undo/Redo and Step Backward/Step Forward commands

- How to use the Undo History palette to go back in time

- How to protect your pictures with layers

How to Keep from Screwing Up

(or How to Protect Your Pictures from Yourself)

ON JUNE 6, 1944, WAR PHOTOGRAPHER ROBERT CAPA joined the troops for D-Day, the invasion of Normandy, where he risked his life to capture the initial battle scenes as the soldiers stormed the beaches. After taking several rolls of film for posterity, Robert Capa sent his pictures back to *LIFE* magazine for developing, where an overeager darkroom worker turned the temperature in the drying cabinet too high and destroyed all but 11 of these historical photographs that could never be replaced.

Now if Robert Capa had been able to use digital photography, he never would have lost his pictures through a darkroom screwup. Instead, he might have lost his pictures through a computer screwup.

In Photoshop Elements, the most common screwup involves changing a picture and suddenly realizing that you made a mistake. Because you often learn from your mistakes (despite getting punished for it in school), Photoshop Elements provides several ways to protect you so each mistake becomes a learning process rather than a fatal error that raises your blood pressure and brings you one step closer to putting your fist through your computer screen.

REMEMBER *The best way to keep from screwing up is to save a separate copy of your picture. That way if you really mess up your picture, you can just delete it and make another copy of the original picture.*

How to Use the Undo and Redo Commands

We've all done something that we later wish we could go back in time and correct. To avoid mistakes, some people choose not to do anything at all, which effectively turns their lives into a lifelong prison sentence of monotony and boredom that they anesthetize with alcohol and drugs. Because you're likely to make mistakes any time you attempt anything new or different, a better solution involves knowing how to recover from your mistakes so they won't discourage you from learning.

To do this, Photoshop Elements offers three different ways to turn back time and return an edited image back to its previous condition. You can use any of these three methods individually or together the next time you do something in Photoshop Elements that you wish you didn't do after all, such as deleting part of a picture or changing a picture's colors.

Method 1: Reverse the Last Command You Chose

If you modify a picture, you may be dismayed to find that your picture now looks worse than ever. Before doing anything else, choose the Undo command right away to take back the last command you chose. To choose the Undo command, click the Edit menu and then click Undo, or press ALT-CTRL-Z (Windows) or OPTION-CMD-Z (Macintosh).

If you choose the Undo command and suddenly decide you want to reverse the Undo command, you can choose the Redo command if you click the Edit menu and then click Redo, or press ALT-CTRL-Z (Windows) or OPTION-CMD-Z (Macintosh).

REMEMBER *The Undo command is handy when you want to test a new tool or technique on an image. If it really screws up your image, just choose the Undo command to return your image back to its previous condition before you messed it up.*

Method 2: Reverse Multiple Commands

One problem with the Undo command is that it can only reverse the last command you chose. If you made several changes to a picture and want to reverse the last two or more commands you chose, you'll have to use the Step Backward command instead.

Each time you choose the Step Backward command, it reverses the previous command. So if you drew a line across your picture and then deleted part of the picture afterwards, the Step Backward command would first reverse the command that deleted part of your picture. The second time, the Step Backward would reverse the command that drew the line across your picture. If you keep choosing the Step Backward command, you can reverse everything you did to a picture up to the point where you first loaded it into Photoshop Elements, as shown in Figure 7.1.

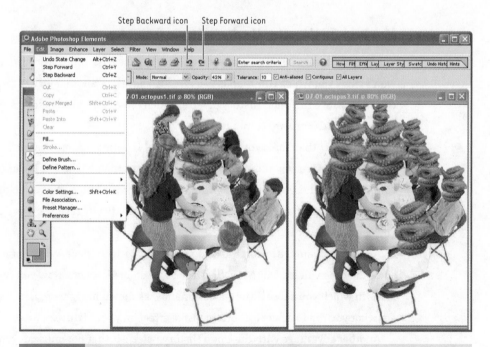

FIGURE 7.1

The Step Forward and Step Backward icons appear on the shortcuts bar (and also on the Edit menu) for easy access with a click of the mouse. The picture on the left shows a family enjoying a Thanksgiving dinner that substitutes turkey with fresh octopus tentacles, because then everyone in the family can have a leg for dinner. The picture on the right shows the octopus latching on to every family member's face like an alien.

To choose the Step Backward command, click the Edit menu and then click Step Backward, press CTRL-Z (Windows) or CMD-Z (Macintosh), or click the Step Backward icon on the shortcuts bar.

If you choose the Step Backward command too many times and suddenly realize that you should have stopped earlier, Photoshop Elements also offers a Step Forward command to repeat your previous commands, one by one. To choose the Step Forward command, click the Edit menu and then click Step Forward, press CTRL-Y (Windows) or CMD-Y (Macintosh), or click the Step Forward icon on the shortcuts bar.

REMEMBER   *You won't be able to choose the Step Forward command if you haven't already chosen the Step Backward command at least once.*

Method 3: Use the Undo History Palette

The Step Backward command offers a quick way to reverse multiple commands, but it won't show you which commands you already chose. For another way to take back any commands, use the Undo History palette, which offers several advantages over the Step Backward/Forward commands.

First, rather than force you to reverse multiple commands one at a time, the Undo History palette lets you jump back to a previous command, whether it was the last command you chose or something you did five commands ago. When you jump back to a previous command, Photoshop Elements automatically reverses every command you chose afterwards.

A second advantage is that the Undo History palette lists every command you chose since the time you loaded the picture into Photoshop Elements. Now you can see the order in which you chose different commands, as shown in Figure 7.2, in case you forgot what you did to achieve a certain visual effect on your picture.

Another advantage with the Undo History palette is that not only can you reverse a previous command, but you can also remove previous commands from the Undo History palette. That way, if you chose certain commands that totally screwed up your picture, you can remove them from the Undo History palette to keep it free of useless commands you'll never want to repeat again.

To use the Undo History list, click the Window menu and then click Undo History, or click the Undo History tab in the Palette Well. The Undo History palette lists all the commands you've chosen. Click the last command that you want to keep. Photoshop Elements dims every command under the one you chose to show you that it has reversed those commands.

If you see a command in the Undo History palette that you don't want to keep on the list, move the mouse pointer over that command and drag it to the Trash icon in the bottom-right corner of the Undo History palette. When you delete a command from the Undo History palette, Photoshop Elements deletes your chosen command and any commands you chose afterwards.

 REMEMBER *Dragging one or more commands from the Undo History palette to the Trash icon is the best way to get rid of those commands you're certain you won't ever want to redo again. In case there's a chance you may want to redo a particular command, it's best not to drag it to the Trash icon because you'll never be able to retrieve it again.*

Palette Well   Trash icon

FIGURE 7.2

The Undo History palette shows you the name of each command you chose. This picture shows a man giving beer to a monkey, which only goes to prove that if you're drunk and horny enough, any mammal can start to look attractive.

In case you're wondering, the Undo History list can display up to 20 of your previous commands. You can always alter this number if you click the Edit menu, click Preferences, and then click General, or just press CTRL-K (Windows) or CMD-K (Macintosh) to display the Preferences dialog box, as shown in Figure 7.3. Then click in the History States text box, type a new number between 1 and 1000, and click OK.

How to Use Layers

The Undo and Step Backward commands and the Undo History palette can help you recover from your mistakes, but digital editing would still be clumsy if you had to keep altering your image and then reversing your last commands when things didn't work out right. So for another way to protect your picture from mistakes, Photoshop Elements offers something magical called *layers*.

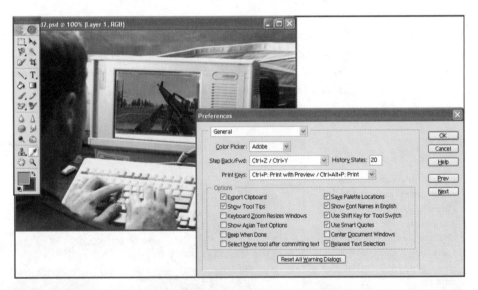

FIGURE 7.3

The Preferences dialog box lets you increase or decrease the number of history states the Undo History list can remember and display. This picture shows a soldier using a laptop computer to play the U.S. Army's free video game called "America's Army," advertising their new slogan, "An Army of One." They had to call it "An Army of One" because that's usually the number of people who prefer enlisting in the Army compared to the Air Force, Navy, or the Marines. (Photo courtesy of the U.S. Department of Defense.)

The idea behind layers is simple. A layer acts like a transparent sheet that protects a picture like a wall of bullet-proof glass protects a cashier in a gas station. If you draw a mustache on bullet-proof glass in just the right position, it can look like you drew a mustache directly on the cashier instead. Similarly, when you paste an image on a layer and move it to the right position, it can look like the pasted image is actually part of the original picture.

By physically storing parts of a picture on different layers, Photoshop Elements can make sure that any changes you make on an image stored on one layer won't accidentally affect any images stored on any other layers.

Because layers physically isolate images from one another, you no longer need to select images carefully when you want to modify them. Without layers, you might have to painstakingly select an image with the Lasso tool to avoid including the background, but with layers, the background rests on one layer and the image you want to select rests on a separate layer, as shown in Figure 7.4. To choose the image, you can just select it much faster using the Rectangular or Elliptical Marquee tool instead.

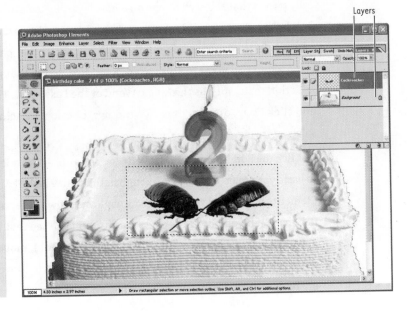

FIGURE 7.4

Isolating images on separate layers makes it easy to select those images later. Although it appears that the Rectangular Marquee tool has selected part of the birthday cake, the candle, and the two cockroaches feasting on the sugar frosting, it has actually only selected the two cockroaches because the cake appears on a separate layer from the cockroaches.

Putting an Image on a Layer

The first time you load a digital picture in Photoshop Elements, that picture just consists of a single layer of your entire image, which Photoshop Elements names *Background*. If you want to edit the entire image, such as changing the lighting or contrast, you could directly modify your original image (and risk screwing it up). As a safer alternative, you can store your entire image on a separate layer and edit the copy of your image on the layer. Now if you screw up, just delete the layer and your original image remains untouched.

To copy an entire image onto its own layer, click the Window menu and click Layers to display the Layers palette. Then double-click the Background layer. When the New Layer dialog box appears, type a name and click OK.

Rather than store an entire copy of your image on a layer, you may just want to store part of an image on a separate layer, which you can do using the ordinary Copy and Paste commands.

Every time you select, copy, and paste an image, Photoshop Elements automatically pastes that selected image on a new layer. By isolating pasted images on their own layers, Photoshop Elements makes it easy to edit part of a picture, such as a person's face, without accidentally modifying any other part of the picture.

So when you want to edit part of a picture, select that part using any of the selection tools, such as the Magic Wand or the Lasso tool. Then click the Edit menu and click Copy, or press CTRL-C (Windows) or CMD-C (Macintosh), to copy your selected image.

Click the Edit menu and click Paste, or press CTRL-V (Windows) or CMD-V (Macintosh), to paste your selected image. Although nothing may look like it has changed, Photoshop Elements has pasted your selected image on its own layer directly on top of the original picture. If you click the Layers palette, you can see that your newly pasted image appears on a separate layer. If you click the Move tool, move the mouse pointer over the newly pasted image, and drag the pasted image to move it, you can see the original image underneath.

Naming a Layer

Every time you paste an image in a picture, Photoshop Elements stores it on a newly created layer with a boring name such as Layer 2 or Layer 5. Generally, you should give your layers descriptive names so you'll know what type of image appears on each layer, such as Sky, Hillside, or Dead Body on the Sidewalk.

To change the name of a layer, click the Window menu and click Layers, or click the Layers tab in the Palette Well. The Layers palette appears.

Double-click the layer you want to rename, and when a pop-up menu appears, click Rename Layer.

A Layers Properties dialog box appears. Click in the Name text box, type a descriptive name for your layer, and then click OK. Your new name for your layer now appears in the Layers Palette.

Switching to Another Layer

At any given time, you can only modify anything that appears on one layer. So if you want to work on an image trapped on a different layer, you'll have to switch to that layer.

To switch to another layer, click the Window menu and click Layers, or click the Layers tab in the Palette Well. The Layers palette appears. Click the layer that contains the images you want to modify. Photoshop Elements highlights your chosen layer.

 REMEMBER *Only one layer can be chosen at a time. You can only select or modify images that appear on the currently chosen layer.*

Rearranging Layers

Besides showing all the layers that make up a picture, the Layers palette also shows you the stacking order of all the layers. The layer at the top of the Layers palette is the top layer, and the layer at the bottom of the Layers palette is the bottom layer. Any images stored on the top layer will be visible but may cover up images stored on any layers underneath.

If you rearrange the stacking order of different layers, you can cause images from one layer to overlap images stored on any layers underneath. To move a layer, click the Window menu and click Layers, or click the Layers tab in the Palette Well. The Layers palette appears.

Move the mouse over the layer you want to move and drag the mouse up or down. Photoshop Elements displays a dotted outline of your chosen layer as you drag the mouse up or down. When the layer appears above or below another layer, let go of the mouse button.

REMEMBER *When rearranging layers, you can create different visual effects by overlapping images over one another.*

Hiding a Layer

Sometimes you may want to know what your picture might look like if you deleted certain images. Rather than delete these images and then deciding that you want to keep them after all, you can just temporarily hide the layers that contain those images.

When you hide a layer, Photoshop Elements temporarily removes all images stored on that layer from view, as shown in Figure 7.5. When you make the layer visible again, all images stored on that layer also magically appear again.

To hide a layer, click the Window menu and click Layers, or click the Layers tab in the Palette Well. The Layers palette appears.

Click in the Layers visibility check box to remove the eye icon. When the eye icon is not visible, the layer is not visible.

To make a layer visible again, click the Layers visibility check box again so the eye icon appears.

Copying a Layer

If you want to edit an image stored on a layer, play it safe and make another copy of that layer. Making copies of layers is easy; wrecking your image beyond repair is hard.

To copy a layer, click the Window menu and click Layers to display the Layers palette. Right-click (Windows) or CTRL-click (Macintosh) the layer you want to copy, and when a pop-up menu appears, click Duplicate Layer. The Duplicate Layer dialog box appears. Type a name for the copy of your layer and then click OK.

REMEMBER *For a quick way to copy a layer, drag the layer you want to copy to the Create a New Layer icon at the bottom of the Layers palette.*

Deleting a Layer

Sometimes you may indeed want to delete a layer when you don't need the images on that layer at all. To delete a layer, click the Window menu and click Layers, or click the Layers tab in the Palette Well. The Layers palette appears.

Move the mouse pointer over the layer you want to delete and then drag the mouse over the Trash icon near the bottom-right corner of the Layers palette.

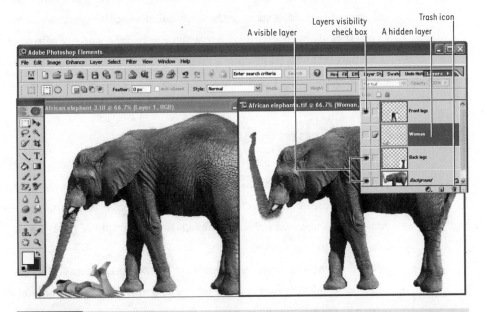

FIGURE 7.5

When the eye icon appears in the Layers visibility check box, you can see the images stored on that layer. When the Layers visibility check box is empty, you won't see any images stored on that layer. The picture on the left shows an elephant standing over a woman in a bathing suit. The picture on the right shows that same elephant after it snorted a pile of powdered Viagra that it mistook for cocaine. Note that in the second picture, the layer containing the woman in the bathing suit is invisible because its Layers visibility check box is empty.

You can also right-click (Windows) or CTRL-click (Macintosh) the layer you want to delete and then click Delete Layer. A dialog box appears and asks if you really want to delete the layer. Click Yes.

REMEMBER *If you suddenly realize you deleted a layer by mistake, you can always choose the Undo command or use the Undo History palette to bring the layer back again.*

Flattening Layers

Although it's possible to create an image with a hundred different layers (depending on the amount of your computer's memory), layers gobble up both memory and disk space. So when you're absolutely certain you're done editing your image, you should "flatten" all your layers, which condenses all your layers into a single layer. This will save memory and disk space, although it will make editing the picture more difficult, so you should only flatten an image when you're done working with it for good.

To flatten the layers in a picture, click the Layer menu and click Flatten Image. Photoshop Elements smashes all your layers into a single layer called *Background*.

Where to Go from Here

Once you understand some of the ways that Photoshop Elements can protect your pictures from accidental and irreversible mistakes, you can freely experiment with the various commands and tools Photoshop Elements offers. Now you won't feel like poor Robert Capa who risked his life to take photographs of the D-Day invasion that somebody else lost forever.

Experiment with every command that Photoshop Elements offers just to see what happens. At the very worse, you'll just be able to reverse that command with the Undo or Step Backward command. At best, you might find some unique command that achieves a certain effect you might never have known you could do before you started experimenting with Photoshop Elements on your own.

So don't be afraid to experiment and make mistakes because that's the only way you can truly learn. (You can bet that the *LIFE* magazine darkroom technician who ruined Robert Capa's irreplaceable photographs never turned up the temperature on the drying cabinets too high again.)

The more you learn about the various commands hidden in Photoshop Elements, the more you'll be able to modify your pictures exactly the way you want.

LESSON 8

What You'll Learn in This Lesson

- How to trim the best part of a picture with the Crop tool

- How to change the size of a picture

- How to use adjustment layers

- How to selectively lighten or darken an image

Fixing Flawed Pictures

(or How to Modify a Picture Without Poisoning Yourself in a Darkroom in the Process)

PERHAPS ONE OF THE STRANGEST DEBATES CURRENTLY RAGING among animal rights activists and sports fishermen is the controversy on whether fish can feel pain. According to a recent study by Edinburgh University and the Roslin Institute, fish do indeed have nervous system receptors, or "polymodal nociceptors," in their heads that respond to damaging stimuli. To test their theory, researchers allowed bees to sting the lips of a trout and recorded how the trout reacted when stung each time. Independent researchers reportedly took the study one step further and poured acid on the trout lips, dipped the trout into molten lead, and smashed the trout face first into the whirling blades of a chainsaw. Each time, these researchers claimed, the trout did indeed exhibit behavior that could possibly be associated as "pain."

The National Angling Alliance (NAA), which represents one million anglers in the United Kingdom, described the conclusions of Edinburgh University and the Roslin Institute as "surprising." An NAA spokesman said, "These findings are in direct contrast to the recent work of Professor James D. Rose of the University of Wyoming, who stated in the *Reviews of Fisheries Science* that fish do not possess the necessary and specific regions of the brain—the neocortex—to enable them to feel pain or, indeed, fear." An unofficial spokesman for the NAA echoed these remarks and said, "How can jabbing a sharp metal hook through your body possibly cause any discomfort? In fact, both of my teenage boys have metal rings through their nose, lips, and cheeks, so not only does that conclusively prove that it's possible not to have pain with a piece of metal through your face, but also that it's also possible not to have any brains when voluntarily shoving a metal hook through your flesh as well."

Until fish can make an evolutionary leap to develop a voice box so they can scream out in agony every time a fish hook slices through their skin, the debate on whether fish can feel pain will likely remain unresolved. However, the debate on whether photography can be a pain or not can soon be settled with the advent of digital photography and a copy of Photoshop Elements.

In the old days of film photography, you had to take your pictures, send your film out for developing, and then wait until you got your pictures back to see whether you captured halfway decent shots or just an expensive series of mistakes—such as your thumbprint or lens cap covering up the lens. The long wait combined with often less than gratifying results made photography a pain for most people.

Although even professional photographers wind up taking rolls of boring pictures that nobody cares about, they also know that they can often salvage a less-than-perfect photograph by touching it up in the darkroom. This can turn a mediocre picture into a good picture, and a good picture into a spectacular one.

Of course, few amateurs own their own darkrooms, but with digital photography, they don't need one. Rather than go through the hassle and expense of setting up a darkroom, digital photographers can just use Photoshop Elements to touch up their pictures without the risk of spilling sodium sulfite into their eyes or inhaling pyrogallic acid fumes into their lungs. Now if they want to poison themselves while developing and touching up their pictures, they can just smoke a cigarette and drink a beer in front of their computer instead.

Trim a Picture

Sometimes you'll capture a great picture but find that you captured too much of the background. So rather than force yourself to stare at an almost-perfect picture, you can just trim away the excess details and essentially recapture the perfect image you really wanted.

To help you trim away excess detail without using scissors or razor blades, Photoshop Elements offers the Crop tool, which lets you tell Photoshop Elements which rectangular part of your picture you want to keep.

To use this tool, click the Crop tool in the Toolbox and then drag the mouse over the part of the image you want to keep. Photoshop Elements draws a marquee around the cropped area of the image and darkens the surrounding area that will be deleted, as shown in Figure 8.1.

Crop tool   Crop area

FIGURE 8.1

You can crop away the extra portion of a picture and just focus on the part you really want to keep. Here, a young child carries a small pumpkin to its doom, where it will be gutted, carved, and illuminated with a toothy grin as a signal to neighborhood children that this particular house has candy. Halloween enthusiasts everywhere have insisted that pumpkins do not feel pain despite the protests of vegetable rights activists who insist that pumpkins do indeed feel pain when sliced apart with a large carving knife.

You can resize the cropped area if you move the mouse pointer over one of the edges of the marquee, wait until the mouse pointer turns into a double-pointing arrow, and then drag the mouse. You can also rotate the cropped area if you move the mouse pointer anywhere outside of the cropped area (so that the mouse pointer turns into a curved double-pointing arrow) and then drag the mouse to rotate the cropped area.

REMEMBER *Even if you rotate a cropped area, Photoshop Elements displays that area tilted to one side in an ordinary window with the edges parallel to the screen edges.*

If you're not happy with the position of the cropped area, move the mouse pointer inside the cropped area to turn the mouse pointer into a black arrow. Then drag the mouse to move the marquee over a different part of your picture.

When you're happy with the size and position of the cropped area, press ENTER (Windows) or RETURN (Macintosh). Photoshop Elements displays your cropped area in a separate window.

Change the Size of a Picture

Sometimes you may capture a perfect picture but it's either too small or too large. For example, a typical 2.0 megapixel digital camera captures images that are 1600 pixels high and 1200 pixels wide. If you send an e-mail with a picture that size, it may appear too large for someone else to see within their e-mail program. Until you get more computer-literate friends who know how to save and display e-mailed images, you may need to reduce the size of your pictures so less knowledgeable computer users can view them within their e-mail programs without having to do anything extra.

Other times, you might have the opposite problem and have a small picture that you'd like to enlarge to use in a flyer or poster. Regardless of whether you need to expand or shrink a picture, you can do so in Photoshop Elements.

Change the Image Size

To enlarge or shrink an image, you can specify the new height and width in pixels, as a percentage of the current image, by resolution, or by unit measurements such as inches or centimeters.

CAUTION *The more you enlarge an image, the blurrier and less detailed that image appears, as shown in Figure 8.2.*

To change the size of an image, load the picture into Photoshop Elements and click the Image menu. From there, click Resize and then click Image Size. The Image Size dialog box appears, as shown in Figure 8.3.

Click one of the text boxes (Width, Height, or Resolution) and type a new value. If you want to change the measurement units, click the measurement unit list box and choose a different unit of measurement, such as pixels or inches.

When you change one of the dimensions of your picture (such as the height, width, or resolution), Photoshop Elements adjusts the other dimensions automatically. If you don't want Photoshop Elements to do this, clear the Constrain Proportions check box by clicking it until the check mark disappears. Click OK when you're done. Photoshop Elements shows your picture at its new size.

FIGURE 8.2

When you enlarge an image, the image gets grainier, such as this picture of what former FBI director J. Edgar Hoover looked like when he was wearing a woman's dress.

(Photo courtesy of the Federal Bureau of Investigation.)

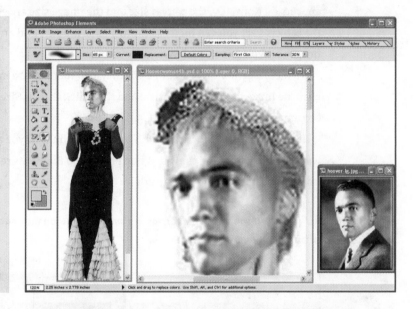

FIGURE 8.3

The Image Size dialog box lets you define how to resize your picture. This picture shows President Bush pardoning the White House turkey right before Thanksgiving. Immediately after this occurred, hundreds of death row inmates in Texas prisons suddenly requested to change their nationality from American to poultry.

(Photo courtesy of the White House.)

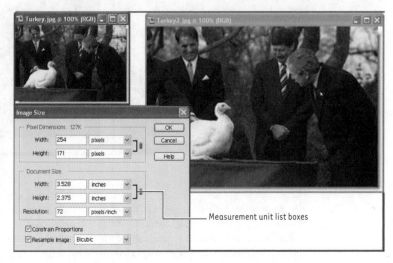

Measurement unit list boxes

Change the Canvas Size

Normally, every picture fills an entire window with no room around the edges. If you want to add text or additional images around the edge of a picture, you can't until you increase the size of the canvas first.

Canvas is just a fancy term that describes the size of the window your picture appears in. Normally, the canvas size and the image size are equal. But if you increase the canvas size, you can increase the available area around an image for adding new images or typing text, as shown in Figure 8.4.

To increase the canvas size of a picture, load that picture into Photoshop Elements, click the Image menu, click Resize, and then click Canvas Size. The Canvas Size dialog box appears, as shown in Figure 8.5.

If you click the Height and Width text boxes, you can type a specific size for the width and height of the canvas. When Photoshop Elements resizes the canvas, your image appears centered in the middle.

REMEMBER *If you shrink the canvas to a smaller size than the image, Photoshop Elements cuts off part of the image from view.*

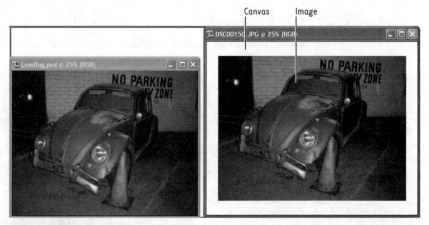

FIGURE 8.4

The canvas defines the area you can edit. This picture shows what happens to washed-up celebrities (in this case, Herbie the Love Bug) after years of drug and alcohol abuse has taken its toll. The alcohol industry would later dispute this photograph and claim that anyone addicted to alcohol can't feel pain because they're usually too busy throwing up and passing out.

For another way to increase the canvas size, click the Relative check box. Photoshop Elements displays zeroes in both the Width and Height text boxes. Click either the Width or Height text box and type a number. If you type **5** in the Width text box and you've defined your measurement units in inches, you increase the width of your canvas by 5 inches.

Every time you increase the size of the canvas, Photoshop Elements centers your image within the new canvas size. If you don't want to increase the canvas size on one or more edges, you can anchor those edges down. For example, if you anchor the left side of a picture, Photoshop Elements only increases the canvas on the top, bottom, and right sides of that picture. If you anchor the upper-left corner, Photoshop Elements only increases the canvas on the bottom and right sides.

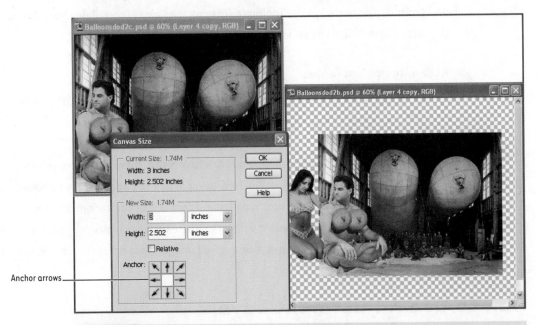

Anchor arrows

The Canvas Size dialog box lets you resize the canvas of any picture. Here we see a team of engineers posing before dual inflatable breast implants which have been surgically implanted in the man to the left. The picture on the right, showing the expanded canvas size, includes a woman rubbing the man's back after having been attracted by the man's breast implants, proving that women can often be just as shallow as men when it comes to treating other human beings solely as objects for their own sexual or financial gratification.

To anchor an edge or corner, click the anchor arrow that points to the edge or corner you want to anchor. The anchor arrows now show you which edges will expand when you increase the width or height of the canvas. When you've defined the height and width of your canvas, click OK.

Choose a Canvas Color

When you increase the canvas size, your image appears with extra space around one or more edges. The current background color displayed in the Toolbox determines the color of this extra space. If the current background color is green, for example, increasing the canvas size displays a green border around your image. Before you increase the canvas size, you may want to select a different color background by clicking on the background color button in the Toolbox to display the Color Picker dialog box. When the Color Picker dialog box appears, select a color and then click OK.

Make a Transparent Canvas

In case you don't want the background color to appear when you increase the canvas size, you can make the background appear transparent instead if you convert the original image to a layer.

To do this, click the Window menu and click Layers to display the Layers palette. Double-click the Background layer. The New Layer dialog box appears. Type a name for your layer and then click OK. Photoshop Elements converts your background image to a layer with the name your chose. Now if you increase the canvas size for your image, the additional canvas space around your original image appears transparent, as shown in Figure 8.6.

How to Use Adjustment Layers

Normally, when you change a picture's contrast, brightness, lighting, and so on, you physically change that image. So what happens if you make several changes, save your picture, and then open it several days or weeks later, only to find that you don't like some of the changes you made? If this happens, you'll just have to try to reverse your changes as best you can because the normal Undo and Step Backwards commands won't help you after you've saved and reopened the file.

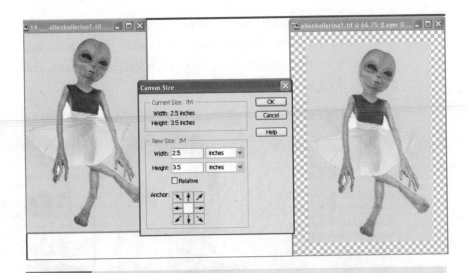

When you increase the canvas size after converting a background image into a layer, Photoshop Elements displays the increased canvas size as a transparent area. This picture shows a transvestite space alien in a ballerina outfit, proving once and for all that the human race isn't the only species that harbors a few individuals who wildly deviate from the norm.

Of course, you can prevent this headache ahead of time if you just use adjustment layers. Like ordinary layers (see Lesson 7), adjustment layers don't physically change the picture. Instead, an adjustment layer only changes an imaginary transparent sheet that lies on top of your picture. Rather than physically change the pixels in your original picture, you just modify the adjustment layer, which gives the illusion that you actually modified the original picture underneath. Now if you suddenly realize you don't like the changes you've made to your picture, you can just delete or modify the adjustment layer, leaving the original picture untouched.

Create an Adjustment Layer

When you create an adjustment layer, you have to choose the type of adjustment you want to make to your picture. Three common types of adjustments include changing the levels, brightness/contrast, or hue/saturation. If you want to change both the brightness/contrast and the hue/saturation, you can just create a second adjustment layer.

To create an adjustment layer, load your picture into Photoshop Elements, click the Layer menu, and then click New Adjustment Layer. A pop-up menu appears. Click Levels, Brightness/Contrast, or Hue/Saturation and the New Layer dialog box appears, as shown in Figure 8.7.

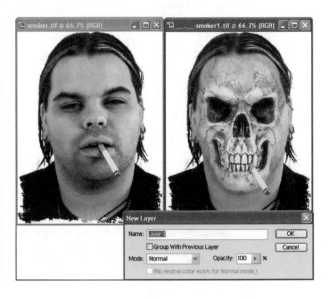

FIGURE 8.7

The New Layer dialog box lets you choose a name, mode, and opacity for your adjustment layer. Here we see a time-lapse image showing what a teenager looked like on the first day he started smoking and another picture showing what he's going to look like on the last day he stops smoking. In the early days of magazine advertising, the tobacco industry actually claimed that smoking relieved pain by soothing a person's digestive system.

REMEMBER *Besides the Levels, Brightness/Contrast, and Hue/Saturation options, Photoshop Elements also offers several other types of adjustment layers, such as Posterize and Invert, which are used to create special visual effects.*

Click the Name text box and type a name for your adjustment layer. To help you identify what different adjustment layers are modifying, Photoshop Elements gives your adjustment layer a generic, descriptive name, such as Brightness/Contrast 1 or Hue/Saturation 3. You may want to give your adjustment layers more distinct names that still help you identify what each adjustment layer modifies.

If you click the Mode list box, you can further modify the way your adjustment layer alters your picture. If you click the Opacity list box, you can change the opacity of your picture. A lower opacity value, such as 25%, makes the adjustment layer more transparent and alters the original picture much less.

Click OK. Another dialog box appears. If you chose to create a Levels adjustment layer, the Levels dialog box appears. If you created a Brightness/Contrast adjustment layer, the Brightness/Contrast dialog box appears. Make any changes needed in this dialog box and click OK. Your adjustment layer then modifies your picture appropriately.

If you want to see what your original picture looks like without the changes you made on the adjustment layer, click the Window menu and click Layers to view the Layers palette. Click the eye icon (the Layers Visibility check box) that appears to the left of your newly created adjustment layer to temporarily hide this layer. Photoshop Elements shows you what your picture looks like without the changes you made in the adjustment layer. Click the Layers Visibility check box again to make your adjustment layer visible once more.

Change an Adjustment Layer

If you create a Hue/Saturation adjustment layer and decide that you really want to adjust the brightness/contrast instead, you could erase your Hue/Saturation adjustment layer and then create a new Brightness/Contrast adjustment layer. Of course, this would be clumsy. Therefore, Photoshop Elements gives you the option to change an existing adjustment layer.

To change an existing adjustment layer, click the Window menu and click Layers to display the Layers palette. Click the adjustment layer in the Layers palette that you want to change.

Click the Layer menu, click Change Layer Content, and then click the option you want the adjustment layer to modify, such as Brightness/Contrast or Levels. A dialog box appears. Make any changes needed in this dialog box. When you're done, click OK.

Make the Dark Look Lighter and the Light Look Darker

Many flawed pictures suffer from lighting problems—either too much light, which makes the picture look washed out and bland, or too little light, which hides the details of the picture in the shadows. If you need to change the lighting of an entire picture, you can use the Fill Flash or Adjust Backlighting command by clicking the Enhance menu and then clicking Adjust Lighting.

However, you may only want to darken or lighten part of an image rather than the entire image. When you want to selectively darken or lighten parts of an image, you can use the Dodge and Burn tools, which mimic the tools photographers use to modify a photograph by changing the exposure. By holding back light (dodging), photographers can lighten areas, and by increasing the exposure (burning), photographers could darken an area.

Use the Dodge Tool (Let There Be Light)

When you choose the Dodge tool, the mouse pointer turns into a brush that you can drag across your picture to "paint" an area that you want to appear lighter, as shown in Figure 8.8. If you want to customize the way the Dodge tool works, you can click any of the four different list boxes that appear in the options bar after you choose the Dodge tool.

If the brush size is too big or too small, click in the Size list box to display a slider. Drag the slider to increase or decrease the size of the brush. A small brush can help you work with fine detail, whereas a large brush can help you change a broad area of your picture. If you click the Brush Preset list box, you can choose both the brush size and the brush type (round, star-shaped, rectangular, and so on) at the same time.

To modify how much (or how little) the Dodge tool lightens up an image, click the Exposure list box and change the percentage (the range is 1% to 100%). The higher the Exposure percentage, the lighter the Dodge tool makes the image.

REMEMBER *You may want to set the Exposure percentage lower than you want because you can then gradually lighten up the image by repeatedly dragging the Dodge tool over the picture.*

If you want to control the Dodge tool even more, click in the Range list box and choose Midtones, Shadows, or Highlights. Midtones changes the gray areas of an image, Shadows changes the dark areas, and Highlights changes the light areas. No matter which range you choose, the Dodge tool still affects every part of your image; it's just that when you choose a range, you're telling Photoshop Elements, "Go ahead and change anything that I drag the Dodge tool over, but emphasize changing the gray, dark, or light areas of my image, depending on whether I chose Midtones, Shadows, or Highlights for the range."

Brush Presets list box   Size list box   Range list box   Exposure list box   Area lightened up by the Dodge tool

Dodge tool

FIGURE 8.8

The Dodge tool can lighten up the dark parts of a picture, such as this poster protesting the Chinese government's oppression of Falun Gong. In their defense, Chinese officials claim that every time they beat a Falun Gong member over the head with a club, they're simply researching whether Falun Gong members can feel pain just like trout.

To use the Dodge tool, load your picture into Photoshop Elements. If you only want to lighten part of your picture, select that part using one of the selection tools, such as the Magic Wand or the Lasso tool. Once you select part of your image, Photoshop Elements won't let you modify anything outside of your selection.

Click the Dodge tool in the Toolbox and make any changes needed, such as choosing a different brush size or increasing the exposure. Drag the mouse to lighten (or "dodge") an area. If you drag the mouse over an area that you previously lightened, the Dodge tool simply lightens up that part of the image even more.

Use the Burn Tool (Let There Be Dark—or What Poor People See Every Time a Conservative Politician Becomes President)

The Burn tool does the opposite of the Dodge tool by darkening parts of an image, as shown in Figure 8.9. Like the Dodge tool, the Burn tool lets you choose a brush size, brush type, range, and exposure percentage to modify the way it works.

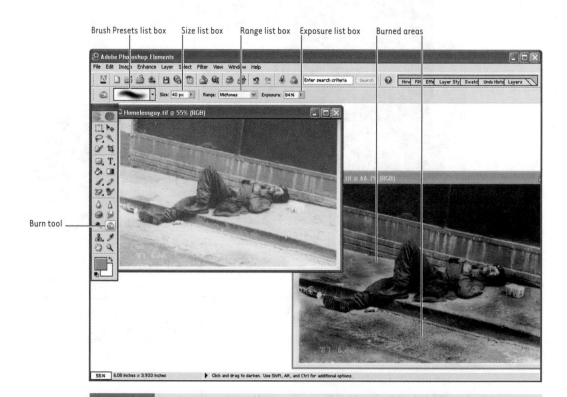

FIGURE 8.9

The Burn tool can darken part of a picture, such as the sidewalk around this homeless man whose presence suggests that maybe this country's welfare system isn't working that well after all. The National Angling Alliance would later claim that homeless people don't feel pain since their bank account lacks the proper receptors to transmit the pain of bankruptcy to their brains. (Photo courtesy of Gracie Vincenza.)

To use the Burn tool, load a picture into Photoshop Elements and click the Burn tool in the Toolbox. Photoshop Elements displays the Brush Presets list box, the Size list box, the Range list box, and the Exposure list box in the options bar. Click any of these list boxes to change the way the Burn tool works. Then drag the mouse across the area you want to darken.

REMEMBER *If you select part of your picture first with a selection tool, such as the Elliptical Marquee tool, you can keep yourself from accidentally darkening anything outside of the area you selected.*

Where to Go from Here

Every picture in the world can be made a little better by touching it up. By adapting darkroom techniques for modifying pictures, Photoshop Elements gives you the power to enhance your digital images without the pain of creating a darkroom and sitting in it for hours at a time to learn photography touch-up techniques. Now if you can't capture a great image right away like the professionals do, you can still fake it by spending a little extra time touching up your images after you've already captured them.

With a little bit of practice, you can turn slightly flawed pictures into works of perfection. Of course, there's a limit to how much touching up can salvage a picture. Just as makeup can't turn a pig into a supermodel (although it's possible to turn supermodels into pigs by overfeeding their inflated egos), Photoshop Elements can't magically convert a lousy picture into a good one.

Then again, sometimes the problem isn't your lack of photography skills but the fact that you're forced to take pictures of really ugly people (otherwise known as your relatives). In case your pictures look great but the subjects in your pictures look like crap, you may want to hurry over to Lesson 11 and find out how to fix common flaws that appear in people's faces, over and over again. Otherwise, skim through Lessons 9 and 10 to learn how to play with different colors in a picture.

LESSON 9

What You'll Learn in This Lesson

- How to turn a color picture into black and white

- How to alter the overall color of a picture

- How to color large areas

Playing with Colors
(or How to Color in a Map Showing the Axis of Evil)

ON JANUARY 29, 2002, PRESIDENT GEORGE W. BUSH warned that "North Korea is a regime arming with missiles and weapons of mass destruction, while starving its citizens. Iran aggressively pursues these weapons and exports terror, while an unelected few repress the Iranian people's hope for freedom. Iraq continues to flaunt its hostility toward America and to support terror. The Iraqi regime has plotted to develop anthrax, and nerve gas, and nuclear weapons for over a decade.... States like these, and their terrorist allies, constitute an axis of evil, arming to threaten the peace of the world."

Fortunately for Iraqis, less than 15 percent of Americans even know where Iraq is on a map. That means if the United States sends oil tankers to Iraq, there's an 85 percent chance the tankers will actually wind up someplace else.

So as a public service to the geographically illiterate that constitute the 11 percent of Americans who can't even find the United States on a map, it's time to learn geography by using the coloring tools Photoshop Elements provides to color in your pictures. With the help of the coloring tools in Photoshop Elements and more exposure to world maps, maybe young Americans will be able to identify at least one of the nations that make up the "axis of evil," even if it means pointing to Iraq on a map as "that pink country next to that blue water over there."

Turn Color into Black and White

The simplest way to play with colors is to remove them altogether by turning a color picture into black and white. Normally, this might seem like a giant step backward, much like former presidential candidate Bob Dole's promise to return the country "back to the past," but unlike Bob Dole's curious remark, there are actually some valid reasons for turning color pictures into black and white.

Sometimes pictures really do look better in black and white than in color. Other times, black and white can give a modern picture a 1950s retro look, when men wore suits to dinner and women slept in separate beds from their husbands. If you're printing a newsletter in black and white, you might also want to convert your pictures to black and white so you can get a more accurate view of how they will look in print. Although black and white might seem like an antiquated concept, such as marital fidelity among congressmen, it can be yet another way to modify your pictures so they look as good as possible.

To turn a color picture into black and white, load the picture into Photoshop Elements. If you just want to turn part of your picture into black and white, select that part using one of the selection tools, such as the Lasso tool. Click the Enhance menu, click Adjust Color, and then click Remove Color. Photoshop Elements turns your color picture into black and white.

Rather than turn a color picture completely black and white, you may want to mix color and black-and-white elements in the same picture. If you turn the background black and white, you can highlight the focus of your picture in color, as shown in Figure 9.1.

To turn your background black and white but leave an object in the foreground in color, select the object you want to remain in color using a selection tool such as the Magic Wand or the Magnetic Lasso tool. Next, click the Edit menu and click Copy. Then click the Edit menu again and click Paste. This copies your selected image on a separate layer.

Click the Window menu and click Layers. The Layers palette appears. Click Background in the Layers palette. Click the Enhance menu, click Adjust Colors, and click Remove Color. Photoshop Elements turns your background black and white while leaving your selected object, on its own layer, in color.

FIGURE 9.1

A full-color picture can appear too cluttered. The same picture, with the background turned black and white, can emphasize the subject in color, such as this street vendor in China, who skins live snakes for food because snake meat has fewer rat hair and insect droppings in it than the average American hot dog.

(Photo courtesy of Richard Hing.)

Tint and Age a Picture

If you want to age a picture so it looks older than it really is, you don't have to wait for the acetate in the photograph to yellow over time. Instead, you can alter the colors in your picture so it looks unnaturally yellow on its own.

To tint a picture to make it look older or faded, you can add or remove a specific color, such as red, green, or blue. To do this, load a picture into Photoshop Elements. If you only want to modify part of your picture, select that part using a selection tool such as the Elliptical Marquee tool or the Magic Wand.

Click the Enhance menu, click Adjust Color, and then click Color Variations. The Color Variations dialog box appears, as shown in Figure 9.2. Click the Midtones, Shadows, or Highlights radio button. (The Midtones option affects the gray areas of your image, the Shadows option affects the darker areas, and the Highlights option affects the lighter areas.)

Drag the Amount slider right or left under the Adjust Color Intensity category. The Color Variations dialog box displays different views of your picture, such as Increase Green and Decrease Blue. Simply click the view you like best.

The Color Variations dialog box shows you the before and after appearance of your picture. You can click additional views to make additional changes to your picture. If you make a change that you don't like, just click the Undo button. If you don't like any changes you made, you can reverse everything by clicking the Reset Image button.

When you're happy with the way your picture looks, click OK and admire the fact that you can see someone's face age right before your eyes without watching them chain-smoke three packs of cigarettes a day to do it.

Play with the Color Cast

Sometimes a picture may appear with an unnatural greenish or purplish tint that wrecks an otherwise decent picture. When a picture contains an unwanted color, you can often remove it by using the Color Cast command.

The Color Cast command works by taking away colors from a picture. Because Photoshop Elements doesn't know what color to take away, you have to click an area that should really be gray, black, or white but currently appears tinted with an unwanted color instead.

FIGURE 9.2

The Color Variations dialog box shows how a picture changes when you increase or decrease certain colors. Here we see drug agents burning confiscated marijuana in Colombia, one of the few countries American teenagers actually know about because it supplies most of their illegal drugs.

(Photo courtesy of the Central Intelligence Agency.)

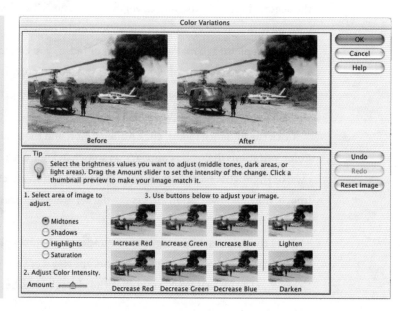

For example, when you click the part of your picture that should be gray, Photoshop Elements removes the color tint or cast from that area so that it appears gray. (If you clicked an area that should be black or white, Photoshop Elements removes the color tint or cast to make that area appear black or white.)

Once Photoshop Elements removes the unwanted color tint from an area, it then removes that color tint from the rest of the picture by the same amount. Unfortunately, this often colors your picture with an even more unnatural tint, but sometimes it actually improves the overall appearance.

To change the color cast of a picture, load that picture into Photoshop Elements, click the Enhance menu, click Adjust Color, and then click Color Cast. The Color Cast Correction dialog box appears and turns the mouse pointer into an eyedropper icon.

Click an area in your picture that should be gray, black, or white. Photoshop Elements immediately alters the color cast of your entire picture, as shown in Figure 9.3. If you don't like the way Photoshop Elements has changed your picture, click the Reset button and try again, or you can click another part of your picture that should be gray, black, or white. When you're finally happy with the way Photoshop Elements has altered the colors in your picture, click OK.

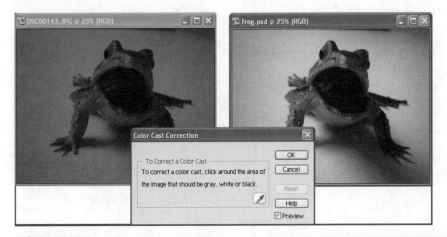

FIGURE 9.3

Before the Color Cast command, a picture can have a strange, unnatural tint. After the Color Cast command removes the tint, the picture looks normal, such as this frog begging for its life before a French chef rips off its back legs and turns them into a fine example of French cuisine.

Color Large Areas

Rather than change the existing colors in a picture, you might want to add new colors to your pictures. The simplest way to color a picture involves the Fill Bucket tool, which acts like a bucket of paint that spills color over your picture. Unlike real paint that indiscriminately drips everywhere, the Fill Bucket tool only fills a specific area with color. So whenever you need to color a large area quickly, use the Fill Bucket tool.

Step 1: Choose the Fill Bucket Tool

To choose the Fill Bucket tool, click it in the Toolbox. Photoshop Elements immediately turns the mouse pointer into a tilted paint bucket icon with paint spilling out, as shown in Figure 9.4. The tip of the spilled paint icon represents the Fill Bucket pointer. When you click the mouse, Photoshop Elements dumps the paint wherever the Fill Bucket pointer appears, based on the Tolerance level you set for the Fill Bucket tool.

FIGURE 9.4

The Fill Bucket tool looks like a can of paint spilling out its contents. Here we see the Fill Bucket tool over a map of France, a country where 24 percent of its young people don't even know their own nation possesses nuclear weapons because French commandos have yet to use nuclear bombs against Greenpeace protesters.

(Map courtesy of the Central Intelligence Agency.)

Fill Bucket tool   Tip of the Fill Bucket mouse pointer

Step 2: Choose a Color

After you choose the Fill Bucket tool, you need to choose a color for your paint. In the name of choice and confusion, Photoshop Elements gives you three different ways to change colors:

- Use the Color Picker dialog box
- Use the Swatches palette
- Use the Eyedropper tool

If you're like most people, none of these choices make any sense right now, so here are the pros and cons of using each method.

Choose the Type of Color Picker Dialog Box to Use

Just to expose you to options you probably don't want, Photoshop Elements gives you a choice of displaying two different types of Color Picker dialog boxes. In Windows, the two choices are Windows and Adobe, whereas on the Macintosh, the two choices are Apple and Adobe, as shown in Figure 9.5.

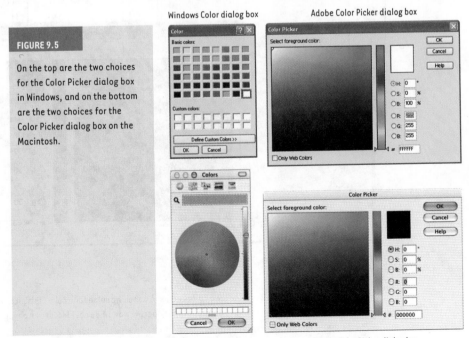

FIGURE 9.5

On the top are the two choices for the Color Picker dialog box in Windows, and on the bottom are the two choices for the Color Picker dialog box on the Macintosh.

Windows Color dialog box

Adobe Color Picker dialog box

Apple Colors dialog box

Adobe Color Picker dialog box

The type of Color Picker dialog box you want to use is purely personal preference. To change the Color Picker dialog box that Photoshop Elements uses, press CTRL-K (Windows) or CMD-K (Macintosh) to display the Preferences dialog box. Click the Color Picker list box and choose Adobe or Windows (or Apple) and then click OK.

Use the Color Picker Dialog Box

The Color Picker dialog box is both a fast and an accurate way to choose a color. You can either click a color or type in the specific value for the color you want. To select a color to use, click the Foreground Color box in the Toolbox. The Color Picker dialog box appears, as shown in Figure 9.6.

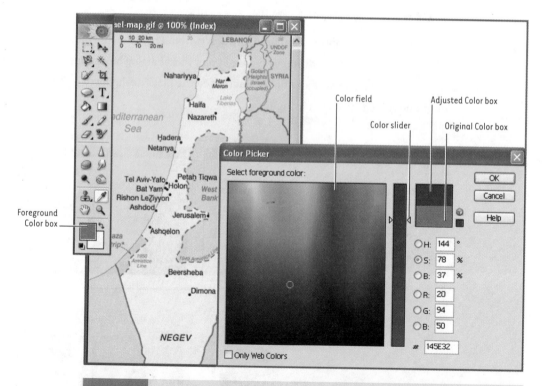

FIGURE 9.6

The Color Picker dialog box lets you click a color or type in a specific value for a color. This picture shows a map of Israel, a country that fewer than 25 percent of young people worldwide could locate on a map.

(Map courtesy of the Central Intelligence Agency.)

REMEMBER *The exact type of Color Picker dialog box that appears depends on which type (Adobe or Windows/Apple) you chose in the Preferences dialog box, as explained in the previous section, "Choose the Type of Color Picker Dialog Box to Use."*

Click the color you want in the Color field. To change the colors displayed in the Color field, drag the Color slider up or down, click in the Color slider, or click one of the radio buttons (H, S, B, R, G, or B).

The Color Picker dialog box displays your currently chosen color (in the Adjusted Color box) along with your previously selected color (in the Original Color box). When you're happy with the color displayed in the Adjusted Color box, click OK. Your chosen color now appears in the Foreground Color box, and you're ready to start painting.

If you have a specific color you want to use and you happen to know the exact RGB (Red, Green, Blue) or HSB (Hue, Saturation, and Brightness) value of that color, you can type the value in the Color Picker dialog box. If you have no idea what the RGB or HSB value of a color might be, you can type different values in the Color Picker dialog box just to see what colors appear.

Use the Swatches Palette

The Swatches palette provides a limited choice of distinct colors to choose from, but it allows you to pick a specific color by name. To choose a color from the Swatches palette, click the Window menu and then click Color Swatches (or click the Swatches tab in the palette well). The Swatches palette appears, as shown in Figure 9.7.

If you click in the Swatches list box, you can choose different palettes that contain different colors. When you hold the mouse pointer over a color, the name of that particular color appears underneath.

Click the color you want to use. The Foreground Color box in the Toolbox displays your chosen color.

Use the Eyedropper Tool

Sometimes you may want to use a color that already appears in your image. In this case, it's easier to tell Photoshop Elements, "See that color there? That's the color I want to use." To use the Eyedropper tool, click it in the Toolbox. The mouse pointer turns into an eyedropper icon, as shown in Figure 9.8.

Move the tip of the eyedropper icon over the color in your image you want to use. To increase the odds you'll choose the color you want, you may want to click the View menu and then click Zoom In.

Click the mouse when the eyedropper icon appears directly over the color you want to use. The Foreground Color box displays your chosen color.

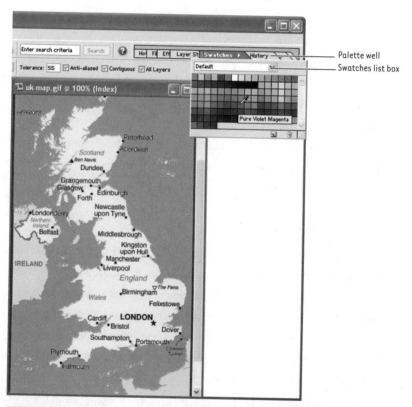

FIGURE 9.7

The Swatches palette lets you choose a color by name. This map shows the United Kingdom, which an astonishing 69 percent of young Americans couldn't find on a map. This makes you wonder whether the same 69 percent of young Americans wouldn't be able to find their heads up their butts if they were detailed on a map, too.
(Map courtesy of the Central Intelligence Agency.)

Step 3: Define the Tolerance

Once you've chosen a color to use, the next step is to define the tolerance for the Fill Bucket tool. The tolerance, which works exactly the same as the Magic Wand tool, defines the area the Fill Bucket tool will cover with paint. A low tolerance tells Photoshop Elements to paint only those pixels that closely match the area you click. A high tolerance tells Photoshop Elements to paint the surrounding pixels that are similar in color. The higher the tolerance, the less picky Photoshop Elements is in painting an area.

Basically, a high tolerance means the Fill Bucket tool generously spills paint all over your picture, including those parts you may not want to paint. A low tolerance means that the Fill Bucket tool confines the paint to a limited area of similar color, which may be too limited. You might need to experiment with different tolerance levels and use the Undo command until you find the right tolerance for your picture.

To define the tolerance, click the Tolerance text box in the options bar, which appears after you click the Fill Bucket tool in the Toolbox. Type a value from 1 to 100.

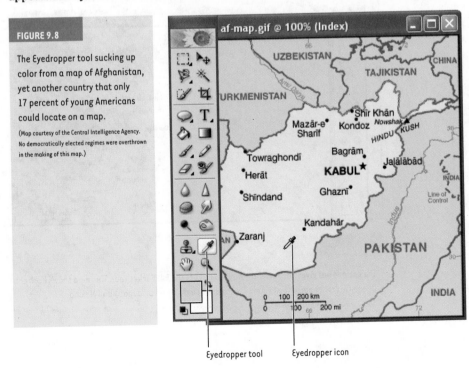

FIGURE 9.8

The Eyedropper tool sucking up color from a map of Afghanistan, yet another country that only 17 percent of young Americans could locate on a map.

(Map courtesy of the Central Intelligence Agency. No democratically elected regimes were overthrown in the making of this map.)

Eyedropper tool   Eyedropper icon

Step 4: Define the Optional Fill Bucket Tool Settings

Once you've defined a color and tolerance level, you're ready to start painting. However, for greater control, you may also want to define the opacity, mode, and fill pattern of the Fill Bucket tool, as shown in Figure 9.9.

The opacity defines how much the paint obscures the picture underneath. A 100% opacity setting completely covers the image underneath, whereas a lower level of opacity, such as 35%, allows you to see the original image underneath the color of your paint.

The Mode list box lets you define different ways for the paint to appear, such as Color Burn or Pin Light. Each mode alters the way the paint appears in slightly different

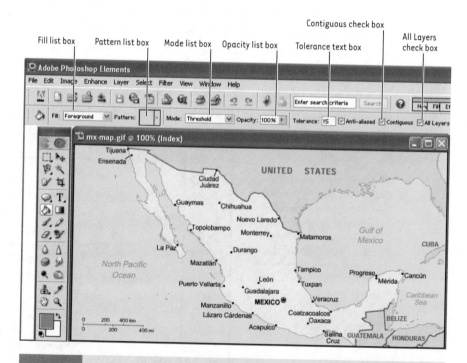

FIGURE 9.9

The options bar gives you different ways to modify the Fill Bucket tool. This map shows both the Pacific Ocean (which 29 percent of young Americans couldn't find on a map) and Mexico.

(Map courtesy of the Central Intelligence Agency, the agency responsible for the 1961 Bay of Pigs fiasco, which most Americans probably know nothing about either.)

ways, so feel free to experiment with each mode until you find the one that creates the effect you want.

The Fill list box gives you two choices: Foreground and Pattern. The Foreground option spills paint in a solid color. The Pattern option displays paint in a pattern, such as bubbles or wood grain, that you can define using the Pattern list box.

Finally, if you only want your paint to fill a contiguous area, make sure the Contiguous check box has a check mark in it. If you clear the Contiguous check box, the Fill Bucket tool not only paints the area where you click but also any other part of your picture (even those parts far away from where you click) where the pixels are similar in color.

Step 5: Protect Your Picture with Layers

In case you don't like the idea of spilling paint directly on your original picture, you can use a layer to protect your picture. That way, any paint you spill with the Fill Bucket tool winds up on your layer and not on your original image. If you suddenly don't like the way the Fill Bucket tool painted your image, you can delete the layer the paint appears on at any time.

To protect a picture with a layer, click the Fill Bucket tool and then click the All Layers check box in the options bar. (If a check mark already appears, don't click the All Layers check box.)

Click the Layer menu, click New, and then click Layer. The Layer dialog box appears. Type a descriptive name for your layer in the Name text box and click OK. Photoshop Elements displays the name of your layer in the title bar.

Although you can't see it, you are now working on your newly created layer instead of the actual picture underneath the layer. Click anywhere in your picture that you want to color with the Fill Bucket tool. Photoshop Elements colors in the area where you click, as shown in Figure 9.10.

Click the Window menu and click Layers. The Layers palette appears. Notice that the paint appears on your layer and not on your original picture. By isolating your paint on a layer, you can delete the paint at any time without messing up your original image.

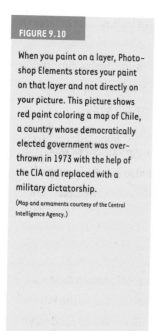

FIGURE 9.10

When you paint on a layer, Photoshop Elements stores your paint on that layer and not directly on your picture. This picture shows red paint coloring a map of Chile, a country whose democratically elected government was overthrown in 1973 with the help of the CIA and replaced with a military dictatorship.

(Map and armaments courtesy of the Central Intelligence Agency.)

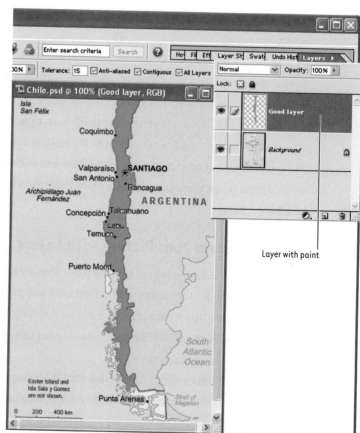

Layer with paint

Where to Go from Here

Now that you know how to add and remove color in a picture, you can start painting your pictures with colors, shades, and tints in a variety of ways. Although color can make a dramatic visual impact, don't overlook the special effect that black and white can give to your pictures, too.

By knowing how to use color, you can fill in a world map to clearly identify every nation that belongs to the Axis of Evil. Considering that nearly every country has engaged in various human rights violations, chemical and biological warfare, and research into weapons of mass destruction to use on helpless civilians, any world map that you color is likely to change from black (evil) and white (good) to multiple shades of pinks, blues, reds, greens, yellows, purples, and oranges that clearly identify the black-and-white nature of the good and evil nations of the world.

Once you've mastered the Fill Bucket tool, the next step is learning to use the Brush tool so you can color smaller areas of your picture with your mouse, which is what you'll learn in Lesson 10.

LESSON 10

What You'll Learn in This Lesson

- How to paint and draw

- How to use the Gradient tool

- How to modify your painting or drawing

Painting and Drawing
(or How to Paint and Draw on a Picture Without Getting Your Butt Caned by the Singapore Police)

IN SEPTEMBER 1993, SINGAPORE AUTHORITIES ACCUSED SEVERAL BOYS, including a 16-year-old Hong Kong resident and an 18-year-old American named Michael Fay, of spray-painting 18 different cars in Singapore. Under Singapore's Vandalism Act of 1966, vandals receive three to eight strokes of a cane for each count of vandalism.

So when the judge ruled that Michael Fay should receive six strokes of the cane, it caused an immediate uproar among American politicians who argued that the punishment was excessive. (Of course, they only argued that Michael Fay's caning sentence was excessive, not the sixteen-year old Hong Kong boy's sentence. Apparently, American politicians felt that only Americans have the right to break another country's laws and escape punishment, just like politicians do all the time with their diplomatic immunity.)

Even then-President Clinton contacted the Singapore government and asked that the sentence be reduced, to which the Singapore government responded by reducing the punishment from six lashes to four, out of respect for the American presidency (which may imply that the Singapore government believes that Bill Clinton deserved the other two lashes just for being stupid).

But imagine how different Michael Fay's fate would have been had he used Photoshop Elements! Armed with a digital camera, Michael Fay could have captured images of his neighbors' cars and then used the paint tools in Photoshop Elements to mark, disfigure, and otherwise deface as many of them as he wished—all without risking the wrath of a single Singapore police officer, who would then be free to enforce Singapore's other laws prohibiting people from spitting gum on the sidewalks and not flushing a toilet in a public restroom instead.

So the next time you want to color a picture with paint but need to be more selective than just spilling paint at random with the Fill Bucket tool (see Lesson 9), you can use the Brush and Pencil tools provided by Photoshop Elements instead.

How to Paint and Draw

When painting or drawing in Photoshop Elements, your mouse pointer acts as your paintbrush or pencil when you drag the mouse across your picture. For greater flexibility (and greater user confusion), Photoshop Elements also gives you several options for modifying your paintbrush or pencil:

- **Color** Determines the color of paint with which your paintbrush or pencil draws.

- **Brush type** Determines how your chosen color appears. Some of the different brush types include round brushes, rectangular brushes, and calligraphy brushes.

- **Brush size** Determines the size of your brush, ranging from small (for painting in fine detail) to large (for coloring a large area quickly).

- **Mode** Determines the way the paint appears. For example, the Hard Light mode creates a sharp, distinct line, whereas the Dissolve mode creates a speckled appearance as if the brush barely had enough paint on it. You may need to experiment with different modes until you find the one you want to use.

- **Opacity** Determines how much the paint covers the image underneath. A 100% opacity setting completely covers an image, whereas a low opacity value allows you to color an image without covering up any details of the image.

REMEMBER *There is no one "best" color, brush type, size, mode, or opacity setting to use. It all depends on your particular image and what type of effect you want to achieve, which means you may have to experiment with different combinations and values until you find what works best for your particular image.*

Once you decide that you need to paint or draw on a picture, you can follow the steps detailed next to choose the tool and settings necessary to add your artistic touch to a picture or to just touch up an existing image so you can paint over any flaws that you don't want anyone else to notice.

Step 1: Choose the Brush or Pencil Tool

The Brush and Pencil tools work in similar ways and appear next to each other in the Toolbox, as shown in Figure 10.1. The main difference is that the Brush tool can mimic brushstrokes that can fade in intensity around the edges, whereas the Pencil tool draws distinct lines that do not fade or dissolve near the edges of the lines you draw.

FIGURE 10.1

The Brush and Pencil tools appear next to each other in the Toolbox, which can be handy when you want to draw a mustache on someone's face, such as this picture of President Bush meeting with President Iliescu of Romania. You can tell these men are important and obviously well qualified to be leaders because both are wearing suits.

(Photo courtesy of the White House.)

To choose either the Brush or Pencil tool, click the appropriate icon in the Toolbox. As soon as you choose the Brush or Pencil tool, the Brush or Pencil Tool options bar appears near the top of the screen.

Step 2: Choose a Color

Painting or drawing would be pointless if you couldn't use colors, so Photoshop Elements provides three different ways to change colors through the Color Picker dialog box, the Swatches palette, or the Eyedropper tool. For more information about using each of these methods for choosing a color, see "Step 2: Choose a Color" under the "Color Large Areas" section in Lesson 9.

Step 3: Choose a Brush Type and Size

After choosing a color, you need to define how your Brush or Pencil tool applies that color to your picture by choosing a brush type. Some brushes are wide, some are narrow, and some appear in bizarre shapes, such as paw prints or smiley faces. To choose a brush type, click the Brush Presets list box, as shown in Figure 10.2. A list of brush types appears.

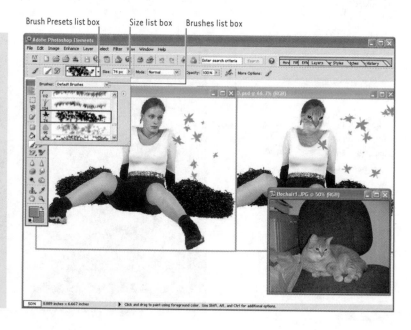

FIGURE 10.2

The Brush Presets list box lets you pick the type of brush you want to use, such as a circle or a leaf shape. The picture on the left shows a bored cheerleader and the picture on the right shows the same bored cheerleader's face after it has been surgically replaced with that of a cat, thus granting her nine lives so she won't die of boredom while watching a game she really doesn't care about.

Click the Brushes list box. A list of other brush type categories appears. Click a brush type category, such as Default Brushes or Pen Pressure. When you choose a different category, the Brush Presets list box displays a different list of brush types.

Double-click the brush type you want to use. The mouse pointer turns into your chosen brush type.

When you choose a brush type, Photoshop Elements automatically chooses a brush size, but you may want to increase or decrease the brush size. Just click the Size list box, and a slider appears underneath. Drag the slider right or left to increase or decrease the brush size. The mouse pointer changes size accordingly.

Step 4: Choose a Mode

The mode determines how the color appears, such as solid, faint, or splattered, as shown in Figure 10.3. To choose a mode, click the Mode list box. A list of different modes appears, including Normal, Darken, and Color Burn. Not all choices may be available for your particular brush type.

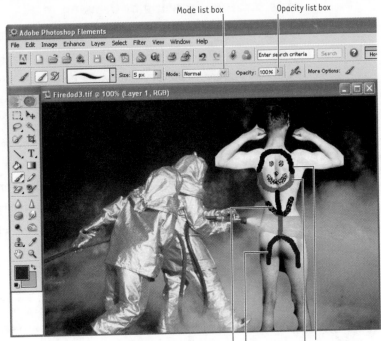

FIGURE 10.3

By changing the mode and opacity, you can alter the way your Brush or Pencil tool paints color on a picture. Here we see a pair of outraged parents attempting to sand-blast a tattoo off their naked teenage boy's back. Like most parents, they believe if children want to express themselves through body mutilation, they should be happy just being circumcised like everyone else.

(Photo courtesy of the U.S. Department of Defense.)

Click a mode (such as Dissolve). When you start painting or drawing, you'll see the results of the mode you chose.

Step 5: Choose the Opacity

The higher the opacity, the more your paint will obscure an image. The lower the opacity, the more faint your paint appears and the more the underlying details of your image will show through the paint. To choose an opacity value, click the Opacity list box. A slider appears underneath.

Drag the slider right or left to increase or decrease the opacity. When you start painting or drawing, you'll see the results of the opacity value you chose. By choosing a low opacity value, you can add color to a picture without making the added color look too obvious. So rather than smear a bright patch of red on a woman's cheek that makes her look like a circus clown, choose a low opacity value to dab color on the picture to subtly enhance the woman's face.

Step 6: Start Painting or Drawing

Once you've chosen different options for the Brush or Pencil tool, such as color and brush size, you can start painting or drawing. Just hold down the mouse button, drag the mouse around, and wherever you move the mouse, that's where Photoshop Elements paints or draws your color. If you want to draw a straight vertical or horizontal line, hold down the SHIFT key and then drag the mouse.

To protect your image, you may want to create and paint on a layer over your original picture. To do this, click the Layer menu, click New, and then click Layer. A Layer dialog box appears. Type a name for your layer and click OK. Now when you use the Brush or Pencil tool, your image appears on the layer instead of the picture itself. By painting or drawing on a separate layer, you can move, resize, and rotate your painting or drawing later, as explained later in the section "How to Modify a Painting or Drawing."

REMEMBER *If you chose the Brush tool, you can click the More Options icon in the options bar to view additional ways to modify the Brush tool, as shown in Figure 10.4.*

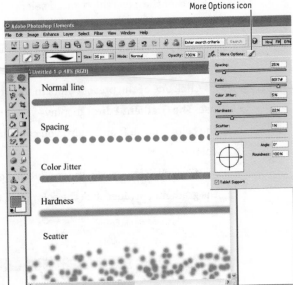

FIGURE 10.4

For people with a lot of free time on their hands, the More Options menu provides still more ways to modify lines you can draw with the Brush tool.

How to Use the Gradient Tool

One colorful way to add color to an image is through the Gradient tool, which blends multiple colors or shades of gray in a pattern across your entire picture or just inside a selected area defined by a selection tool such as the Rectangular Marquee tool, as shown in Figure 10.5.

Step 1: Choose the Gradient Tool

To use the Gradient tool, you need to click its icon in the Toolbox. The Gradient Tool options bar appears near the top of the screen.

Step 2: Choose the Colors for Your Gradient

After you choose the Gradient tool, you need to choose the colors you want to use from the Gradient Picker list box. When you click the Gradient Picker list box, Photoshop Elements displays a list of different gradient colors, such as Red and Green or Violet, Green, Orange. Just click the gradient colors you want to use and skip to Step 3.

Rather than use the limited selection of color gradients offered by Photoshop Elements, you can customize your own colors instead. To do this, click the Gradient Editor in the options bar. The Gradient Editor dialog box appears, as shown in Figure 10.6.

Click one of the preset colors in the Presets box to choose some colors you want to use. The Gradient Editor displays your chosen colors in the gradient bar. If you slide the color stops left and right, you can define where the gradient changes from one color to another.

If you click anywhere underneath the gradient bar, you can add a new color stop to the gradient bar. Just click the color stop, and the Gradient Editor displays a Color list

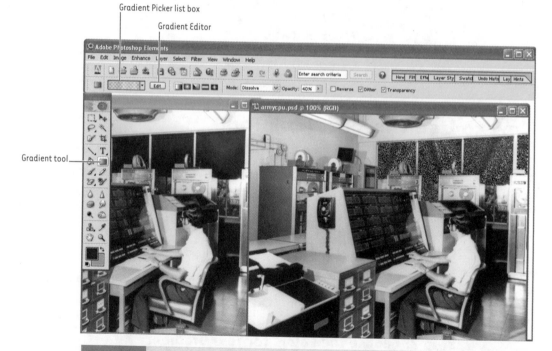

Gradient Picker list box

Gradient Editor

Gradient tool

FIGURE 10.5

The Gradient tool can be used to create a unique visual effect with colors or shades of gray, such as coloring the blacked out windows in this picture showing a BRLESC-II computer, which required the use of vacuum tubes and punch cards just to download a single pornographic image off the Internet. (Photo courtesy of the U.S. Army.)

box. If you click the color currently displayed, you can view the Color Picker dialog box to choose a different color to use.

If you click an opacity stop, the Gradient Editor displays an Opacity list box so you can change the opacity level to a value between 1% and 100%. Then you can drag the opacity stop left or right on the gradient bar to define the opacity of a certain part of your gradient, such as the end of the middle.

Step 3: Choose a Gradient Type

Once you have chosen your gradient colors, you need to choose how you want your gradient to appear, such as a band of different colors (linear gradient) or a circular band of colors (radial gradient), as shown in Figure 10.7. Just click the gradient type you want to use and then skip to Step 5 or choose some additional options in Step 4.

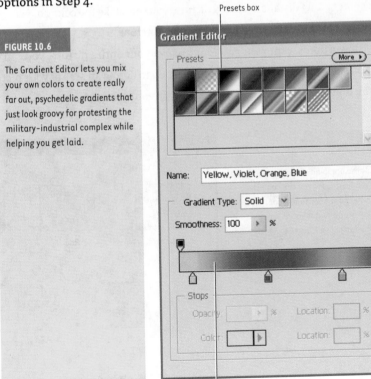

Presets box

FIGURE 10.6

The Gradient Editor lets you mix your own colors to create really far out, psychedelic gradients that just look groovy for protesting the military-industrial complex while helping you get laid.

Gradient Bar

Color Stop

Opacity Stop

Step 4: Choose a Mode and Opacity

For one final way to modify your gradient, you can modify the mode and opacity. The Mode list box gives you different ways to alter your gradient—from Normal to Soft Light or Color Burn. (You'll have to experiment with these options to find the one you like best.)

If you click the Opacity list box, you can define the opacity for your entire gradient. A 100% opacity value makes your gradient completely cover up your picture, whereas a low value simply tints your picture with the gradient.

Step 5: Draw Your Gradient

When you draw a gradient, you need to define the start and end points. The start point is where the mouse pointer appears when you first start to drag the mouse. The end point is where you release the mouse button after dragging the mouse. By dragging the mouse a short or long distance across a picture, you can make the colors of your gradient look smashed together or stretched across your picture.

If you don't want your gradient to cover your entire picture, you can use a selection tool, such as the Rectangular Marquee tool, to define an area of your picture. Now when you draw your gradient, it only appears in your selected area.

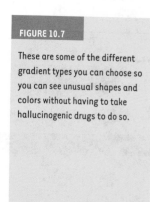

FIGURE 10.7

These are some of the different gradient types you can choose so you can see unusual shapes and colors without having to take hallucinogenic drugs to do so.

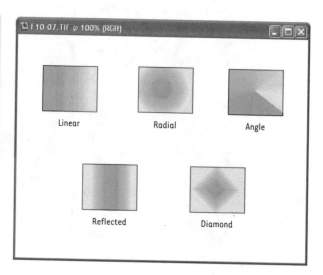

For greater flexibility, you may want to draw your gradient on a separate layer. That way, you can delete, move, or resize it later. To create a layer, click the Layer menu, click New, and click Layer. The Layer dialog box appears. Type a name for your layer and click OK.

How to Modify a Painting or Drawing

One of the biggest advantages of drawing or painting on a layer is that you can modify your painting or drawing later, or even temporarily hide it from view. By storing images on separate layers, you can modify them later without worrying about accidentally modifying any other part of a picture.

To modify an image stored on a layer, click the Window menu and then click Layers. The Layers palette appears. Click the layer that contains the image you want to modify. Click the Move tool in the Toolbox. Photoshop Elements displays handles around the image stored on that layer, as shown in Figure 10.8.

FIGURE 10.8

The Move tool can be used to resize, move, and rotate an image stored on a layer, such as this image of an animal rights activist training lobsters to attack people. These lobsters would later be smuggled into seafood restaurants all over the world to cause havoc when unsuspecting cooks try to pick one out of a lobster tank.

If you have two or more images stored on the same layer, Photoshop Elements displays handles around every image stored on the same layer. To solve this problem, select an image, choose the Cut command from the Edit menu, and then choose the Paste command from the Edit menu to paste that image on a separate layer.

Photoshop Elements won't automatically display handles around any image stored on the Background. To solve this problem, click the Background in the Layers palette, click the Layers menu, and then click Duplicate Layer. When a Duplicate Layer dialog box appears, click OK. Now click on the layer called Background Copy in the Layers palette, click the Move tool, and Photoshop Elements displays handles around the images stored on the Background copy layer.

If you plan to manipulate the images stored on this Background copy layer, you may want to click in the Background's visibility check box in the Layers palette to make the Background invisible.

REMEMBER *Make sure that both the Auto Select Layer and the Show Bounding Box check boxes are selected. If the Auto Select Layer check box is clear, you won't be able to click an image stored on another layer. If the Show Bounding Box check box is clear, you won't be able to see the box and handles around an image in your picture.*

Drag the handles to resize the image. To move the image, move the mouse pointer over it and then drag the mouse. If you move the mouse pointer near one of the handles, the mouse pointer turns into a curved arrow. If you drag the mouse when the curved arrow pointer appears, you can rotate your image.

Where to Go from Here

By painting or drawing on your pictures or applying gradients to them, you can create unique visual effects that turn ordinary-looking pictures into ordinary-looking pictures with special visual effects on them—all without upsetting the authorities like Michael Fay did in Singapore. With a little practice and a lot of time, you can also use the painting tools to touch up your pictures by adding color.

Although the painting, drawing, and gradient tools give you new ways to express yourself with color, you may want to know more about touching up your pictures to make them look more natural. In that case, move along to Lesson 11, where you'll learn how to fix pictures of people's faces without expensive plastic surgery, Botox injections, or skin-stretching facelifts that can make a normal, older person look like a younger freak of nature.

Part

Three

Digital Editing Techniques

LESSON 11

What You'll Learn in This Lesson

- How to change colors with the Red Eye tool

- How to enhance colors with the Sponge tool

- How to use the Sharpen and Blur tools

Fixing Flawed Faces and Other Parts of a Picture
(Without the Scar Tissue)

MANY WOMEN DEVELOP FEELINGS OF INFERIORITY AND LOW SELF-ESTEEM every time they see photographs of glamorous women gracing the covers of their favorite magazines. The problem isn't that the fashion models are young, thin, and gorgeous. The real problem is that even fashion models don't look as good as their own photographs.

Makeup artists and professional photographers spend countless hours trying to create that one perfect shot of a skinny model that will cause girls across America to throw up their dinners on a daily basis. Fashion models can always look their best, especially after someone airbrushes their photographs before releasing them to the general public.

Such airbrushing can remove anything that might detract from a fashion model's nonexistent perfect look, such as slightly blurring portions of the model's face so you can't see her skin pores, whitening or straightening her teeth, or coloring and enlarging her lips to fit some ideal of perfection that fashion models themselves can't even meet in real life.

So the next time you take pictures of people who don't look perfect, you could either try to take pictures of people who look better than your friends or relatives, or just touch up your existing photographs using the magic of Photoshop Elements. Best of all, if you use Photoshop Elements, other people won't have to develop an eating disorder to look good in your pictures either.

REMEMBER *The tools discussed in this lesson work in similar ways:*
1. *Choose the tool you want to use.*
2. *Define the brush size. Small brush sizes are great for altering fine details, whereas large brush sizes are better for making changes quickly.*
3. *Define any additional features of the brush based on the particular tool you chose, such as the color or the physical shape of the brush.*

If you can remember these three basic steps to using each tool, you can focus more of your time being creative with each tool and less time being confused how to use it to do something useful.

How to Change Colors with the Red Eye Tool

The eyes are supposed to be the windows to the soul, which may explain why so many super models have such a vapid stare.

Look at any great photograph of a person, and one of the first parts of the body that catches your attention will be the eyes. (Unless, of course, you're looking at a picture of a scantily clad man or woman, in which case other body parts are likely to take precedence.)

Because the eyes can define the way a person looks in a photograph, you can often improve or change the mood of a photograph just by using the many tools Photoshop Elements provides for coloring a person's eyes.

Fixing Red-Eye

One common flaw with photographs of people, taken indoors, is red-eye, which occurs when the light from the camera's flash reflects off the back of a person's eyes. This causes a person's eyes to appear with a red, demonic look like they're either possessed by the devil or an extreme right-wing conservative religious organization. Although red-eye can ruin an otherwise decent picture of a person, it can also be fixed rather easily.

To fix red-eye, Photoshop Elements provides a special tool called the Red Eye brush tool. Basically the Red Eye tool lets you tell Photoshop Elements what color you want to replace and then automatically change it to a different color.

Step 1: Choose the Red Eye Tool

The Red Eye tool turns your mouse pointer into a brush that serves two purposes. First, it lets you click the color you want to remove, such as the red tint in someone's eye. Second, it lets you drag the mouse and click to paint an area with a new color.

To choose the Red Eye tool, click the Red Eye tool icon in the Toolbox. As soon as you choose the Red Eye tool, the Red Eye tool's options bar appears near the top of the screen, as shown in Figure 11.1.

FIGURE 11.1

The Red Eye tool lets you correct red eye, whether it appears in a person or in an animal, such as this Red Eye Tree Frog from the rainforests of Central America. To the right is a genetically modified Red Eye Tree Frog that not only tastes more like chicken but is more adaptable to pollution and toxic wastes, which will be its new environment after all the rainforests get burned down.

Step 2: Choose a Brush Type and Size

Because no two red eyes in a picture may look alike, Photoshop Elements lets you define the brush type and size of the Red Eye tool. A large brush type and size can be handy for rapidly fixing red-eye, whereas a smaller brush type and size can be useful for touching up a picture to make sure no traces of red-eye still remain.

To choose a brush type, click the Brush Presets list box. A list of brush types appears, as shown in Figure 11.2.

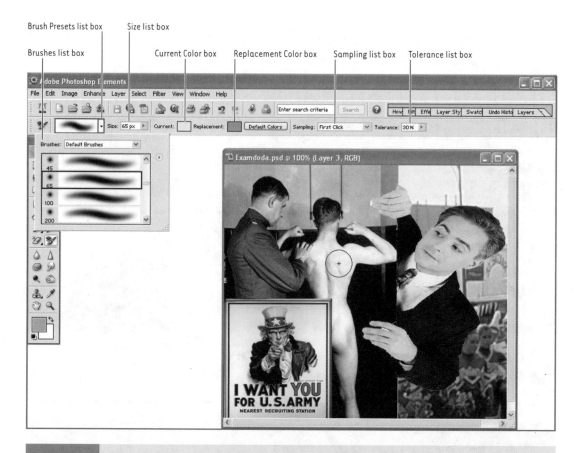

FIGURE 11.2

The Brush Presets list box lets you choose a brush type and size all at once. Here we see a military recruiting poster geared toward enticing more homosexuals to join the armed services. (Photo courtesy of the U.S. Department of Defense.)

Click the Brushes list box. A list of other brush type categories appears. Click a category, such as Default Brushes or Pen Pressure. When you choose a different category, the Brush Presets list box displays a different list of brush types.

Double-click the brush type you want to use. The mouse pointer turns into your chosen brush type.

When you choose a brush type, Photoshop Elements automatically chooses a brush size, but you may want to increase or decrease the brush size anyway. Just click in the Size list box. A slider appears underneath. Drag the slider right or left to increase or decrease the brush size. The mouse pointer changes size appropriately.

Step 3: Identify the Color to Replace

To use the Red Eye tool, you need to identify two colors: the color you want to replace (the red tint in someone's eye) and the color you want to use in its place.

To choose the color you want to replace, click in the Sampling list box and choose First Click. This tells Photoshop Elements that the first color you click will be the color you want to replace.

Click the Replacement Color box. A Color Picker dialog box appears. Click the color you want to appear in place of the red tint in someone's eye and then click OK. Your chosen color appears in the Replacement Color box.

Step 4: Set the Tolerance Level

When you first click the Red Eye tool over part of a picture, you're telling Photoshop Elements, "See this color I just clicked? That's the color I want you to replace when I drag the mouse around."

If you set the tolerance level low, such as 4%, then the Red Eye tool won't replace any color in your picture unless it almost exactly matches the first color you clicked. If you set the tolerance level high, such as 86%, then the Red Eye tool is more lenient and replaces colors that are similar but not exactly identical to the color you first clicked.

In general, a high tolerance lets you change colors easily, but at the risk of changing parts of your picture that you don't want to recolor. A low tolerance prevents you from coloring parts of your picture by mistake, but it may require that you click and drag the Red Eye tool over and over again.

To set the tolerance for the Red Eye tool, click in the Tolerance list box in the options bar. A slider appears. Drag this slider left to right to change the tolerance level from 1% to 100%.

Step 5: Use the Red Eye Tool

Once you've defined the color to use and the tolerance level of the Red Eye tool, move your mouse pointer over the red eye and then click and drag the mouse over the red tint that you want to replace. Depending on the tolerance level you chose, you may need to keep clicking and dragging the mouse pointer over the red eye until you've replaced all the red color with a new color.

REMEMBER *If you find the Red Eye tool is replacing too little or too much color with each mouse click, you may need to adjust the tolerance level by clicking in the Tolerance list box.*

Coloring Hair (and Everything Else as Well)

Although designed to replace the red tint in someone's eye, the Red Eye tool can also be used to replace the color of anything else in a picture, such as the color of someone's hair, skin, or clothes. Unlike the Brush tool, which simply covers part of a picture over with paint, the Red Eye tool replaces color while leaving the details untouched, as shown in Figure 11.3.

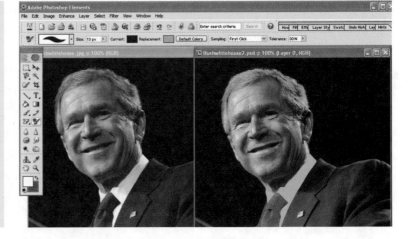

FIGURE 11.3

The Red Eye tool can be used to replace the color in any part of a picture, such as giving George W. Bush a punk makeover to make him more appealing to younger voters. Unfortunately, most younger voters still prefer Bill Clinton, because Clinton's denial of illicit sex is something that more young people can actually relate to.

(Photo courtesy of the White House.)

For example, if you colored someone's shirt with the Brush or Fill Bucket tool, the paint would cover the wrinkles in the shirt. But with the Red Eye tool, you can change the colors in someone's shirt and still leave the wrinkles and any other details untouched.

Coloring Black and White Pictures

In case you have a bunch of old black-and-white pictures hanging around, you can also use the Red Eye tool to add color to boring black-and-white images. When coloring a black-and-white picture, you may first need to convert the picture from Grayscale mode to RGB mode. To do this, click the Image menu, click Mode, and then click RGB Color.

When you use the Red Eye tool on a black-and-white picture, it replaces different shades of gray with your chosen color, as shown in Figure 11.4. The higher you set the tolerance level for the Red Eye tool, the more area the Red Eye tool colors your picture with each click or drag of the mouse. You may need to experiment with different toler-ance levels until you find what works best for your particular image.

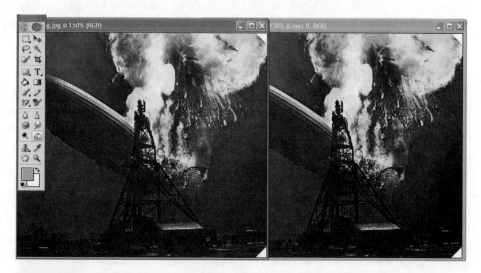

FIGURE 11.4

The Red Eye tool can be used to color a black-and-white picture, such as making the explosion of the Hindenburg look more colorful and exciting. Who would have guessed that when you enclose flammable hydrogen gas inside fabric coated with a layer of iron oxide, cellulose acetate butyrate, and powdered aluminum (a mixture used to create solid fuel for rockets), you could create such a spectacular explosion that would one day look great for the cover of Led Zeppelin's debut album?

Coloring with the Sponge Tool

The Red Eye tool can be great for replacing one color with another, but what if you simply want to brighten or mute an existing color instead? Although you could still use the Red Eye tool, it's much easier to use the Sponge tool instead.

Step 1: Choose the Sponge Tool

The Sponge tool turns your mouse pointer into a brush that lets you drag the mouse around part of your picture to make the colors underneath appear brighter or duller.

To choose the Sponge tool, click the Sponge tool icon in the Toolbox. As soon as you choose the Sponge tool, the Sponge tool's options bar appears near the top of the screen, which displays the Brush Preset, Size, Mode, and Flow list boxes.

Step 2: Choose a Brush Type and Size

Depending on what you want to color with the Sponge tool, you need to define the brush type and size through the Brush Preset list box. To choose a brush type, click in the Brush Presets list box. A list of brush types appears.

Click in the Brushes list box, and a list of other brush type categories appears. Click a brush type category, such as Default Brushes or Square Brushes. When you choose a different category, the Brush Presets list box displays a different list of brush types.

Double-click the brush type you want to use. The mouse pointer turns into your chosen brush type.

When you choose a brush type, Photoshop Elements automatically chooses a brush size, but you may want to increase or decrease the brush size anyway. Just click in the Size list box. A slider appears underneath. Drag the slider right or left to increase or decrease the brush size. The mouse pointer changes size appropriately.

Step 3: Choose the Mode to Use

The Mode list box gives you two choices: Saturate and Desaturate. Choose Saturate if you want to flood part of your picture with more color. Choose Desaturate to soak up excess color from an image and give it a duller appearance.

Step 4: Set the Flow Level

The flow level determines how quickly the Sponge tool sucks up color (in Desaturate mode) or floods a picture with color (in Saturate mode). The flow level can range from 1% to 100%, where a low flow level means you may need to drag the Sponge tool over and over to achieve the effect you want, whereas a high flow level means the Sponge tool adds color to (or soaks up color from) your picture quickly, which may be too quick if you set the flow level too high.

To set the flow level, click in the Flow list box in the options bar. A slider appears. Drag this slider left to right to change the tolerance level from 1% to 100%.

Step 5: Use the Sponge Tool

After you've defined the mode and flow level for the Sponge tool, move the Sponge tool over the part of your picture that you want to change, hold down the mouse button, and then drag the mouse. If you set the flow level low, such as 5%, you may barely see any change, but if you set the flow level high, such as 90%, you should see a change in the color right away, as shown in Figure 11.5.

REMEMBER *To make teeth look whiter, use the Dodge tool, as explained in Lesson 8.*

Smoothing Wrinkles and Other Flaws with the Blur Tool

One reason why centerfolds and super models look so good in every photograph (besides the fact that they're hardly wearing any clothes) is that most of their pictures mask their flaws, whether it be unsightly moles, tattoos, scars, or just less-than-perfect facial features. If people only saw your best features every time they looked at you, they'd think you were a perfect specimen of the human race, too.

In a society that worships youth and beauty, it's no surprise that many people resort to face-stretching plastic surgery in a desperate attempt to stave off the inevitable wrinkles that sprout across their face like cracks in a drying river bed. So to smooth out wrinkles and other types of facial flaws, Photoshop Elements offers the Blur tool.

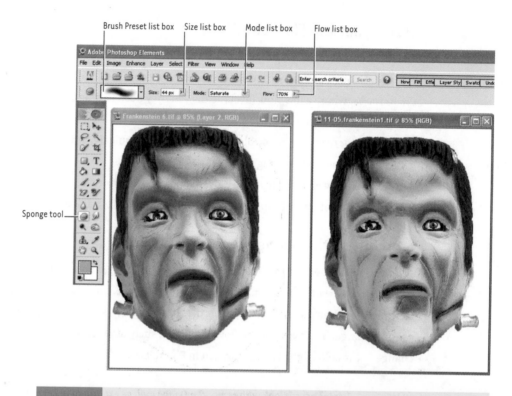

Brush Preset list box   Size list box   Mode list box   Flow list box

Sponge tool

FIGURE 11.5

The Sponge tool can brighten the colors of somebody's face so that every picture makes a person look like a movie star before alcohol and drugs ravish their faces and make them look like washed-up celebrities who will soon be wanted by the police. The picture on the left shows Frankenstein in his prime while the picture on the right shows Frankenstein turning green after ingesting too much alcohol.

REMEMBER *If you want to blur an entire picture rather than just a select part of a picture, click the Filter menu, click Blur, and click Blur once more. Once you've chosen this command, you can repeat it to keep blurring your picture by pressing* CTRL-F.

The Blur tool lets you drag the mouse across an area that you want to appear out of focus, which can hide surface flaws and make the image look softer with fewer distracting details. By using the Blur tool on select portions of your picture, you can hide flaws while leaving the bulk of your picture untouched, which can create the illusion that the image in the picture is completely natural when it isn't.

Step 1: Choose the Blur (or Sharpen) Tool

The Blur tool turns your mouse pointer into a brush that lets you drag the mouse around your picture to smear parts of it, making them look out of focus and fuzzier. (The opposite of the Blur tool is the Sharpen tool, which works the same way, except it lets you sharpen the focus of parts of an image.)

To choose the Blur tool, click the Blur tool icon in the Toolbox. As soon as you choose the Blur tool, the Blur tool's options bar appears near the top of the screen, which displays the Brush Preset, Size, Mode, and Strength list boxes.

Step 2: Choose a Brush Type and Size

To choose a brush type, click in the Brush Presets list box. A list of brush types appears. Click in the Brushes list box, and a list of other brush type categories appears. Click a brush type category, such as Default Brushes or Square Brushes. When you choose a different category, the Brush Presets list box displays a different list of brush types.

Double-click the brush type you want to use. The mouse pointer turns into your chosen brush type. If necessary, you can change the brush size if you click in the Size list box. A slider appears underneath. Drag the slider right or left to increase or decrease the brush size. The mouse pointer changes size appropriately.

Step 3: Choose the Mode to Use

The Mode list box gives you several different ways in which the Blur tool affects your image, such as Darken (which darkens your image as it blurs it), Lighten (which lightens your image as it blurs it), and Saturation (which blurs the brightness of colors).

Click in the Mode list box and choose a mode. You may need to experiment with different modes to find which works best on your particular image.

Step 4: Set the Strength

The strength level ranges from 1% to 100% and determines how easily the Blur (or Sharpen) tool affects your image as you drag the mouse over it. A high strength, such as 98%, means that you only need to drag the mouse over an image once to see the effect right away. This can make blurring (or sharpening) an image easier, but it may make too drastic of a change.

A low strength, such as 4%, means that you may need to drag the mouse over part of an image several times before you can see any visible changes. This can give you more control over blurring (or sharpening) an image, but it can be more time-consuming.

To set the strength level, click in the Strength list box in the options bar. A slider appears. Drag this slider left to right to change the strength level from 1% to 100%.

Step 5: Use the Blur (or Sharpen) Tool

After you've defined the mode and strength level for the Blur or Sharpen tool, move the Blur or Sharpen tool over the part of your picture you want to change, hold down the mouse button, and then drag the mouse, as shown in Figure 11.6.

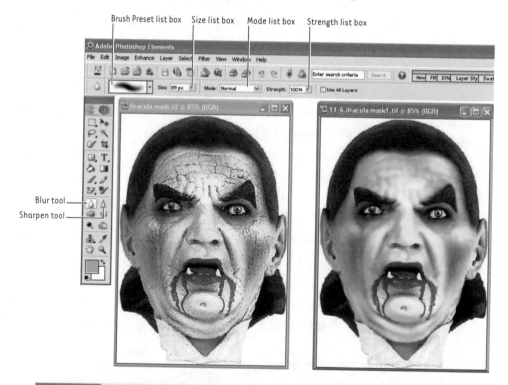

FIGURE 11.6

The Blur tool can smooth out the wrinkles in a face so that a person can look 20 years younger. Of course, the person in the picture will still look like hell in real life. Here we see the Blur Tool magically erasing the wrinkles from Dracula's face so he looks nearly two hundred years younger or approximately the same age as Joan Collins.

Where to Go from Here

To fix people's faces in your pictures, be ready to use the Red Eye tool (to replace colors in eyes, hair, and clothes), the Sponge tool (to enhance or mute colors), the Blur tool (to hide details), and the Dodge tool (to make teeth look brighter). The next step from here is to learn how to physically alter faces and other body parts, which you'll read about in Lesson 12.

Now that you understand the basic tools you can use to alter someone's face and warp reality into fantasy, you can study the latest pictures of a super model or centerfold and see how someone may have altered them to make the models look better. Even if you still feel a twinge of envy over a particular model's looks, just remember that you're probably much smarter than they are. If in doubt, just remember the immortal words of model Brooke Shields, who once said, "Smoking kills. If you're killed, you've lost a very important part of your life."

What You'll Learn in This Lesson

- How to change objects and body parts with the Liquify filter

- How to alter objects with the Warp tool

- How to resize things with the Bloat and Pucker tools

Rearranging Faces, Body Parts, and Other Objects

(Without Hiring a Hit Man to Do It for You)

DURING WORLD WAR II, THE AMERICAN GOVERNMENT contracted General Electric to develop an inexpensive substitute for synthetic rubber. While working on this project in 1943, a scientist named James Wright accidentally dropped boric acid into silicone oil, which created a strange gooey substance that could be molded into different shapes and bounced around on the floor.

General Electric tried for years to find a use for this strange substance, but it took an unemployed marketing consultant named Peter Hodgson to see its potential as a toy. Despite being nearly $12,000 in debt, Peter Hodgson borrowed $147 to buy the production rights from General Electric and soon began marketing the strange substance under the name *Silly Putty*.

Part of Silly Putty's worldwide appeal stems from its malleable nature that lets you mold it into any shape and then smash it all back together again when you're finished playing with it. Although many people's ethics and morals are just as malleable as Silly Putty, their faces unfortunately are not. So until plastic surgery can seamlessly reshape someone's face, the next best solution is to mold someone's face using a special tool in Photoshop Elements called the Liquify filter. By using the Liquify filter, you can turn any image into a blob of digital Silly Putty to reshape objects and body parts into any form you desire.

Use the Liquify Filter

Unlike most of the tools provided in Photoshop Elements, the Liquify filter tools appear in a separate toolbar inside the special Liquify window. To load the Liquify Filter, click the Filter menu, click Distort, and click Liquify. The Liquify window displays your image with the Liquify filter tools arranged on the left side of the window, as shown in Figure 12.1.

REMEMBER *If your picture consists of two or more layers, click the layer that contains the image to which you want to apply the Liquify filter. Then open the Liquify window by following the instructions listed previously.*

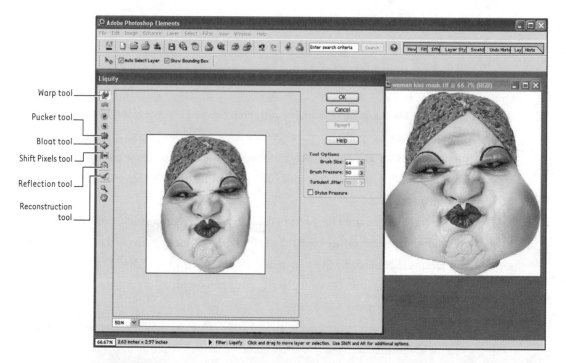

FIGURE 12.1

The Liquify window is where you can modify any part of your picture with the mouse, such as slimming down Anna Nicole Smith's face so you can't see the two cheeseburgers stuffed inside her cheeks.

Step 1: Choose a Tool

After you have opened the Liquify window, you need to choose which tool to use. Just click the tool icon that appears on the toolbar to the left of the Liquify filter, and Photoshop Elements highlights that tool icon to let you know which tool you're currently using. Once you choose a tool, the mouse pointer turns into a circle. (If you chose the Hand tool or the Zoom tool, the mouse pointer turns into a hand or magnifying glass icon, respectively.)

CAUTION *While you have the Liquify window open, you won't be able to access any of the other Photoshop Elements tools or menus.*

Step 2: Choose a Brush Size

After you have chosen a tool, you need to define the size. Just click the Brush Size list box so a slider appears underneath. Then drag the slider left or right to define a size. As an alternative, you can type a value between 1 and 600 into the Brush Size list box instead.

REMEMBER *You do not need to choose a brush size for the Hand tool or the Zoom tool.*

Step 3: Choose a Brush Pressure

After you choose a size for your brush, you need to define the brush pressure to use, which can range in value from 1 to 100. The higher the brush pressure, the easier the mouse pointer can warp your image. The lower the brush pressure, the less your image warps. Generally, it's a good idea to start out with a high brush pressure value to make big changes to your picture and then lower the brush pressure value so you can make finer, more subtle changes. After you have chosen a brush pressure, you're ready to start reshaping your image.

REMEMBER *You do not need to choose a brush pressure value for the Hand tool or the Zoom tool.*

Reshape Objects with the Warp Tool

The Warp tool lets you reshape any part of your image by dragging the mouse to smear the image underneath, much like pushing your finger into a picture captured on a blob of Silly Putty. The more you push in one direction, the more you distort the image, as shown in Figure 12.2.

Besides enabling you to give someone's picture a nose job, the Warp tool can also be handy for correcting dental problems without Novocain or laughing gas. The Warp tool can straighten teeth or soften particularly sharp teeth to reduce the points and make fangs look flat and straight, as shown in Figure 12.3.

REMEMBER *The Warp tool can do anything that the other Liquify filter tools can do. The other tools, such as the Turbulence tool, just make it easier to accomplish certain visual effects.*

Shrink Items with the Pucker Tool

The Pucker tool shrinks or puckers images much like a sour lemon puckers the face of a person. As you hold the mouse pointer over an image and hold down the mouse button, the Pucker tool shrinks the image from the center of the mouse pointer, as shown in Figure 12.4.

Used with exaggerated effect, the Pucker tool can create bizarre visual effects, as shown in Figure 12.5, but used sparingly, the Pucker tool can diminish the size of moles or birthmarks from someone's face or body.

FIGURE 12.2

The Warp tool can perform rhinoplasty, also known as a nose job, on any face, such as fixing this mad scientist's prominent chin and nose to make him look a lot less like Jay Leno.

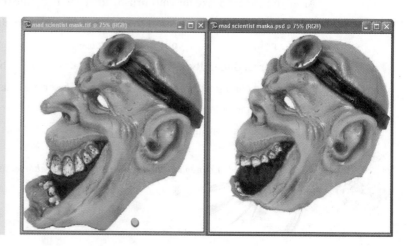

FIGURE 12.3

The Warp tool can reshape teeth easily, such as filling in the gaps and reducing the fang-like effect of the teeth on this Tyrannosaurus Rex, which underwent dental work without using laughing gas and risking sexual assault by an unscrupulous dentist.

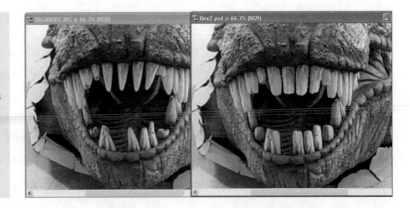

FIGURE 12.4

The Pucker tool can shrink an object, such as the head of Senator Trent Lott of Mississippi. The picture on the left shows the senator with his head at normal size, whereas the picture on the right shows his head shrunken to his brain's normal size.

(Photo courtesy of National Aeronautics and Space Administration.)

FIGURE 12.5

The picture on the right depicts a typical young Viking. The picture on the left depicts that same young, strong Viking if he subjected himself to twelve hours of watching MTV during his adolescent years and subsequently turned himself into a moron.

Enlarge Items with the Bloat Tool

On the opposite end of the spectrum from the Pucker tool is the Bloat tool, which lets you move the mouse pointer over an object and expand whatever appears in the center of the mouse pointer, as shown in Figure 12.6.

Not surprisingly, the Bloat tool can be especially useful to expand an object like a balloon, as shown in Figure 12.7, or to enlarge a woman's breasts without the use of silicone implants, which can leak and cause medical complications sometime in the future.

FIGURE 12.6

The Bloat tool can expand a body part, such as this woman's lips puffed up without the use of collagen or an unknown strain of a sexually transmitted disease contracted by sailors in the Philippines.

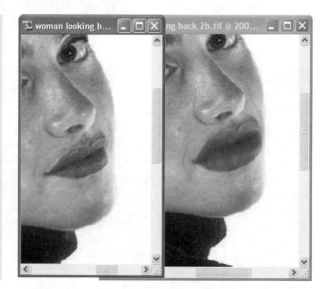

FIGURE 12.7

The Bloat tool can expand an object like a balloon. In the picture on the right, a man's eyes appear enlarged, as if in shock after he witnessed the rare occurrence of a militant feminist admitting that sometimes a man's behavior can actually be more socially and politically acceptable than a woman's behavior.

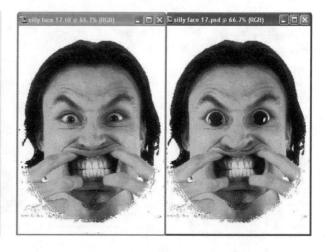

Have Fun with the Turbulence and Twirl Tools

Although less useful than the Warp and Bloat tools for modifying faces, the Turbulence and Twirl tools can come in handy for creating interesting visual effects. The Turbulence tool turns the mouse pointer into a miniature tornado that can scramble any part of the image that appears directly underneath it, which can be useful to create ripples in still water or to rearrange clouds in the sky to give them a stormier and more threatening appearance.

When you click the Turbulence tool, you can define a value from 1 to 100 in the Turbulent Jitter list box. A high value creates a smoother change in your image, whereas a low value creates a more radical change in your image.

The Twirl tools rotate any image underneath the mouse pointer when you hold down the mouse button or drag the mouse, as shown in Figure 12.8. One Twirl tool twirls an image clockwise, whereas the other one turns it counterclockwise.

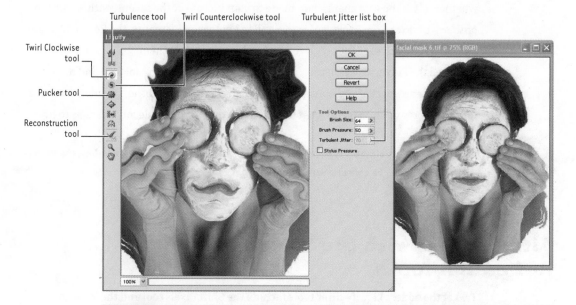

FIGURE 12.8

The Turbulence and Twirl tools can create unusual visual effects, such as messing up the hair and fingers of this mime, taunting a blind man by putting cucumbers over his own eyes. Not being amused, the blind man later had his guide dog maul the mime to death. Fortunately, as he died, the mime stayed true to his craft and didn't make a sound.

Fix Mistakes with the Reconstruction Tool

With so many different tools available through the Liquify filter, it's inevitable that you'll choose a tool and find that it didn't quite do exactly what you thought it would do. To fix any mistakes you make using the Liquify filter, Photoshop Elements offers two ways to fix any changes you made.

The first method is the Revert button. Just click this button at any time, and Photoshop Elements returns your image back to its original condition before you opened the Liquify window. Although the Revert button can reverse any number of changes you may have made, it can be somewhat drastic to use if you only want to reverse a single change or two. In case you don't want to reverse everything you've done, you can use the Reconstruction tool instead.

The Reconstruction tool lets you drag the mouse pointer over any change you made with any of the Liquify filter tools, and the Reconstruction tool reverses that change, whether it was the first change you made to your picture or the seventeenth. Unlike the ordinary Undo or Step Backward command in Photoshop Elements, the Reconstruction tool can reverse changes out of the order in which you made them.

To use the Reconstruction tool, just click the Reconstruction tool icon and drag the mouse over any part of your image that you had changed. Photoshop Elements miraculously restores your image to what it looked like before you made any changes to it.

 CAUTION *Once you click OK to accept any changes you made in the Liquify window, the Reconstruction tool won't be able to reverse those changes ever again.*

Alter Images with the Shift Pixels and Reflection Tool

Two of the oddest Liquify filter tools include the Shift Pixels tool and the Reflection tool. The Shift Pixels tool moves pixels perpendicular to the direction you drag the mouse. So if you drag the mouse to the right, any pixels that you drag the mouse over get pushed up. If you drag the mouse to the left, any pixels that you drag the mouse over get pushed down.

If you drag the mouse up, the pixels get pushed to the left. Drag the mouse down and the pixels get pushed to the right, as shown in Figure 12.9. To reverse this effect, hold down ALT (Windows) or OPTION (Macintosh) before you drag the mouse.

The Reflection tool creates a mirror reflection of an image. Drag the mouse to the right, and the area immediately under the path of the mouse appears reflected wherever you dragged the mouse. Drag the mouse to the left, and the area immediately over the path of the mouse appears reflected wherever you dragged the mouse, as shown in Figure 12.10.

FIGURE 12.9

The Shift Pixels tool affects your image depending on which way you drag the mouse.

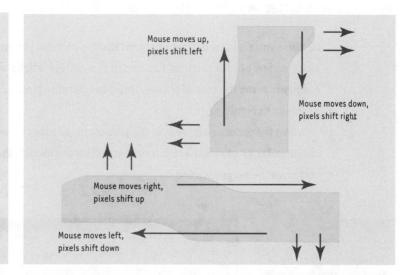

Mouse moves up, pixels shift left

Mouse moves down, pixels shift right

Mouse moves right, pixels shift up

Mouse moves left, pixels shift down

FIGURE 12.10

Dragging the Reflection tool to the left directly underneath this wooden shed creates a reflection of that wooden shed underneath. This picture shows what happens when an outhouse gets clogged and overflows after people use too many discarded corn cobs as a substitute for toilet paper.

(Photo courtesy of National Aeronautics and Space Administration.)

If you drag the mouse up, the area to the right appears reflected wherever you dragged the mouse. Drag the mouse down, and the area to the left appears reflected wherever you dragged the mouse. To reverse this effect, hold down ALT (Windows) or OPTION (Macintosh) before you drag the mouse.

REMEMBER *Although neither the Shift Pixels tool nor the Reflection tool is terribly useful for touching up a person's face, it can be handy for creating interesting visual effects for your pictures.*

View Details with the Zoom Tool

Because you may need to touch up details in a picture, you may want to zoom in to see a larger view of your picture. To zoom in to a picture, click the Zoom tool. Photoshop Elements turns the mouse pointer into a magnifying glass icon with a plus sign inside, as shown in Figure 12.11.

Move the mouse pointer over the part of the picture you want to examine in closer detail and click the mouse. Each time you click the mouse, Photoshop Elements increases the magnification.

Zoom tool

FIGURE 12.11

The Zoom tool and the Zoom list box let you change the magnification of an image, such as this photograph capturing the Great Pumpkin sitting on the toilet, catching up on the latest financial news from the *Wall Street Journal*.

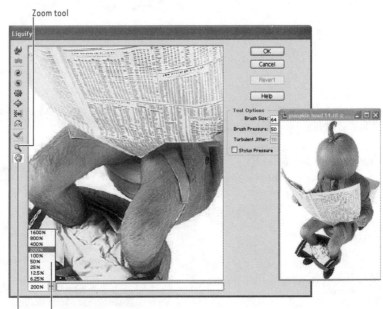

Hand tool   Zoom list box

To zoom out of a picture, hold down ALT (Windows) or OPTION (Macintosh) while clicking the mouse. When you hold down ALT or OPTION, the magnifying glass icon displays a minus sign inside. Then, each time you click the mouse, Photoshop Elements decreases the magnification.

 REMEMBER *You can also change the magnification if you click the Zoom list box and click a magnification level, such as 50%.*

Move Pictures with the Hand Tool

The Hand tool lets you slide your picture around the Liquify filter so you can move your picture to the part of the screen where it's most comfortable for you to view and edit. For example, if you want to change something in the upper-right corner of the Liquify window, just use the Hand tool to move this part of the image closer to the center of the screen so you can see more of the area surrounding that part of the image.

To use the Hand tool, click the Hand tool icon. The mouse pointer turns into a hand icon. Move the mouse pointer over any part of your picture, hold down the mouse button, and drag the mouse to move the image around. Release the mouse button when you're happy with the position of your image.

 REMEMBER *For a fast way to access the Hand tool, simply hold down SPACEBAR, and the mouse pointer turns into the Hand tool right away.*

Where to Go from Here

Reshaping body parts and any other animate or inanimate objects can be easy with all the special tools available through the Liquify filter. Combined with the tools you learned in Lesson 11, you have all the basic tools you need to rearrange a picture of anything as if it were a blob of Silly Putty, whether it be your mother-in-law's face or a panorama of the Grand Canyon. By combining the tools you learned in Lessons 11 and 12 with the new tools you'll learn in Lesson 13, you'll know enough to manipulate and alter practically anything you want.

LESSON 13

What You'll Learn in This Lesson

- How to use the Clone Stamp tool

- How to remove flaws such as wrinkles and tears

- How to erase people, places, or things from a picture

Making People, Places, and Things Disappear

(or The Ministry of Truth Meets the Warren Commission with the Man on the Grassy Knoll)

THE ASSASSINATIONS OF ABRAHAM LINCOLN AND JOHN F. KENNEDY have fascinated people for years because of the potential conspiracy surrounding the suspicious circumstances of their deaths. Although the various conspiracy theories may never be proven right or wrong, the odd coincidences that link these two Presidents in their place in history can never be doubted.

Abraham Lincoln was elected to Congress in 1846. John F. Kennedy was elected to Congress in 1946. Abraham Lincoln was elected President in 1860. John F. Kennedy was elected President in 1960. The names Lincoln and Kennedy each contain seven letters. Lincoln's secretary was named Kennedy. Kennedy's secretary was named Lincoln.

Andrew Johnson, who succeeded Lincoln, was born in 1808. Lyndon Johnson, who succeeded Kennedy, was born in 1908. Booth ran from the theater and was caught in a warehouse. Oswald ran from a warehouse and was caught in a theater. Booth and Oswald were assassinated before their trials. A week before Lincoln was shot, he was in Monroe, Maryland. A week before Kennedy was shot, he was in Marilyn Monroe.

Perhaps the most constant element of any conspiracy revolves around the never-ending stream of photographic "evidence" used to bolster the claims of the conspiracy advocates. Some of these photos are undoubtedly genuine, whereas many are simply fabricated to support a specific point of view. In the old days, faking photographic evidence was mostly limited to government agencies, but now with the power of Photoshop Elements, anyone can doctor up their own photographs to promote whatever strange ideas may be lodged somewhere inside their heads.

How the Clone Stamp Tool Works

The Clone Stamp tool is one of the more versatile tools available in Photoshop Elements. Basically, the Clone Stamp tool copies (clones) your entire picture and gives you the option to paste all or part of it over your original picture, but in a different location. By using the Clone Stamp tool, you can copy and paste part of your picture over any undesirable image to make it disappear, as if it never existed in the first place.

Using the Clone Stamp tool requires three basic steps. First, you have to define something called a "source point," which sounds technical and important but simply means that the first thing you click the mouse pointer on will be the first part of the image that the Clone Stamp tool will paste somewhere else. So if you click a patch of skin next to a tattoo, the Clone Stamp tool copies that patch of skin, as shown in Figure 13.1.

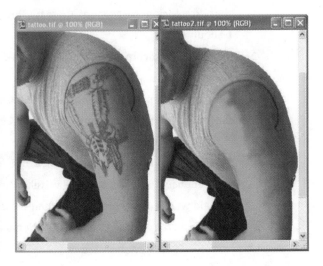

FIGURE 13.1

The Clone Stamp tool can be handy for covering up physical defects or flaws, such as digitally erasing the tattoo off this man's arm. In the old days before Photoshop Elements, removing a tattoo often meant expensive laser surgery or outright amputation, and if you were lucky, the doctor might actually amputate the correct limb as well.

The second step to using the Clone Stamp tool involves clicking the mouse to paste your source point image. So if your source point image is a patch of skin, a click of the mouse over part of a tattoo makes the Clone Stamp tool cover that part of the tattoo with the source point image (the patch of skin), giving the illusion of making part of the tattoo disappear.

The third and final step to using the Clone Stamp tool involves dragging the mouse to paste more of your cloned picture over the original picture. To help you see what the Clone Stamp tool will paste, look at the reference pointer, which looks like a crosshair icon over the original, cloned image, as shown in Figure 13.2.

FIGURE 13.2

The three steps to using the Clone Stamp tool. Step 1: Hold down the **ALT** or **OPTION** key and click over a picture to define your source point. Step 2: Click anywhere to paste your source point image. The total amount pasted depends on the brush size of the Clone Stamp tool. Step 3: Drag the Clone Stamp tool brush to paste your cloned picture. In this picture, dragging the Clone Stamp tool around the source point pastes the rest of the face of what is either the pickled body of an alien from outer space or the next mutant baby fathered by Michael Jackson.

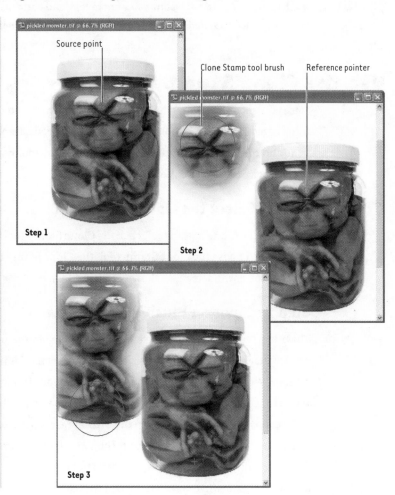

The reference pointer always moves in the same direction as you drag the Clone Stamp tool. Whatever the reference pointer moves over on your original picture, that's what the Clone Stamp tool pastes as you drag the mouse.

So if you click a monster's face to define your source point, the first place where you click pastes your source point (the monster's face). If you drag the mouse down, the reference pointer moves over the monster's chin, hands, and feet, which means that the Clone Stamp tool also pastes the monster's chin, hands, and feet.

REMEMBER *The Clone Stamp tool always copies your entire picture. The source point defines what part of your original picture you want to copy and paste first. Dragging the Clone Stamp tool determines what additional parts of the cloned picture to paste.*

Use the Clone Stamp Tool

Once you understand how the Clone Stamp tool works, you need to learn how to customize the Clone Stamp tool for your particular needs. Depending on what you want to do and the particular picture that you're editing, you may need to alter the Clone Stamp tool's brush size or behavior.

Step 1: Select the Clone Stamp Tool

To choose the Clone Stamp tool, click the Clone Stamp tool icon in the Toolbox. As soon as you choose the Clone Stamp tool, the Clone Stamp tool's options bar appears near the top of the screen, as shown in Figure 13.3.

Step 2: Choose a Brush Type and Size

The brush type determines the shape of the Clone Stamp tool, which can be round or rectangular shaped. The brush size simply makes the Clone Stamp tool bigger or smaller. When you need to cover up large areas, you'll want to use a larger brush size. When touching up finer details, you'll want to use a small brush size.

To choose a brush type, click in the Brush Presets list box and click a brush type. When you choose a brush type, Photoshop Elements automatically chooses a size, but you can modify the brush size at any time by clicking in the Size list box. When a slider appears underneath, drag it left or right to change the size of the brush.

Step 3: Choose a Mode and Opacity

The mode determines how the Clone Stamp tool pastes your cloned image back in your picture. For example, if you choose the Dissolve mode after you copy an image with the Clone Stamp tool, Photoshop Elements pastes your cloned image starting from the center and slowly dissolving outward to give the cloned image a frayed appearance, as shown in Figure 13.4.

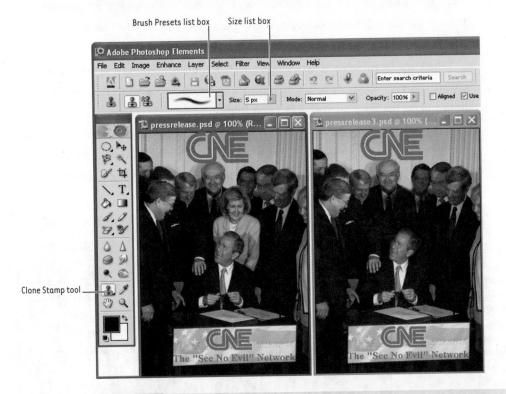

FIGURE 13.3

The Clone Stamp tool lets you wipe out an object by copying over it. At the press conference shown in this picture, President Bush signs into law the creation of a new government-sponsored news network dubbed CNE (short for "Censored News Entertainment" or "See No Evil"). The CNE network will censor anything that anyone might find offensive, such as removing the woman in pink to avoid offending right-wing, conservative females who find the image of a woman outside of the home extremely disturbing. The CNE network will later have to censor this censored image to avoid offending women who find the thought of right-wing, conservative females censoring other women extremely offensive. (Photo courtesy of the White House.)

The opacity level ranges from 1% to 100%, where a 100% opacity level pastes a cloned image exactly as it originally appeared, whereas a lower opacity level, such as 34%, pastes the cloned image much fainter. By lowering the opacity level, you can create a "ghost-like" effect for your pasted images.

Step 4: Choose the Aligned and Layers Options

The Clone Stamp tool's options bar displays two check boxes that can further define the way the Clone Stamp tool works: the Aligned check box and the Use All Layers check box.

When the Use All Layers check box is selected, the Clone Stamp tool can copy multiple images, even if they're stored on separate layers, such as a man's face stored on one layer and the background sky behind him stored on a second layer.

If the Use All Layers check box is clear, you can only copy images stored on the currently selected layer. (To select a different layer, just click the Window menu, click Layers, and when the Layers palette appears, click the layer you want to select.)

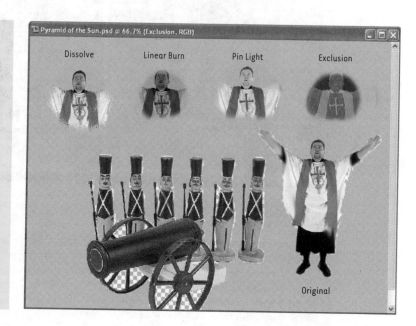

FIGURE 13.4

The mode you choose for the Clone Stamp tool determines how your cloned image appears when pasted back onto a picture. In this picture, we see the cloned face of a minister conducting services before sending troops into battle. To avoid offending his military superiors, this minister has tastefully omitted any reference to the biblical commandment "Thou shalt not kill," replacing it with the more practical one that urges soldiers to kill as many strangers wearing differently colored uniforms as possible.

Whether the Use All Layers check box is clear or checked, when you paste a cloned image back onto your picture, Photoshop Elements will always paste it on the currently selected layer.

The Aligned option determines how the Clone Stamp tool behaves after you click it once to paste your original source point image. If a check mark appears in the Aligned check box, you can paste your cloned picture by either dragging or clicking the mouse, as shown in Figure 13.5.

Step 5: Choose a Source Point

The source point tells Photoshop Elements, "This is the part of the image I want to copy and paste somewhere else." To choose a source point, hold down the ALT key (Windows) or the OPTIONS key (Macintosh). The mouse pointer turns into a circle with a crosshairs icon inside. Move this mouse pointer over the image that you want to clone and click the mouse.

FIGURE 13.5

With the Aligned option turned off, clicking in two different areas pastes the source point image (the face) twice. With the Aligned option turned on, clicking in two different areas pastes two different parts of the same cloned image, in this case the face and shirt of a man who insists that it's perfectly safe to drive drunk without wearing any seat belts.

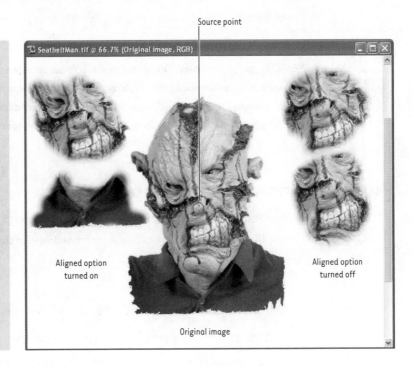

Source point

SeatbeltMan.tif @ 66.7% (Original image, RGB)

Aligned option turned on

Aligned option turned off

Original image

Step 6: Paste Your Source Point

After you have cloned a source point, you can paste it anywhere on the same picture or on a different picture stored in another file altogether. The next place where you click the mouse is where Photoshop Elements will paste your source point, as shown in Figure 13.6.

Step 7: Paste the Rest of Your Cloned Image (Optional)

After you paste your source point somewhere else by clicking the mouse, you can drag the mouse to paste the rest of your cloned image. If the Aligned check box has a check mark in it, the Clone Stamp tool pastes a different part of the cloned picture no matter how many times you release the mouse button and drag the mouse somewhere else. If you clear the Aligned check box, then every time you release the mouse button and drag the mouse again, Photoshop Elements pastes your original source point.

So if you want to paste multiple copies of the source point, clear the Aligned check box. If you want to paste a single copy of your cloned image somewhere else, make sure a check mark appears in the Aligned check box, as shown in Figure 13.7.

 REMEMBER *You can use the Clone Stamp tool as a faster version of the ordinary Copy and Paste commands. Unlike the Copy and Paste commands, you don't have to select an image to copy first. However, the Copy and Paste commands store pasted images on a separate layer automatically, whereas the Clone Stamp tool stores pasted images on the same layer.*

Put the Clone Stamp Tool to Work

The Clone Stamp tool is one of the most powerful Photoshop Elements tools you can use to modify your digital images. Some common uses for the Clone Stamp tool include

- Fixing tears in a scanned picture
- Hiding wrinkles, scars, tattoos, and other unwanted body flaws
- Removing undesirable people, places, and things from a picture
- Copying images from one picture and pasting them in another

FIGURE 13.6

Once you define a source point, you can paste that source point somewhere else with a click of the mouse. In this picture, a soldier, patrolling the demilitarized zone between North and South Korea, looks down with thanks for the protection of a police dog that will keep him from getting captured by the North Koreans. In return, the police dog looks up with thanks for the protection of the soldier who will keep it from becoming the dinner of the North Koreans.

(Photo courtesy of the U.S. Department of Defense.)

Cloned image of the source point

Source point

FIGURE 13.7

When you drag the Clone Stamp Tool around, you can paste your cloned image somewhere else, which gives the illusion of copying and pasting part of your original picture to a new position, such as copying the faces of the Joint Chiefs of Staff as they would have appeared in George Orwell's novel *Animal Farm* and pasting them in the lower-right corner of the picture.

(Photo courtesy of the U.S. Department of Defense.)

Source point

Cloned image of the source point

Surrounding image pasted from around the source point

Fix Tears and Flaws in a Picture

One way to use the Clone Stamp tool is to cover up small flaws in an image, such as a wrinkle on a face, a birthmark on an arm, or a rip in a scanned picture. Because the Clone Stamp tool directly manipulates images, you may want to protect yourself by creating a layer to paste your cloned image on.

First, choose the Clone Stamp tool and click to define your source point. Then create a layer by clicking the Layer menu, clicking New, and then clicking Layer. When the New Layer dialog box appears, type a name for your layer and click OK.

REMEMBER *By pasting your cloned image on a layer, you can easily modify the appearance of your picture without physically altering it.*

Now click the Clone Stamp tool over the flaw you want to hide. Photoshop Elements pastes your source point image over the flaw. Because you probably won't be able to cover up the entire flaw with one click of the mouse, you may need to define another source point to paste over a different part of the flaw. By carefully choosing different source points and pasting them over a flaw, you can make that flaw disappear, as shown in Figure 13.8.

REMEMBER *The key to hiding flaws is to choose a source point that can replace part of the flaw and still look natural in its new location.*

Remove Objects and People from a Picture

Rather than cover up a tiny part of an image, you may need to cover up a much larger portion to remove a person, building, tree, lawyer, or other undesirable object. Although you could copy different source points and paste them over the unwanted item, you might find it faster to choose a source point and surrounding area that could blend in with the background near the object you want to remove, as shown in Figure 13.9.

By doing this, you just need to copy a source point once and drag the mouse to wipe out your undesirable object. Not only is this method faster but it creates a more natural appearance as well.

FIGURE 13.8

By using the Clone Stamp tool, you can copy parts of a picture to cover up any flaws, such as this image on the left of a man who broke out in a horrifying rash as a result of contracting a mutant strain of a venereal disease after having unprotected sex with Madonna. The picture on the right shows what happens when the Clone Stamp tool and a shot of penicillin clears up these flaws.

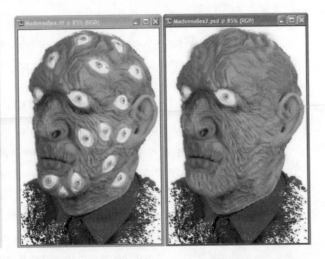

FIGURE 13.9

By copying a source point that blends in with the background, the Clone Stamp tool can be used to paste over an object and make it disappear, such as removing a disabled UFO from its crash site on a beach. Like the incident in Roswell, New Mexico, the official Air Force report concluded that not only did witnesses mistake military space research vehicles and test dummies for a UFO and space aliens, but they also mistook a test dummy found in Roswell, New Mexico, in 1947 for a man on the grassy knoll in Dallas, Texas, in 1963. (Photo courtesy of the U.S. Air Force.)

Because your cloned image may not exactly align over the original picture, create a layer and paste your cloned image on this layer. Now you can move the pasted image on its separate layer to align it over the original picture so it looks flawless.

Copy an Image from One Picture to Another

Not only can the Clone Stamp tool copy an image and paste it over itself, but it can also copy an image and paste it over a picture stored in a different file, which can give you a quick way to copy and paste images from one file to another, as shown in Figure 13.10.

To do this, you just define the source point in the picture that you want to copy and then create a layer in your second picture before you click the Clone Stamp tool and drag the mouse around. By storing your cloned picture on a layer, you can later use the Move tool to adjust the pasted image so it looks natural over the other picture.

FIGURE 13.10

You can copy a source point from one picture and then clone and paste it over another picture to create unusual special effects. In the gorilla picture on the far right, by using the Clone Stamp tool with the Aligned option checked, you can drag the mouse to draw the gorilla face over the man's face (far left) to create the image in the middle. The CNE network would later have to censor this image to avoid offending fundamentalist, religious groups who object to the idea that a gorilla might actually be smarter than they are.

Where to Go from Here

The Clone Stamp tool can be one of the most valuable tools to fix torn images, remove scratches and flaws, or just eliminate distracting or objectionable people or items from a picture altogether so you can protect yourself and others from having to deal with reality. Of course, anyone else can use the same Clone Stamp tool to alter (censor) the same picture so it doesn't offend them (although their altered version may wind up offending you if you don't agree with the way they censored the image). For the ultimate politically correct, censored image, take a look at Figure 13.11.

Now that you know how to use the copy and paste capabilities of the Clone Stamp tool, the Silly Putty molding techniques of the Liquify filter (Lesson 12), and the color-altering capabilities of the Red Eye tool and Sponge tool (Lesson 11), you know how to use most of the tools you need to touch up or modify your own digital images.

Of course, for more fun, you may also want to alter the lights and add motion to your pictures, which you'll learn about in Lesson 14.

FIGURE 13.11

The CNE network displays this completely blank image to avoid showing anything that might possibly offend anyone. Unfortunately, the CNE network must also censor this image because it offends anyone who finds censorship of any kind highly offensive.

What You'll Learn in This Lesson

- How to change the sky in a picture

- How to play with lighting effects

- How to create the illusion of movement

Playing with Skies, Lights, and Motion

(or Making Your Own UFO Without the Wreckage of an Air Force Balloon)

IN JULY 1994, THE OFFICE OF THE SECRETARY OF THE AIR FORCE ended an exhaustive search to determine if any government agency possessed information regarding the recovery of a UFO that supposedly crashed near Roswell, New Mexico in 1947. According to this report, government officials concluded that the incidents at Roswell could be directly linked to a then top-secret project dubbed Project MOGUL.

Project MOGUL involved lifting multiple acoustic sensors and radar tracking devices in the air using up to two dozen weather balloons. When lofted to a great height by these balloons, the Project MOGUL sensors could detect blasts from nuclear bomb tests, specifically those exploded by the former enemy known as the Soviet Union. (Not to be confused with previous former enemies, such as Spain, England, Germany, Japan, and Vietnam, or current former enemies, including North Korea, Iraq, and Iran.) Since the United States didn't want the Soviet Union to know their nuclear tests could be monitored, the United States kept Project MOGUL a closely guarded secret.

So when Mac Brazel found debris from a Project MOGUL balloon on his ranch near Roswell, New Mexico, in 1947, military officials tried to hide Project MOGUL's existence by claiming it was a flying disc, and they later switched their story to say it was nothing more than a weather balloon.

The "alien" bodies that witnesses supposedly saw were nothing more than anthropomorphic test dummies carried aloft for scientific research. Other witnesses, who claimed they saw alien bodies at the Roswell Army Air Field hospital, were most likely confused by a 1956 KC-97 aircraft accident in which 11 Air Force members lost their lives and by a 1959 manned balloon accident that injured two Air Force pilots.

Of course, UFO critics question how witnesses in 1947 could look at human bodies that wouldn't arrive until nearly ten years later and mistake them for alien carcasses. Also puzzling is how witnesses could mistake the wreckage of a weather balloon and test dummies for the crashed remnants of a flying saucer and alien occupants.

Because no official government answer, short of parading the wreckage of a crashed flying saucer, will likely satisfy anyone, the mystery of Roswell still lingers in the minds of many. Of course, if these people owned a copy of Photoshop Elements, they could create their own UFO pictures using trick lighting or models doctored up with Photoshop Element's tools to make them look like they're moving. By learning to use the various Photoshop Elements tools discussed in this lesson, you can make any picture look like there's a UFO in the background, and with a little bit of work, you can even make the UFO look like it's about to abduct your ex-spouse or mother-in-law.

How to Change the Sky

In the world of UFO sightings, the sky often plays a big role in the background, because UFO photographs have yet to capture a flying saucer on the ground. Although you could modify the existing sky by changing its brightness, contrast, or colors, you may prefer to create a more dramatic image for your sky by either creating a more exciting sky yourself or copying an existing sky from another picture.

Method 1: Create Clouds with the Render Command

In case a picture has a blank sky in the background, you can use Photoshop Elements to create your own randomly drawn clouds using the colors currently displayed in the Foreground Color and Background Color boxes. To begin, choose the foreground and background colors for Photoshop Elements to use when creating your clouds.

(See Lesson 9 for more information about choosing colors.) Next, select the background sky using a selection tool such as the Magic Wand, and then click the Filter menu, click Render, and click Clouds. To create a more vivid cloud pattern, hold down the ALT (Windows) or OPTION (Macintosh) key and then click Filter | Render | Clouds. You can see results in Figure 14.1.

REMEMBER *If you don't first select an area before choosing the Clouds command, Photoshop Elements will draw clouds over your entire picture.*

Method 2: Create a Sky with the Gradient Tool

The Gradient tool (which you first learned about in Lesson 10) can be another way to create an unusual image for the skies in your pictures. Gradients are most useful for either enhancing an existing background or creating a dramatic effect to enhance the mood of a picture.

FIGURE 14.1

By adding clouds, the picture on the right can appear more sinister, as we see a proctologist show students how to insert a rectal thermometer through a protective radiation body suit. By the way, is that a black helicopter in the background or a UFO coming to abduct another person living in a trailer park?

(Photo courtesy of the U.S. Department of Defense.)

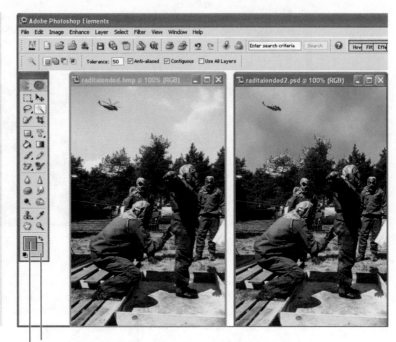

Background Color box

Foreground Color box

To use the Gradient tool, click the Gradient tool icon in the Toolbox, click in the Gradient Picker list box to choose a gradient type (as shown in Figure 14.2), select the sky in the background using a selection tool such as the Magic Wand, and then drag the mouse in the selected area to draw the direction in which you want your gradient to appear.

Method 3: Copy and Paste a Sky with the Copy and Paste Into Commands

If you already have an image of a sky that would look good in the background of another picture, you can copy it and then use the Paste Into command to paste it into a select area of another picture, such as the sky. (To learn more about the Paste Into command, see Lesson 6.)

Gradient Picker list box

Gradient Tool icon

FIGURE 14.2

Gradients can create interesting visual effects in a picture, such as this image of the U.S.S. Maine before it myste-riously blew up in a Cuban harbor. When correspondents for William Randolph Hearst's *New York Journal* investi-gated and found no evidence of Spanish sabotage, Hearst replied, "You furnish the pictures, I'll furnish the war." In honor of the long-standing tradition of fabricating "evidence" to justify starting a war, government historians are now calling William Randolph Hearst a "trailblazer."

(Photo courtesy of the Library of Congress, Prints and Photographs Division, Detroit Publishing Company Collection.)

To copy a sky from another picture, select that portion of the image to copy using a selection tool such as the Magic Wand, click the Edit menu, and then click Copy. Open your second picture, select the area you want to paste the copied image into, such as the sky, click the Edit menu, and then click Paste Into, as shown in Figure 14.3. After you paste an image into an area, you may need to drag the mouse over the copied image so it looks just right in its new location.

Method 4: Copy a Sky with the Clone Stamp Tool

Another way to copy images of a sky from one picture to another involves the Clone Stamp tool (see Lesson 13 for more information). Just click the Clone Stamp tool icon in the Toolbox, hold down the ALT (Windows) or OPTION (Macintosh) key, and click anywhere on the image that you want to copy. Then open a second picture and drag the mouse around the sky area to draw the cloned image of the sky from the first picture, as shown in Figure 14.4.

FIGURE 14.3

The Paste Into command can paste a copied image inside a selected area. The picture on the left shows an Iraqi boy holding up a yellow package of military rations given to him by U.S. Marines. Upon the boy's first taste of military rations, he exclaimed (roughly translated), "You mean you guys actually eat this @#$&?" The picture on the right shows the same boy standing in front of a ravaging tornado that will cause less damage to his town than a whole mob of Iraqi looters. (Photos courtesy of the U.S. Department of Defense and the National Oceanic and Atmospheric Administration.)

The Clone Stamp tool can copy part of an image from one picture to another. Here we see Santa Claus posing next to two girls he crossed off his naughty list after the three of them got drunk and plowed his sleigh through the side of a house in Oklahoma. (Photo courtesy of the National Oceanic and Atmospheric Administration.)

Play with Lighting Effects

One reason why professional photographers can capture portraits so well time and time again has nothing to do with experience, equipment, or skill. It simply has to do with lighting. When amateurs take a picture indoors, their pictures must rely on whatever lighting might be around, plus the effects of the camera's flash, which means that nine times out of ten, an amateur's indoor photograph will probably look awful.

Professionals don't take such chances with the lights because they supply their own in the form of portable and adjustable lights that can be aimed from any direction. Because you may not be able to control the lights when you take a picture, you can do the next best thing and control the lights within Photoshop Elements.

Shine Lights on a Picture

Rather than lug around heavy portable lights to brighten up your pictures, you can mimic heavy and expensive lighting equipment through the Lighting Effects filter in Photoshop Elements, as shown in Figure 14.5. When you use the Lighting Effects filter, you can specify the following:

- The type of light to use, such as a single spotlight, lights shining down from the ceiling, or lights shining up from the floor.

- The direction, distance, and width of the light beam. The closer the light appears, the brighter your picture will be. The wider the light, the more lit up the edges of your picture will be.

- The intensity of the light—whether it's very bright or dim.

 REMEMBER *The Lighting Effects filter works only on the currently selected layer. If you want the Lighting Effects filter to affect your entire picture, you may need to click the Layer menu and then choose Flatten Image first.*

The Lighting Effects filter can mimic a variety of different types of lights shining on a subject, such as this exhibit depicting what the Rolling Stones might look like if they performed in the year 2153.

To create a lighting effect for your picture, click the Filter menu, click Render, and click Lighting Effects. The Lighting Effects dialog box appears, shown in Figure 14.6, which will likely overwhelm you with multiple details, so here's how to make sense of them all:

- **Style list box** Lets you choose to mimic different physical types of lights to use, such as Floodlight, RGB Lights, and Triple Spotlight.

- **Light Type list box** Lets you choose how your specific lights shine on your picture: Directional (lights up your entire picture), Omni (lights up a circular area), or Spotlight (lights up a narrow beam on your picture).

- **Intensity slider** Determines the brightness of the light.

- **Focus slider** Determines the width of the light.

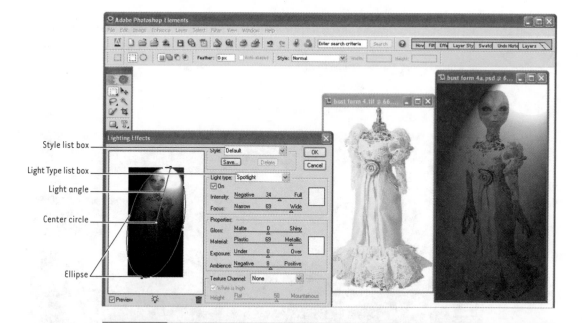

FIGURE 14.6

The Lighting Effects dialog box lets you customize the way your lights brighten up a picture, such as the way the lights shine on this mannequin, which the Air Force claims people mistook for an alien in 1947. After the Air Force released this photograph, thousands of people reported sighting space aliens, dressed in the latest fashions, in department store windows all over the country.

- **Gloss slider** Determines how much the surface reflects light, from low (Matte) to high (Shiny).

- **Material slider** Determines how the light reflects off the object. Moving the slider toward the Plastic setting means that the object reflects the color of your light; moving the slider closer to the Metallic setting means that the light reflects the object's color.

- **Exposure slider** Yet another way to brighten or darken the light.

- **Ambience slider** Increases or decreases the amount of light.

- **Center circle** Defines the point that the light shines on.

- **Light angle** Determines both the angle of the light and how near (or far) the light shines on the center circle.

- **Ellipse** Defines the width of the light beam.

Click in the Style list box and choose a lighting style you want to mimic, such as Five Lights Down. Click in the Light Type list box and click the type of light you want to use, such as Spotlight.

REMEMBER *Some of the light options in the Style list box may display multiple lights that you can configure individually.*

Drag the center circle to change the point at which you want your light aimed. Drag the light angle to change the direction your light hits the center circle and the distance at which the light appears (closer or farther) from the center circle. Drag the handles on the side of the ellipse to widen or narrow the area on which the light shines.

Drag any of the sliders, such as the Intensity, Material, or Exposure, to alter the way your light appears. Click OK when you're done experimenting (a fancy term for "goofing around").

Create Lens Flare

Sometimes when you take a picture outdoors, the sunlight reflects off the lens, creating a flash of light in your picture known as *lens flare*. Although lens flare can often be unwanted, you may want it occasionally to spice up the appearance of your pictures, as shown in Figure 14.7.

FIGURE 14.7

Lens flare can brighten up any image, such as this painting of a space-based missile defense system designed to knock down enemy missiles before they reenter the atmosphere. In preliminary tests, the missile defense system missed its targets but did shoot down Santa Claus in his sleigh, a cartoon beagle wearing a World War I flying helmet on a dog-house, and an Air Force weather balloon that it mistook for a flying saucer. (Artwork courtesy of the Defense Intelligence Agency.)

REMEMBER *The Lens Flare command works only on the currently selected layer. If you want the Lens Flare command to affect your entire picture, you may need to click the Layer menu and then choose Flatten Image first.*

To create lens flare, click the Filter menu, click Render, and then click Lens Flare. The Lens Flare dialog box appears, which lets you specify the following:

- **Brightness** Defines the (what else?) brightness of the lens flare.

- **Flash Center** Defines the center where you want the lens flare to appear.

- **Lens Type** Defines the type of lens flare, either 50–300mm Zoom (creates a bright flare at the flash center and an additional, bright glare nearby), 35mm Prime (creates a bright flare at the flash center and an additional, weaker glare), or 105mm Prime (creates a bright circle at the flash center).

Drag the flash center (which appears as a crosshair, shown in Figure 14.8) where you want the lens flare to appear. Then click a radio button in the Lens Type group, such as the 50–300mm Zoom radio button.

To adjust the brightness of your lens flare, either type a value from 1 to 100 in the Brightness text box or slide the Brightness slider left or right. Figure 14.9 shows the result when 105mm Prime is selected in the Lens Type list. When you're done trying out different values for your lens flare, click OK when you're happy with the lens flare you've created.

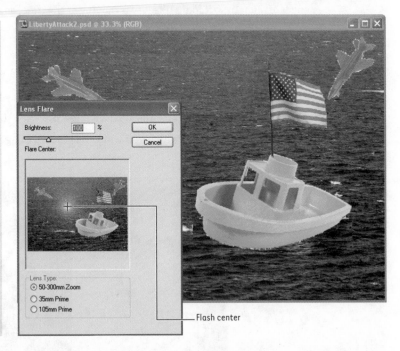

FIGURE 14.8

The Lens Flare dialog box lets you define a specific type of lens flare for your pictures, such as in this picture of plastic toy boats and airplanes simulating the 1967 Israeli attack on the U.S.S. Liberty, one of the few times a foreign country has attacked and killed American servicemen without causing a war to break out soon afterwards.

FIGURE 14.9

Lens flare (such as 105mm Prime) can be particularly useful for creating the illusion of light shining from an object in a picture, such as creating headlights shining from a car wreck. By digitally modifying car photographs, used car salesmen can now alter reality with fantasy and become as untrustworthy as a UFO investigator working for the U.S. Air Force.

Create the Illusion of Movement with the Motion Blur Filter

When you capture a moving image on film, that image tends to look slightly blurred. So if you want to create the illusion of movement in your own pictures, you can blur the edges of an item so it looks like it was moving at the time, as shown in Figure 14.10.

Method 1: Blur an Image the Simple Way

To blur an image, select an edge using a selection tool such as the Lasso tool. Then click the Filter menu, click Blur, and click Motion Blur to display the Motion Blur dialog box.

Click in the Angle text box and type a value from −360 to 360, or drag the Blur Angle line to define an angle at which you want the blurred image to appear. Click in the

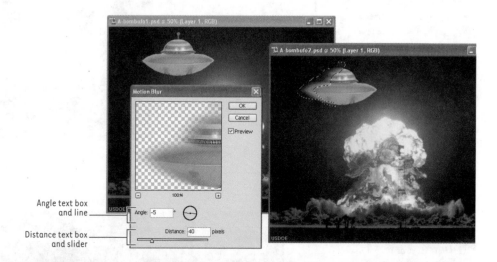

Angle text box and line

Distance text box and slider

By selecting the edge of an object and then using the Motion Blur filter, you can create the illusion that you captured the image as it moved, such as this flying saucer hovering near an atomic bomb blast in the Nevada desert. Like other UFO sightings, Air Force officials studying this photograph concluded that this flying saucer was actually a flock of birds that passed unscathed through the million degree heat and blast from the nearby atomic explosion.

(Photo courtesy of the U.S. Department of Energy.)

Distance text box or drag the Distance slider to define how much you want to blur your image. The greater the distance value, the blurrier your image will appear. Click OK when you're happy with the way the blurred image looks.

Method 2: Blur an Image with Multiple Layers

The previous method blurs an edge, but if you want to create a more dramatic blur, you can make multiple copies of an image, position each copy a specific distance from the original image, blur each copy, and then change the opacity value of each copy so that the farthest copy from the original appears with the lowest opacity and the copy closer to the original appears with a higher opacity. In case this brief description makes no sense whatsoever, follow these steps to see how it's done.

Step 1: Make Multiple Copies of an Image

Use a selection tool, such as the Lasso Tool, to select the image you want to blur, choose the Edit menu, and click Copy. Now choose the Edit menu and click Paste several times to display multiple images of the object you want to blur. Position these copies to one side of the original image so they overlap, as shown in Figure 14.11.

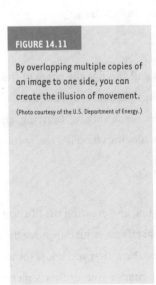

FIGURE 14.11

By overlapping multiple copies of an image to one side, you can create the illusion of movement.

(Photo courtesy of the U.S. Department of Energy.)

Step 2: Change the Opacity of Each Copy

By changing the opacity of each image, you can further create the illusion of movement. To change the opacity of an image, choose the Window menu and click Layers so the Layers palette appears.

Click a layer and then click the Opacity list box that appears in the top of the Layers palette. Either drag the Opacity slider or type a value in the Opacity text box, such as **15** or **35**. The copy of the image farthest from the original should appear with the lowest opacity value, whereas the copy nearest the original should appear with the highest opacity value, as shown in Figure 14.12.

Step 3: Merge All the Layers and Apply the Motion Blur Filter

Choose the Window menu and click Layers in case the Layers palette isn't visible. Then click a layer that contains the copy of the image, choose the Layer menu, and click Merge Down to merge your chosen layer with the layer directly underneath it. Repeat this process until you have merged all the layers that contain the copies of your image.

Choose the Filter menu, click Blur, and click Motion Blur. The Motion Blur dialog box appears. Click in the Angle text box and type an angle. Then drag the Distance slider to blur the copies of the image, as shown in Figure 14.13.

Step 4: Touch Up with the Smudge Tool

Finally, click the Smudge tool in the Toolbox and smudge the edges of the original image so that it blends in with the blurred multiple copies of your image, as shown in Figure 14.14. Through the combination of creative smudging, blurring, and opacity values, you can make any object appear to be moving when it's really standing still.

Where to Go from Here

By altering the background sky, providing lights, and creating the illusion of motion in your pictures, you can create unusual visual effects or just improve the existing appearance of any objects in your photographs. Now that you know some of the ways to modify your pictures, you can learn how to change your ordinary pictures into creative works of art through panoramas, filters, and special effects, which you'll learn about in Lesson 15.

The copy farthest from the original should have the lowest opacity value.

(Photo courtesy of the U.S. Department of Energy.)

When you use the Motion Blur filter, the multiple copies appear as a single blur.

(Photo courtesy of the U.S. Department of Energy.)

The Smudge tool lets you touch up and blur the edges of your original image to complete the blurred effect simulating movement.

(Photo courtesy of the U.S. Department of Energy.)

LESSON 15

What You'll Learn in This Lesson

- How to create a panorama

- How to create a collage

- How to use filters to modify your pictures

Playing with Collages, Panoramas, and Special Effects

(or How to Profit from Pollution and Traffic Congestion with the Blessings of the Government)

IN THE 1920S, GENERAL MOTORS HAD A PROBLEM. Although gasoline was cheap (12 cents a gallon) and automobiles popular, few people would buy a car if they lived in one of the larger cities. The problem wasn't the lack of parking spaces or congested roads (which never stops people from buying cars today). Instead, the problem was that in most major American cities at the time, private companies ran profitable, pollution-free electric street cars and trolleys that went nearly everywhere.

Faced with competing against a cheap, reliable, and convenient public transit system, General Motors knew they would have a hard time selling many cars. So rather than compete, General Motors (along with Firestone and Standard Oil) created a company called National City Lines, which invested in the companies that ran the different public transportation systems. Once National City Lines gained control of these public transit systems, they raised fares to discourage riders and systematically dismantled the street car and trolley systems in every city to force residents to rely on either buses or private automobiles. No matter what choice people made, the end result would be the same: General Motors would ultimately profit from selling either buses or automobiles.

Of course, buses weren't really an option either. Unlike streetcars and trolleys, which had an exclusive right-of-way, buses had to share the road with automobiles, which meant that taking a bus would almost always take longer than driving a car. This, combined with reduced bus schedules, left people with little choice but to shun any form of public transportation that involved buses and opt for their own car instead.

Taken individually—the growth of the automobile industry, the dismantling of city streetcar and trolley systems, and the growing traffic congestion and pollution that clogs every city's highways—you may think that each event is separate from the others. But when you combine each event and trace the connection between each one, you can see the whole picture.

In the world of Photoshop Elements, combining individual pictures to make one big picture is called either a collage or a panorama. A *collage* simply consists of separate pictures pasted side by side. A *panorama* consists of multiple pictures of the same object that, when pasted together, display the big picture that each individual picture is unable to show by itself, such as a panorama of the Grand Canyon or the real reason why few cities in America have a decent, inexpensive, profitable mass transit system any more.

How to Create a Panorama

Sometimes you may want to take a picture of an object but find that it's too big. You can try stepping back or zooming out, but then a majestic image such as the Empire State Building or Niagara Falls winds up looking like a little speck in the distance.

As an alternative, you can take a picture showing part of a large object, take another picture showing a slightly different part of the same object, and keep repeating this process until you've taken several pictures of the same object, but each showing a slightly different part. Although you could print these different pictures out and then cut and paste them together, it's much easier to do this digitally using a special feature of Photoshop Elements called Photomerge. As the name suggests, Photomerge takes multiple images and aligns them together, creating a single large picture of a wide or tall object that a single shot couldn't capture by itself.

REMEMBER *When taking pictures for a panorama, make sure the images in your pictures overlap so that Photoshop Elements can find the common objects in two different pictures and paste them together.*

To use the Photomerge feature, open all the pictures that show a different part of the same object. Then click the File menu and click Create Photomerge. The Photomerge dialog box appears, as shown in Figure 15.1, listing the file names of all the pictures currently displayed.

REMEMBER *As an alternative to loading all your pictures ahead of time, just click the File menu and then click Create Photomerge. When the Photomerge dialog box appears, click the Browse button, and when the Open dialog box appears, click the images you want to merge.*

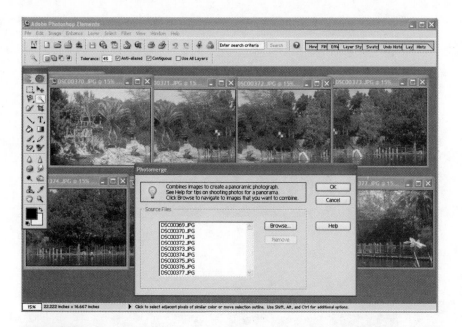

FIGURE 15.1

The Photomerge dialog box lets you add (or remove) images to combine them into a single picture. These pictures show a Congo fishing village where the main form of public transportation involves walking. The National City Lines would later tear up all footpaths and force people to buy automobiles they can't afford so they can become dependent on cheap, foreign, imported oil like any modern society on this planet would want to do.

Click OK when you're done adding or removing images from within the Photomerge dialog box. Photoshop Elements tries to find common images between each picture and align them up properly. After a few seconds, Photoshop Elements proudly displays the result, as shown in Figure 15.2.

Although Photomerge takes most of the effort out of aligning multiple pictures together, the alignment won't always be perfect. In case you see a picture in your panorama that appears slightly crooked or out of place, just click it. Photoshop Elements displays a red box around your chosen picture. Now drag the mouse to move your picture to a new position.

In case you want to examine your panorama in more detail, click the Zoom In or Zoom Out button to increase or decrease the magnification. As an alternative to clicking the Zoom In and Zoom Out buttons, you can also drag the Navigator slider right or left to increase or decrease the magnification.

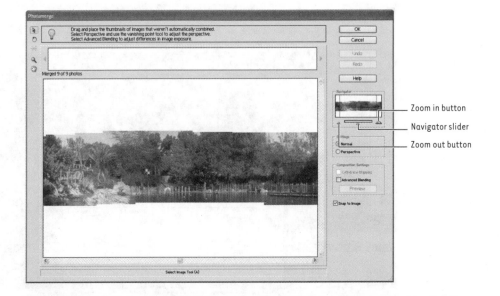

FIGURE 15.2

Photomerge combines multiple pictures into a single panoramic image that you could never capture in a single shot, such as a panoramic view of a Congo fishing village or a panoramic view of your mother-in-law's wide butt trying to squeeze through a narrow revolving door.

If Photomerge did a horrible job of stitching together your multiple pictures, as shown in Figure 15.3, don't worry. Sometimes when you take a picture of a wide or tall object, the perspective changes from one picture to another. For example, a picture taken straight on the middle of a wall will look flat, whereas a picture taken of another part of the same wall, but farther away, will look slightly distorted because of the angle and distance at which you captured the picture.

To fix perspective problems, just click the Perspective radio button in the Settings category. Photomerge alters the perspective and tries to stitch your pictures back together again correctly, as shown in Figure 15.4.

When you're happy with the way your merged photographs look, click OK. Photoshop Elements displays your brand-new, merged picture in a separate window. At this point you need to save this new picture by clicking the File menu and clicking Save, or by pressing CTRL-S (Windows) or CMD-S (Macintosh).

FIGURE 15.3

In this picture, Photomerge did a clumsy job aligning the multiple pictures together of African tribesmen paintings on a wall. Fortunately, archeologists discovered these paintings on a wall, because if they had discovered them on a freeway overpass, they would have called them graffiti.

FIGURE 15.4

With the perspective altered, Photomerge correctly aligns the African tribesmen paintings. Now they look just like they did in real life, but without the annoyance of waiting for other people to get out of the way so you could take some pictures.

REMEMBER *After you save your panorama, Photoshop Elements may still display multiple windows of all the pictures you loaded first to use in your panorama. Although you could close each window individually, it's easier to let Photoshop Elements do it for you. If you're running Windows, just hold down SHIFT, click the File menu, and then click Close. Photoshop Elements will then close every open window on the screen. If you're running a Macintosh, just click the File menu and click Close All.*

How to Create a Collage

Unlike a panorama, which consists of multiple images of the same object pasted together, a collage often consists of completely different images pasted together that are still related somehow, such as a picture of workmen tearing up a street car track combined with an image from the 1988 movie *Who Framed Roger Rabbit?*, where the detective hero, Eddie Valiant, makes an offhand comment to a kid who asks if he has a car. "Who needs a car in L.A.?" Valiant says. "We've got the best public transportation system in the world." Across the road, the sign above the tram station that reads THE WORLD'S BEST PUBLIC TRANSPORTATION SYSTEM is being replaced by that of Clover Leaf Industries.

Unlike a panorama that Photoshop Elements can automatically create for you, a collage consists of multiple pictures that you must arrange yourself. The steps to creating a collage are similar to those in creating a panorama. You can either load all the pictures you want to use in your collage and then click the File menu followed by the Create Photomerge command, or you can just click the File menu, click the Create Photomerge command, and then click the Browse button in the Photomerge dialog box to load all the pictures you want to use.

Click OK in the Photomerge dialog box when you've loaded all the images you want to use in your collage. Photoshop Elements displays a dialog box informing you that it's unable to match your pictures together in a panorama. Click OK. The Photomerge window appears with all your chosen images at the top of the window.

Drag each image from the top to the large white area underneath. If a picture overlaps, Photoshop Elements makes the edges blend together, as shown in Figure 15.5.

FIGURE 15.5

The Photomerge feature can create a collage showing what the Grand Canyon could look like after real estate developers and corporations exploit it with the aid of local politicians, who will gladly rewrite laws to favor development in return for a cut of the profits.

(Photos courtesy of the National Park Service and the Environmental Protection Agency.)

How to Modify a Picture with Filters and Effects

When seen through the eyes of someone who grew up thinking that government officials always work for the public good and corporations always try to compete fairly, the scandal of the American public transportation system might seem horrifying. But if you look at this same scandal through the eyes of someone who believes that there's no such thing as honesty or ethics in either politics or business, the scandal simply looks like a shrewd and profitable strategy. It all depends on how you look at it.

Just as you can view the same historical events through different perspectives, so can you do the same with your pictures by viewing them through different filters or effects. Both filters and effects can subtly or drastically modify your pictures and turn them from realistic images into stylistic works of art (or total garbage if you're not careful).

Use a Filter

Photoshop Elements provides 12 different types of filters:

- **Artistic** Turns pictures into works of art, such as watercolors or fresco.
- **Blur** Makes an image look (what else?) blurrier in different ways.
- **Brush Strokes** Makes a picture appear to be created out of unique brush strokes, such as spray or splatter.
- **Distort** Warps a picture (see Lesson 12 for specific information about using the Liquify filter).
- **Noise** Adds or removes scratches, dust, and speckles from a picture.
- **Pixelate** Modifies the appearance of the pixels that make up an image.
- **Render** Creates clouds, lens flare, and lighting effects (see Lesson 14).
- **Sharpen** Tries to improve the quality of your pictures by making images look sharper.
- **Sketch** Converts your pictures into an image as if drawn using various sketching tools, such as charcoal or a graphic pen.
- **Stylize** Alters an image in various ways, such as dividing an image into tiles or making it glow.

- **Texture** Changes the material that the image appears on, such as making the image appear as if it were on stained glass or mosaic tiles.

- **Video** Provides filters specifically designed to improve the quality of frames captured from a video.

You can apply a filter to your entire picture or just to a portion of a picture you've selected using a selection tool such as the Lasso tool or the Magic Wand. If you don't select part of your picture, Photoshop Elements assumes you want to apply the filter to your entire picture.

Click the Window menu and then click Filters to display the Filters palette, as shown in Figure 15.6. (You can also click directly on the Filters palette tab.)

Click in the Filters type list box and choose a filter type to use, such as Sketch or Artistic. The Filters palette then displays all the options for that particular filter type. Click the filter you want to use.

Depending on which filter you choose, a dialog box may appear, giving you additional ways to modify how the filter will change your picture. Make any modifications to your filter and then click OK. Photoshop Elements shows your picture as seen through your chosen filter.

Filters Type list box

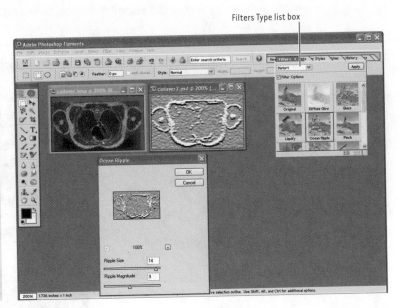

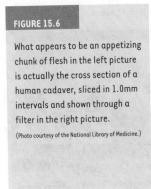

FIGURE 15.6

What appears to be an appetizing chunk of flesh in the left picture is actually the cross section of a human cadaver, sliced in 1.0mm intervals and shown through a filter in the right picture.

(Photo courtesy of the National Library of Medicine.)

REMEMBER *If you click the Filters menu, you can see the same filter options as you can on the Filters palette. The big difference is that the Filters palette visually shows you how each filter may change your picture, whereas the Filters menu does not.*

Use an Effect

Photoshop Elements provides four different types of effects:

- **Frames** Provides different ways to put a frame around your pictures.
- **Image Effects** Changes the appearance of an image, such as making the image look like it was made out of neon lights or in the middle of a blizzard.
- **Text Effects** Changes the way text appears (see Lesson 16).
- **Textures** Creates different images, such as wood grain or brick.

Like a filter, you can apply effects to your entire picture or just to a portion of a picture selected with a selection tool such as the Lasso tool or the Rectangular Marquee tool. If you don't select part of your picture, Photoshop Elements assumes you want to apply the effect to your entire picture.

Click the Window menu and then click Effects to display the Effects palette, as shown in Figure 15.7. (You can also click directly on the Effects palette tab.)

Effects Type list box

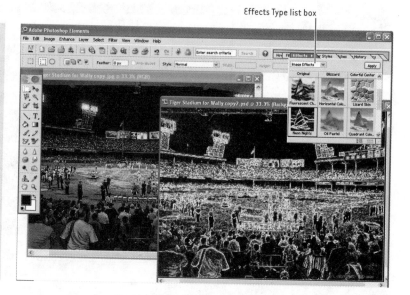

FIGURE 15.7

The left picture shows the last baseball game at historic Tiger Stadium, whereas the right picture shows the same image after a special visual effect is applied so that you can see the same image through the eyes of a sports fan after indulging in one too many beers.

(Photo courtesy of the Robert Cherewick.)

Click in the Effects Type list box and choose an effects type to use, such as Image Effects. The Effects palette then displays all the options for that particular effects type. Click the effect you want to use. Photoshop Elements shows your picture modified by your chosen effect.

CAUTION *You won't be able to use some types of effects, such as Cut Out and Recessed, until you select part of an image first.*

Where to Go from Here

By using Photoshop Elements' Photomerge command, filters, and effects, you can turn ordinary pictures into extraordinary works of art. By using the Photomerge feature to create collages, you even salvage pictures that you might normally just erase. With all these Photoshop features at your fingertips, you can take sweeping panoramic views of all the traffic jams, smog, and urban sprawl scarring cities across America.

As you put together your pictures of cars jammed across highways while spitting out poisonous carbon monoxide, you can rest assured that the perpetrators of the electric street car and trolley scandal were justly punished by the always-fair American legal system.

On March 13, 1949, Attorney General Clark convicted nine corporations (National City Lines, Inc., American City Lines, Inc., Pacific City Lines, Inc., the Standard Oil Company of California, the Federal Engineering Corporation, the Phillips Petroleum Company, the General Motors Corporation, the Firestone Tire & Rubber Company, and the Mack Manufacturing Corporation) and seven individuals (E. Roy Fitzgerald and Foster G. Beamsley of NCL; H.C. Grossman, GM; Henry C. Judd, Standard Oil of California; L.R. Jackson, Firestone Tire & Rubber; Frank B. Stradley and A.M. Hughes, Phillips Petroleum) on one count of conspiring to monopolize a part of the trade and commerce of the United States.

The corporations were convicted and fined $5,000 each. The individuals were convicted and fined $1 each, thereby proving that crime really does pay, just as long as it's done by a white man committing a white collar crime with the aid of friendly politicians.

LESSON 16

What You'll Learn in This Lesson

- How to add text to a picture

- How to twist text into different shapes

- How to add and modify text on a picture

Playing with Text
(or What to Do When a Picture Isn't Worth a Thousand Words)

UNLIKE ENGLISH, THE CHINESE WRITTEN LANGUAGE DOES NOT USE AN ALPHABET. Instead of symbols that represent sounds, the Chinese language uses symbols that represent objects. So early versions of the Chinese word for "man" actually looked like a drawing of a man. Because drawing a complete stick figure of a man took too much time, people eventually simplified the symbol to its most prominent characteristics. The word for "man" now looks like a torso with two legs that can be drawn with two simple strokes of a pen.

Obviously, creating separate characters to represent every possible object in the universe would make a written language nearly impossible to learn, let alone use, so many Chinese words consist of multiple symbols. For example, the word for "university" consists of two symbols that mean "big" and "school." The word for "sunrise" consists of two symbols that mean "sun" and "horizon." So following this logic, you could create a new word to describe someone like Adolf Hitler with the two Chinese symbols that represent an "ass" (donkey) and a "hole."

So although a picture may be worth a thousand words (or in the Chinese language, a picture literally is a word), sometimes a picture can benefit from a little explanatory text typed directly over the image. Such text can provide a short description ("John's 4th Birthday – May 9, 2003"), a caption ("Photo by Walter Bowman"), or a headline ("John Makes a Wish! Mean Aunt Eaten by Goldfish!").

Whether you plan to create posters, advertisements, or just family portraits, you can always use text to make your pictures look even more inviting and memorable.

How to Add Text to a Picture

When you type text on a picture, Photoshop Elements stores your text on a separate layer (see Lesson 7 for more information about layers). To add text to a picture, click the Text tool in the Toolbox. Photoshop Elements displays the Text tool's options bar, as shown in Figure 16.1.

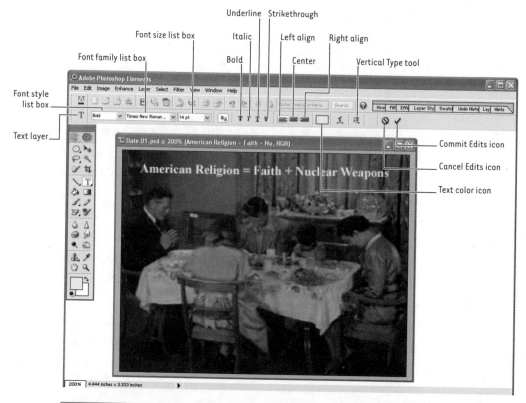

The Text tool lets you type text, and the Text tool's options bar lets you modify the appearance of that text. In this picture, we see a family praying before a meal. Despite their fervent prayers, the mother made them all go to church the next morning anyway. (Archival footage supplied by Archives.org.)

REMEMBER *If you click the Vertical Type tool, you can type text that appears up and down instead of left to right.*

Click in the area where you want your text to appear. (Don't worry about getting the text to appear exactly right since you can always move, edit, or resize it later.) As soon as you click the mouse, Photoshop Elements displays a cursor.

To choose a font, click in the Font family list box and click a font such as Times New Roman. To choose the size of your text, click the Font size list box and click a size such as 12. To change the appearance of text, click in the Font style list box or click the Bold, Italic, Strikethrough, or Underline icon on the options bar. To change the alignment, click the Left Align, Center, or Right Align icon on the options bar. If you click the Text Color icon on the options bar, the Color Picker dialog box appears, which lets you click the color you want to use for your text.

When you're done selecting different options for your text, start typing, and Photoshop Elements displays your text with the options you chose. After you type text, you can always modify it later if you highlight it and then change any options, such as choosing a different font or alignment.

REMEMBER *Unlike a word processor, Photoshop Elements won't wrap your words to the next line when the text reaches the right edge of your picture. To display text on the next line, you must press ENTER (Windows) or RETURN (Macintosh).*

Edit Text

To edit text that you already created, you have two choices. First, you can click the Text tool in the Toolbox and then click anywhere on the text that you want to edit. Photoshop Elements displays a cursor near the text that appears on your picture.

Second, you can click the Window menu and click Layers to display the Layers palette. Then you can double-click the big *T* symbol displayed on the Layers palette, which appears on the layer that you want to edit. Photoshop Elements highlights your chosen text, as in the picture shown in Figure 16.2. Anything you type will replace all the text currently stored on that specific layer.

Whether you click directly on text that appears on the picture or double-click the T symbol that appears on the Layers palette, the next step is to use the ordinary editing keys, such as DELETE, BACKSPACE, and the arrow keys, to delete text or move the cursor around and then type any new characters.

CAUTION *Not all text can be edited. If you apply an effect on some text (see the section "Apply Effects and Gradients" later in this chapter), such as making the text look like the letters were carved out of metal, Photoshop Elements treats your text as any other part of your picture, which means you can modify it using any of the Toolbox tools, such as the Eraser Tool, but you won't be able to edit that text with the keyboard. To show you which text can be edited and which text cannot, Photoshop Elements displays the letter* T *on the Layers palette, next to any text that can be edited. If a* T *does not appear, that text cannot be edited, as shown in Figure 16.3.*

Move, Resize, and Rotate Text

After you have typed some text on a picture, you can move, resize, or rotate it later. Just click the Move tool and then click over the text that you want to alter. Photoshop Elements displays a box around your chosen text with tiny squares, known as *handles*, around the edges.

Text layer

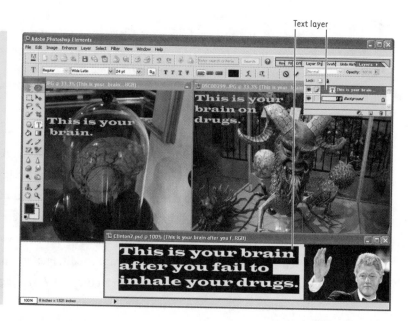

To move text, move the mouse pointer over the text and then click and drag the mouse. Then release the mouse button when the text appears in a position you like.

To resize text, move the mouse pointer directly over a handle until the mouse pointer turns into a double-pointing arrow. Then click and drag the mouse to stretch or shrink the text. Release the mouse button when you're happy with the size of your text.

To rotate text, move the mouse pointer near the outside edge of a handle until the mouse pointer turns into a curved double-pointing arrow. Then click and drag the mouse to rotate the text. Release the mouse button when you're happy with the rotation of your text.

Delete Text

In case you created text and then later decide you don't need it after all, click the Window menu and click Layers. The Layers palette appears. Click the layer that contains the text you want to delete.

REMEMBER *As a shortcut, you can delete a layer if you right-click that layer (Windows) or hold down the CTRL key and click (Macintosh) in the Layers palette. When a pop-up menu appears, click Delete Layer.*

Text that can be edited   Simplified text that can no longer be edited

FIGURE 16.3

The Layers palette can show you which text can be edited (identified with a *T*) and which text cannot be edited (lacking a *T*). This picture shows a successful crash landing at a flight school designed to teach future airline pilots how to get drunk and still fly a plane afterwards.

(Photo courtesy of the U.S. Department of Defense.)

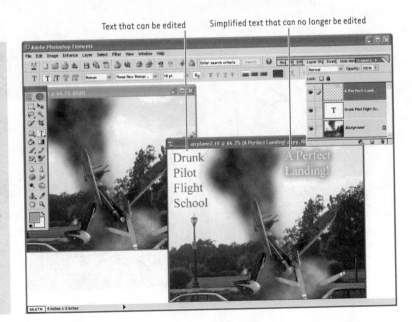

Now click the Layer menu and click Delete Layer. A dialog box appears, asking if you really want to delete your chosen layer. Click Yes. Photoshop Elements deletes your chosen layer.

Twist Text into Different Shapes

No matter what color or font you use for your text, it may still look too plain. So for more fun, Photoshop Elements lets you curve text in different shapes so you can achieve more interesting effects, such as a wavy effect. Two ways you can twist text involves the Warp Text dialog box and the Liquify filter (see Lesson 12 for more information about the Liquify filter).

The Warp Text dialog box can bend text quickly while still allowing you to edit it later. The Liquify filter can create more unusual effects but takes time and won't let you edit your text afterwards.

Shape Text with the Warp Text Dialog Box

To twist text, click the Text tool on the Toolbox and then click the text you want to warp. Click the Warp Text icon on the options bar. Photoshop Elements displays a Warp Text dialog box, as shown in Figure 16.4.

Warp text icon

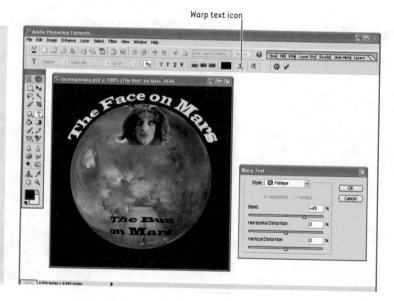

FIGURE 16.4

The Warp Text dialog box lets you warp your text into different shapes, such as curves. This pictures show a NASA photograph conspiracy theorists have uncovered that clearly shows the famous "Face on Mars" and its lesser known counterpart on the other side of the planet, the "Butt on Mars."

(Photo courtesy of the National Aeronautics and Space Administration.)

Click in the Style list box and click a warp style to use, such as Arc or Wave. The Bend, Horizontal Distortion, and Vertical Distortion sliders appear. Drag these sliders to change the way your text appears. Click OK when you're happy with the twisted shape of your text.

Bend Text with the Liquify Filter

If you want to modify the appearance of individual letters, you'll have to use the Liquify filter instead of the Warp Text dialog box. To bend characters with the Liquify filter, click the Window menu and then click Layers to display the Layers palette. Click the layer that contains the text you want to warp.

Click the Layer menu and then click Simplify Layer. After you simplify a layer, Photoshop Elements treats your text as just another part of your picture, so you can't edit that text anymore.

REMEMBER *As a shortcut, you can simplify a layer if you right-click that layer (Windows) or hold down the CTRL key and click (Macintosh) in the Layers palette. When a pop-up menu appears, click Simplify Layer.*

Click the Filter menu, click Distort, and click Liquify. The Liquify window appears, displaying your text. Click in the Brush Size or the Brush Pressure list box to modify how the Liquify brush (mouse pointer) works.

Move the mouse pointer over the text and drag the mouse to warp, twist, and otherwise deform individual letters, as shown in Figure 16.5. Click OK when you're done.

FIGURE 16.5

The Liquify window lets you bend the individual characters of your text to your will in strange and unique ways, in much the same way that Uri Geller can bend spoons with his mind.

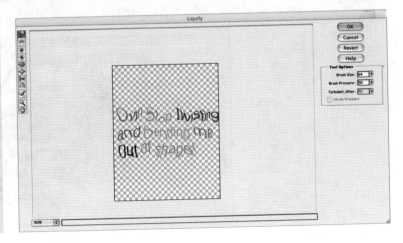

Apply Effects and Gradients

Although coloring your text and using bizarre fonts can make your text stand out, you may want to create more interesting visual effects to make your text grab a viewer's eyes even more. Two additional ways to modify text is to use a special text effect and a gradient.

Text effects alter the appearance of text, such as making letters appear as if they were carved out of metal or spray-painted with a stencil. A gradient can display colors within the characters that make up your text.

CAUTION *When you apply an effect or gradient to text, Photoshop Elements simplifies that text, which means you won't be able to edit it later. So make sure you spelled everything correctly before applying an effect or gradient; otherwise, you may create a beautifully designed typo for everyone to see. For additional protection, make a copy of the layer containing text and then work on that copy. Now if you mess up the copy, you can just delete that layer and still have the original text to work with all over again.*

Apply Effects on Text

Click the Window menu and click Effects. The Effects palette appears. Click in the Effects list box and click Text Effects. The Effects palette displays all the available effects you can apply to your text, as shown in Figure 16.6.

FIGURE 16.6

The Effects palette displays all the unique effects you can apply to your text. This picture shows graffiti written by street gang members if they actually knew how to spell.

REMEMBER *Make sure you don't need to make any changes to your text because once you apply an effect, you won't be able to edit your text again.*

Click the effect you want to use, such as Wood Paneling or Running Water. Photoshop Elements alters the appearance of your text. Figure 16.7 shows different types of text effects you can use.

Color Text with a Gradient

You can color your text by clicking the Text Color icon on the options bar, but coloring your text this way gives every letter the same uniform color. If you want to display different colors for your text, you have to highlight letters individually and then click the Text Color icon to choose a different color.

For variety, you may want to use a gradient, which can display a range of colors that blend from one to another like a rainbow.

To use a gradient on text that you already typed, click the Window menu and click Layers. The Layers palette appears. Click the Layer menu and then click Simplify Layer.

REMEMBER *As a shortcut, you can simplify a layer if you right-click that layer (Windows) or hold down the CTRL key and click (Macintosh) in the Layers palette. When a pop-up menu appears, click Simplify Layer.*

FIGURE 16.7

Photoshop Elements offers a variety of different effects to alter the way your text appears, so you can be as creative or just plain weird as you like.

Hold down the CTRL key (Windows) or the CMD key (Macintosh) and click the layer that contains the text you want to fill with a gradient. Photoshop Elements displays a marquee around all the text on your chosen layer.

Click the Gradient tool on the Toolbox. You may want to change some of the gradient options in the options bar (see Lesson 10 for more information about modifying the Gradient tool).

Move the mouse pointer to one side of your selected text and then click and drag the mouse across your text. Release the mouse button, and Photoshop Elements displays your chosen gradient inside your text.

Press CTRL-D (Windows) or CMD-D (Macintosh), or click the Select menu and click Deselect, to see how your gradient looks, as shown in Figure 16.8.

Fill Text with an Image

Filling text with color or a gradient can make your text look more interesting, but for really wild effects, you can also fill text with part of an image, as shown in Figure 16.9.

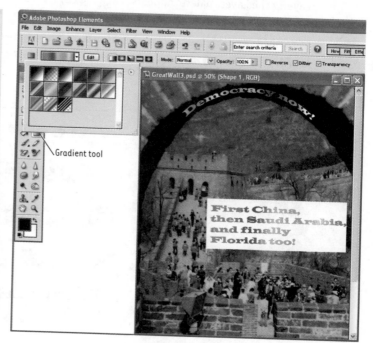

REMEMBER *For best results, pick a background with different dark colors so they'll show up within the inside of your text. If you choose light colors or a background with little diversity, the image will look plain and dull inside your text.*

To create text that displays an image inside each character, click the Text tool on the Toolbox so that the Text tool's options bar appears. Then click the Horizontal or Vertical Mask tool.

Click a picture that contains an image you want to appear inside your text. Photoshop Elements masks your entire picture in red and displays a blinking cursor. Click in the Font Family and Font Size list boxes to choose a font and a size. You may also want

Vertical Mask tool

Horizontal Mask tool

FIGURE 16.9

When you fill text with a background image, you can create interesting visual effects, such as this picture showing how the words "black power" can use the background image from an African painting to promote the black cause without using four-letter words or anything that begins with "mother" and rhymes with "sucker."

to click in the Font Style list box and choose Bold or Bold Italic to make your letters wider so they can display more of the image inside.

Type your text. As you type, your letters appear without the red mask so you can see what part of the background image will appear inside each character. If you don't like the way your text appears, click the Cancel Edits icon in the options bar and start over. If you're happy with the way the text looks, click the Commit Edits icon on the options bar (refer back to Figure 16.1 for the location of the Cancel Edits and Commit Edits icons).

As soon as you click the Commit Edits icon, Photoshop Elements removes the red mask and selects your text with a marquee. Press CTRL-C (Windows) or CMD-C (Macintosh), or click the Edit menu and click Copy, to copy your selected text.

Open another picture (or just use the same picture you typed on with the Horizontal or Vertical Mask tool) and press CTRL-V (Windows) or CMD-V (Macintosh), or click the Edit menu and click Paste. Photoshop Elements pastes your text on your new picture.

Click the Move tool on the Toolbox to move or resize the text. When you're happy with the way your text looks, click anywhere away from the text. Your newly pasted text now appears on a separate layer, as shown in Figure 16.10.

FIGURE 16.10

Text containing an image appears on its own layer. This picture shows beautiful, snow-covered mountains along highway I-15, which inexplicably leads travelers past pristine mountain ranges towards Barstow, California, a city better known for its rest-rooms than anything else.

Where to Go from Here

Text can enhance your pictures and make them more visually interesting. With special effects, gradients, colors, fonts, and images, you can make your text as plain or as colorful as you want. Of course, text can't always salvage every picture, so use it sparingly. You may be surprised at how a subtle change such as adding text can make any picture worth looking at more than once without having to show someone naked in the picture to do it.

Part

Four

Where to Go from Here

LESSON 17

What You'll Learn in This Lesson

- How to print a picture

- How to print thumbnails of multiple pictures

- How to create a Picture Package

Publishing Your Pictures

(or How to Suck Your Inkjet Printer Dry by Printing Color Photographs)

SINCE ANCIENT TIMES, SCHOLARS HAVE LAMENTED the loss of countless invaluable manuscripts that were once housed in the Library of Alexandria. According to one legend, Julius Caesar supported Cleopatra against her brother Ptolemy XIV, and was besieged by Ptolemy's army and fleet in the city of Alexandria. To block Ptolemy's fleet, Caesar reportedly set fire to the docks, which consumed the ships, the docks, and then spread to the famous Library of Alexandria itself, destroying the most complete collection of all Greek and Near Eastern literature in the world. Of course, losing vast storehouses of knowledge is much easier today because instead of burning down libraries to keep people ignorant, we just let them watch television instead.

The problem with the Library of Alexandria was that it held all its manuscripts in one location, which meant the destruction of that one location meant the loss of all the valuable books housed inside. Similarly, all your pictures, carefully modified using the various tools in Photoshop Elements, remain housed on a single hard disk. If that hard disk crashes, it could be a personal catastrophe similar to losing the Library of Alexandria.

So after you spend your valuable time doctoring up your pictures to make them look pretty, it's time to share them with others. If you don't have a printer, you can grab your relatives and have them crowd around your computer monitor every time you want them to admire your work. Obviously, this isn't practical because most people don't want their relatives around in the first place. So as an alternative to viewing your pictures on a computer monitor, take some time to print them out so you will always have a hard copy of your work.

With printed copies of your photographs, you can share your pictures with others without letting them get near you or your computer. If you want to get fancy, Photoshop Elements can even save your pictures in an Adobe Acrobat PDF (Portable Document format) file that you can share on disk.

How to Print a Single Picture

Basically, there's no real mystery in printing out a picture from Photoshop Elements. Just as long as your printer works with your computer, you can just give the usual Print command if you just click the File menu and then click Print.

However, before you print, you may want to take some time to define how you want your picture to print (landscape or portrait), how big your picture appears on a printed page, or whether you want the picture to appear centered or off to one edge.

Position Your Picture on a Page

If you just tell Photoshop Elements to print your picture, your picture will likely appear in the center of the page. Although this might be fine for some people, others might want more control over both the placement of their picture on a page and the size of their picture when it's printed out.

To define the size and position of your picture on a page, click the File menu and then click Print Preview. The Print Preview dialog box appears, as shown in Figure 17.1.

To resize your picture, move the mouse pointer over the black border that appears on the corners of your picture. If you can't see a black border, make sure a check mark appears in the Show Bounding Box check box. When you move the mouse pointer over the black border, the mouse pointer turns into a double-pointing arrow. Click and drag the mouse to resize your picture.

If you want to be precise about the size of your picture, click in the Height and Width text boxes and type specific values for the size of your picture. If you click in the measurement unit list boxes, you can change the measurement units to inches, centimeters, picas, or millimeters.

If you want your picture to fill your entire page, just click in the Scale to Fit Media check box and Photoshop Elements will magically enlarge your picture to fill the entire page with no extra effort involved on your part.

Normally, Photoshop Elements centers your picture on a page, but if you don't want your picture centered, click in the Center Image check box to clear it. Then move the mouse pointer over your picture and drag it to a new location. In case you want to be specific about the position of your picture, click in the Top and Left text boxes and type values to define how far from the top of the page your picture appears and how far from the left your picture appears on the page.

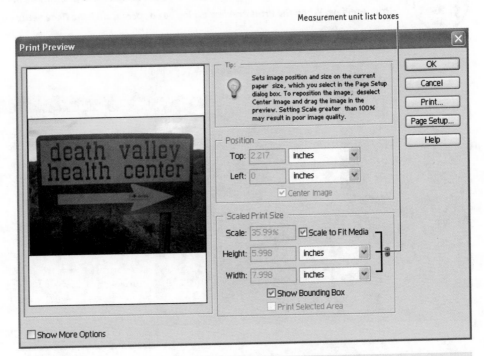

FIGURE 17.1

The Print Preview dialog box lets you define the size of your picture and its position on the page. This picture shows the most inappropriately named health facility, available only in Death Valley.

Define the Size and Orientation of Your Pages

You can just shove an ordinary-size piece of paper in your printer and print out your pictures, but if you want to use unusual-size paper or want more control over the way your pictures appear on a page, you have to use the Page Setup command.

The Page Setup command lets you define the size of the paper to use, such as an envelope or a letter-size piece of paper, whereas the orientation determines whether your picture prints sideways or up and down.

To choose the Page Setup command, click the File menu and click Page Setup. The Page Setup dialog box appears, as shown in Figure 17.2.

REMEMBER *You can also access the Page Setup command if you click the File menu and click Print Preview. When the Print Preview dialog box appears, click the Page Setup button.*

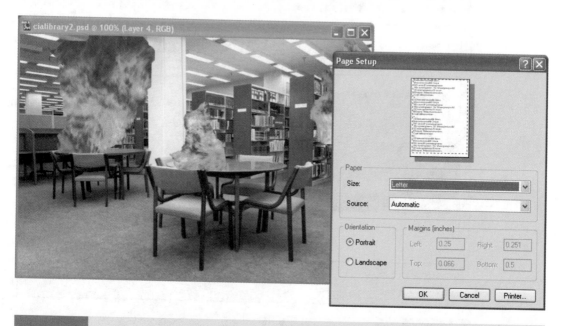

FIGURE 17.2

The Page Setup dialog box lets you define a paper size and orientation. In this picture, right-wing conservatives and left-wing liberals have banded together to burn any books that offend them, which include the dictionary, the encyclopedia, and every translation of the Bible.

Click in the Size list box and click a paper size, such as Envelope or Letter. Then click either the Portrait or Landscape radio button in the Orientation category. Portrait orientation means that the height of the page is greater than its width. Most programs, such as word processors, print everything in portrait orientation by default. Landscape orientation means that the width of the page is greater than its height, which means that the image prints sideways on a page.

If you're ready to start printing, click the Printer button, and when another Page Setup dialog box appears, choose the printer you want to use (if you have a choice) and then click OK.

How to Print Thumbnails of Multiple Pictures

If you have many images stored in a folder, you may find it difficult to keep track of exactly which pictures you have stored in which folder. Although you could use the Browse command to view the images stored in a folder, Photoshop Elements also gives you the choice of printing out a contact sheet.

A contact sheet consists of miniature thumbnail images. When you print one out, you can see, at a glance, which pictures you've stored in a specific folder. If you have many pictures stored in a single folder, Photoshop Elements may create multiple contact sheets, as shown in Figure 17.3.

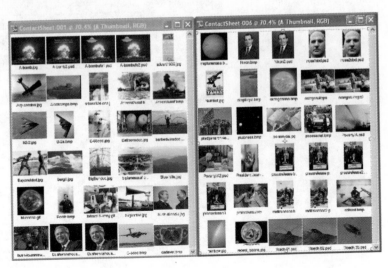

FIGURE 17.3

Contact sheets display thumbnail images of all the pictures stored in a single folder. Now you can see, at a glance, in which folder your teenage boy has stored all his pornographic images.

To create a contact sheet, click the File menu, click Print Layouts, and then click Contact Sheets. The Contact Sheet dialog box appears, as shown in Figure 17.4.

Click the Browse button (Windows) or the Choose button (Macintosh). Another dialog box appears. Click the folder that contains the images you want to use in your contact sheet and click OK (Windows) or Choose (Macintosh).

Click in the Width and Height text boxes and type values to define the size of your contact sheet.

REMEMBER *If you chose a really bizarre size for your contact sheet, you may not be able to print it correctly.*

Click in the Columns and Rows text boxes and type the number of columns and rows you want. Click OK when you're done. Now sit back and watch Photoshop Elements create your contact sheet right before your eyes.

FIGURE 17.4

The Contact Sheet dialog box lets you define the number of rows and columns in which to arrange your thumbnail images.

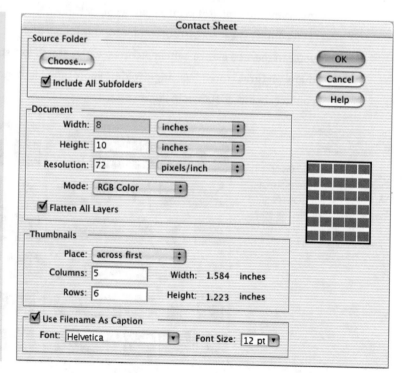

To print your contact sheet, click the File menu and click Print Preview. When the Print Preview dialog box appears (refer to Figure 17.1), click the Scale to Fit Media check box so all your thumbnail images fit on your page. If the Scale to Fit Media check box is blank, Photoshop Elements may not be able to print all your thumbnail images on a single page.

REMEMBER *You don't need to save your contact sheets because they may change if you add or delete images at a later time.*

How to Create and Print a Picture Package

Rather than print one picture on a page or a bunch of little thumbnails of multiple pictures on a page, you may want to create a Picture Package instead. A Picture Package takes multiple pictures and stores them in a new file that displays those pictures multiple times, as shown in Figure 17.5. Picture Packages can be particularly handy when you want to print as many pictures as possible on a single sheet of expensive photo paper.

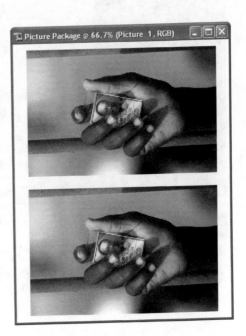

FIGURE 17.5

A Picture Package displays a single picture multiple times in a window or on a page when printed out. This Picture Package shows a man holding a trading card of his favorite corrupt politician. By collecting trading cards of corrupt politicians, ordinary citizens can pretend to buy and sell politicians just like the rich people do.

(Photo courtesy of the U.S. Department of Defense.)

To create a Picture Package, load the picture you want to use, click the File menu, click Print Layouts, and then click Picture Package. The Picture Package dialog box appears, as shown in Figure 17.6.

Click in the Page Size list box and choose a size for the paper you want to use for printing. Click in the Layout list box and choose how many pictures you want to cram on a single sheet of paper, such as one 5x7 picture and two 3.5x5 pictures.

When you first create a Picture Package, the Picture Package dialog box displays the same picture multiple times. If you want, you can add different pictures to a Picture Package, as shown in Figure 17.7. Just click the picture in the Picture Package dialog

FIGURE 17.6

The Picture Package dialog box lets you define a page size and layout for your pictures. This picture shows what happens when you combine truth in advertising with legal prostitution and wind up showing how ugly most hookers really are, proving that some things in print may really be better off being burned after all.

box you want to replace with another picture. The Select an Image File dialog box appears. Click the file containing the picture you want to put in your Picture Package and click OK when you're done.

If you want, you can have text appear directly on each picture in your Picture Package. Just click in the Content list box under the Label category and click Custom Text. Then type your text in the text box labeled Custom Text and make any changes to the font, size, color, and so on.

Finally, click in the Position list box and choose where you want the text to appear, such as Centered or Top Left. If you want, click in the Rotate list box and choose an angle to rotate your text.

When you're done creating your Picture Package, click OK. Photoshop Elements creates a new file that contains multiple copies of your pictures crammed in a single window. At this point you can print your Picture Package or save it, although you don't need to save it if you don't want to.

A Picture Package can display several different pictures, such as these various pictures of a little boy's birthday party. Note that the little boy is wearing a pirate hat because the theme of the party was "Come as your favorite corporate CEO."

Where to Go from Here

Printing out your pictures gives you a way to share your photographs with others. Because photographs can look slightly different when viewed on a monitor compared to holding an actual photograph in your hands, you may want to print your photographs to study them for flaws before you hand them out to others. If you use a high-quality inkjet printer with special photography paper, you can make your pictures look nearly as good as if you had them professionally developed.

If the printed copies of your photographs start to fade, just print out some more. The more you print, the more likely you will never lose a particular image. Best of all, you can make as many printed copies of your pictures as you like. That way, if your computer goes up in flames like the Library of Alexandria, you'll still have copies of all your precious photographs. (Unless, of course, all the copies of your photographs happen to be next to your computer when it bursts into flames.)

Who knows what information may have been lost when the Library of Alexandria burned down? Perhaps the library contained the recipe for creating Greek Fire, a secret weapon of the Eastern Roman Emperors. Greek Fire was hurled on to enemy ships and burst into flames on contact. Supposedly the fire was inextinguishable and burned even on water, thus causing panic and dread among its victims. The secret recipe for Greek Fire had been handed down from one emperor to the next for centuries, but even today, its exact composition remains a mystery, which shows you that today's scientists aren't really that smart after all.

The Library of Alexandria may have also held the secret to how ancient civilizations moved heavy rocks and boulders across great distances to create the pyramids of Egypt, the stone formation at Stonehenge, and the statues of Easter Island. Although the secret to how ancient civilizations transported boulders may have been lost forever because nobody printed it out for future civilizations to study, that secret may have actually been rediscovered by a 5-ft.-tall, 100-pound Latvian immigrant named Edward Leedskalnin.

From 1920 to 1940, Leedskalnin worked alone to build his home in Florida City. Unlike other men who have built their homes, Leedskalnin built his home out of an estimated 1,000 tons of coral rock, which includes the following features:

- An obelisk weighing 28 tons.
- An 8-foot-tall wall that consists of large blocks, each weighing several tons.
- Large stone crescents perched atop 20-foot-high walls.
- A 9-ton swinging gate that moves at the touch of a finger.

After building his home by himself for 16 years, a new subdivision being built nearby threatened Leedskalnin's privacy, so he decided to move his entire coral house, furniture, and walls ten miles to Homestead, Florida, where it now rests as a tourist attraction called Coral Castle. How a single man moved so many tons of coral rock by himself remains yet another mystery that today's scientists can't answer either.

Curious neighbors claimed they saw Leedskalnin place his hands on stones and sing, which somehow levitated the rocks. Local teenagers claimed they spied on him one night and saw him floating "coral blocks through the air like hydrogen balloons."

Leedskalnin explained his secret simply as "leverage" and even wrote down possible hints of his secret in booklets and clues scattered around his Coral Castle, but unless he printed out additional instructions for how he managed to move tons of coral rock by himself, the secret Leedskalnin discovered has long since disappeared when he died in 1951.

LESSON 18

What You'll Learn in This Lesson

- How to e-mail a picture

- How to use your pictures for a web page

- How to create a slideshow

- How to share your pictures with other programs

Adobe Web Photo Gallery
4/24/2003

Sharing Your Pictures Electronically

(or How People Can See Pornography Without Looking at a Magazine)

"A 44-GUN FRIGATE LIKE OUR CHERISHED OLD IRONSIDES took over 60 tons of hemp for rigging, including an anchor cable 25 inches in circumference. The Conestoga wagons and prairie schooners of pioneer days were covered with hemp canvas. Indeed the very word "canvas" comes from the Arabic word for hemp. In those days hemp was an important crop in Kentucky and Missouri.... In 1942, patriotic farmers at the government's request planted 36,000 acres of seed hemp, an increase of several thousand percent. The goal for 1943 is 50,000 acres of seed hemp."

—Excerpt from the 1942 U. S. Department of Agriculture film *Hemp for Victory*

Just as alcohol has been alternately banned and then legalized again through the whims of government laws, so has hemp been legalized and later banned because of equally fickle government legislation that views hemp with suspicion due to its close relation to marijuana. Despite its current ban, hemp has actually played a major role in American history. Benjamin Franklin started one of America's first paper mills using cannabis hemp because he wanted to have a free colonial press without having to beg for paper or books from England.

Although Franklin had to resort to using hemp for producing paper, he could have saved himself the hassle of printing at all if he had just had a personal computer and a copy of Photoshop Elements instead. Rather than print anything out the old-fashioned way on paper, Franklin could have printed and distributed information electronically.

Distributing files electronically can vary—from sending pictures to friends as e-mail attachments, to posting pictures on web pages for anyone to see, to storing multiple pictures in a special slideshow file that people can view on wildly different computers. With so many ways to electronically distribute your pictures, you can find the way that you like best without having to waste paper or break the law using hemp to do it.

(In case you want to use hemp paper to print out your pictures from Photoshop Elements, you can buy laser and inkjet hemp paper from Rawganique at http://www .rawganique.com or Grass Roots Natural Goods at http://www.grassrootsnaturalgoods.com.)

How to E-mail a Picture

One of the most popular ways to share your pictures with others is through e-mail. Although you could open up your e-mail program and then attach a file containing your picture, Photoshop Elements offers another way to e-mail a picture from within Photoshop Elements itself. By sending a picture by e-mail through Photoshop Elements, you can first see the picture that you're sending without worrying about choosing the cryptic file name of your particular picture.

CAUTION *If you're using America Online, you won't be able to send e-mail directly from Photoshop Elements.*

To e-mail a picture, load the picture you want to send. Then click the File menu and click Attach to E-mail. If the picture you chose is not stored in the JPEG file format, a dialog box appears and asks if you want to convert the file to JPEG format first. Click Auto Convert if you want to convert the file to JPEG format or click Send As Is if you want to send the file without converting it.

REMEMBER *If you send a picture without converting it to JPEG format, the file size of that picture may be extremely large. If a picture is too large, you may have trouble sending it by e-mail.*

Your e-mail program displays a blank message window with your chosen picture already attached to your message, as shown in Figure 18.1. At this point, you can type an e-mail address, a brief description of your message in the Subject text box, and any message you want to send along with your picture. Then click Send.

Put Your Pictures on a Web Page

Sending pictures to others by e-mail can be fun, but if you want everyone to see your pictures, it's much easier to post them on a web page that the whole world can access whenever they want.

Photoshop Elements gives you two ways to post pictures on a web page. First, you can save a picture in the JPEG file format and then manually add that picture to a web page. Second, you can have Photoshop Elements create a web page for you automatically that displays every picture stored in a specific folder.

REMEMBER *When you're posting pictures on a web page, they must be stored in either the GIF or JPEG file format because these are the two universal graphic file formats that most computers and browsers can recognize and display. The GIF file format is most commonly used for simple graphics, such as logos and drawings. The JPEG format is most often used for photographs.*

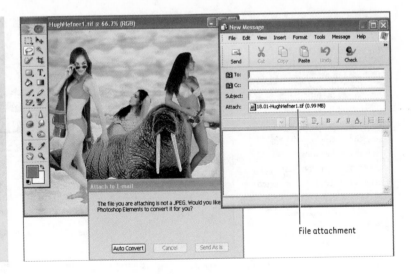

FIGURE 18.1

When you choose the Attach to E-mail command from the File menu, a Message window pops up that automatically attaches your chosen picture to a blank e-mail message. This picture shows the latest girlfriend of *Playboy* founder Hugh Hefner, standing in front of Hugh's wrinkled, gray, flabby skin that still manages to attract 20-year-old women by virtue of the size of his bank account. (Photo courtesy of the National Oceanic and Atmospheric Administration.)

File attachment

Save a Single Picture for a Web Page

If you have a single picture that you'd like to post on a web page, you must convert it to a JPEG file first. Photoshop Elements actually provides two ways to do this. One way involves clicking the File menu and then clicking Save As. When the Save As dialog box appears, click in the Format list box and click JPEG.

If you want, you can also type a new name for your picture to help you recognize the JPEG file format of a picture and the original. For example, your original picture might be called MyDog, whereas the JPEG version of that same picture might be called MyDog.JPG. When you're done typing a name and choosing the JPEG file format, click Save.

REMEMBER *When you save a picture in the JPEG file format, Photoshop Elements adds the .jpg file extension to the picture's name.*

For a second way to convert your pictures into the JPEG file format that gives you more options for determining the file size and quality of your images, click the File menu and then click Save for Web. A Save for Web dialog box appears, as shown in Figure 18.2.

Click in the compression quality list box and choose Maximum, High, Medium, or Low. When you choose a compression option, the Save for Web dialog box displays the estimated file size and download time for someone to view your file using a 28.8 Kbps

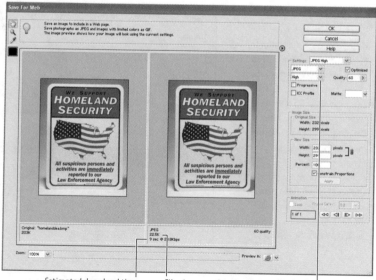

FIGURE 18.2

The Save for Web dialog box shows how different options can change the size of your file. Here we see the official U.S. Government Homeland Security sign, warning people that all suspicious activities will be reported to the local authorities, unless, of course, that suspicious activity happens to be conducted by the local authorities.

(Photo courtesy of the U.S. Drug Enforcement Agency.)

Estimated download time   File size   Compression quality list box (kilobytes per second) modem. You want your file sizes to be as small as possible without sacrificing image quality so people won't have to wait too long to view your pictures over the Internet.

If you want to change the size of your picture, click in the Width or Height text box and type a new value. When you're done, click OK. The Save Optimized As dialog box appears.

Type a name for your JPEG file in the File Name text box and click the folder where you want to store to the JPEG version of your picture. Click Save. Photoshop Elements saves your picture as a JPEG file in your chosen folder. Now you can add this picture to a web page and post it on the Internet for everyone to look at and admire.

Save Multiple Images on a Web Page

If you want to create a gallery of multiple images on a web page, you could save each picture individually as a JPEG file and then post it on a web page by hand. But for a faster alternative, Photoshop Elements can automatically yank out every picture stored in a folder, convert them to JPEG format, and display them on a web page at the blink of an eye—a handy feature known as a Web Photo Gallery.

To create a Web Photo Gallery, move all the pictures you want to put on a web page into a specific folder (and remember the name of that folder). Then switch to Photoshop Elements, click the File menu, and click Create Web Photo Gallery. The Web Photo Gallery dialog box appears, as shown in Figure 18.3.

FIGURE 18.3

The Web Photo Gallery dialog box lets you define the way you want your web pages and your images to appear, such as a simple layout, a pretentious theater-like layout, or a playful childhood layout with cartoon bears and balloons. Noticeably missing from the options is the ability to display your boss's face on a web page as the bull's-eye of a target.

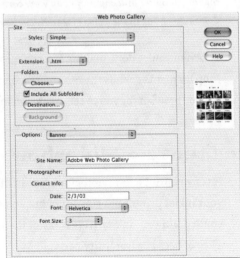

Click in the Styles list box and choose a style such as Museum or Theater. Click Browse (Windows) or Choose (Macintosh). A dialog box pops up for you to choose the folder that contains the images you want to put on your web page. Click a folder and then click OK (Windows) or Choose (Macintosh).

Click Destination. A dialog box pops up for you to choose the folder where you want Photoshop Elements to store your Web Photo Gallery. You can always create a new, empty folder if you click the Make New Folder (Windows) or New Folder (Macintosh) button. Click a folder and then click OK (Windows) or Choose (Macintosh).

If you want to include text on your web page, click in the Option list box and choose Banner. The bottom part of the Web Photo Gallery dialog box changes to allow you to type text and a date, along with choosing a font and a font size.

If you want to change the colors of your web page, click in the Option list box and choose Custom Colors. The bottom half of the Web Photo Gallery dialog box displays different colors for various parts of your web page, such as the background, link text, and ordinary text. When you click a color that appears next to a Web page item such as Active Link or Text, the Color Picker dialog box appears. From within the Color Picker dialog box, you can click the color you want to use for your chosen option.

REMEMBER *When choosing colors for your web page, it's a good idea to use web-safe colors that any browser and computer can view correctly. To view web-safe colors, click the Only Web Colors check box in the Color Picker dialog box.*

When you're done making any changes to define your web page, click OK. Photoshop Elements spends the next few seconds creating your web page and displaying it in your browser for you to see, as shown in Figure 18.4.

How to Create a Slideshow

After you print a few photographs on an inkjet printer, you may be shocked to find that your inkjet printer has run out of ink. In general when you print color photographs, you'll drain your ink cartridges faster than a member of the Kennedy family emptying a keg of beer at a fraternity party.

Examples of some of the different types of web pages the Web Photo Gallery dialog box can create. Because it's so easy to create web pages that display multiple images automatically, look for some of Photoshop Elements' web page designs to start popping up on pornographic web sites all over the Internet in the near future.

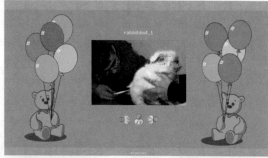

So as an alternative to sucking the ink out of your own inkjet printer by printing your photographs, you may want to print your pictures to an Adobe Acrobat PDF (Portable Document Format) file instead. When someone opens a PDF slideshow file, the file displays your pictures one at a time on the screen. Because every Windows, Macintosh, and Linux computer can view PDF files, you can share your pictures as a PDF file and let other people print them out as their leisure (and suck the ink out of their printers instead).

To create a PDF slideshow, click the File menu, click Automation Tools, and then click PDF Slideshow. The PDF Slideshow dialog box appears, as shown in Figure 18.5.

Click the Browse button. The Open dialog box appears. Click the files you want to include in your PDF slideshow file.

REMEMBER *To choose multiple files, hold down* CTRL *(Windows) or* CMD *(Macintosh) and click each file you want to use. To choose a group of files in sequence, click the first file you want to choose, hold down* SHIFT, *and then click the last file you want to choose. Photoshop Elements highlights the first and last files you clicked and every file in between.*

Click the Choose button. The Save dialog box appears. Type a name for your PDF slideshow file and click Save.

REMEMBER *If you click the Add Open Files check box, the PDF Slideshow dialog box automatically adds any pictures currently displayed within Photoshop Elements.*

To customize your slideshow, click the options under the Slide Show Options category. If you click the Advance Every check box, you can specify how many seconds your slideshow waits before displaying the next picture automatically.

If you click the Loop After Last Page check box, your PDF slideshow will keep displaying your images indefinitely. If you click in the Transition list box, you can define different transitions that define how the various pictures in your PDF slideshow file appear, such as Dissolve or Wipe Down.

CAUTION *If you're using Mac OS X, you may have to run Adobe Acrobat under "Classic Mode" so that any PDF slideshow transitions appear correctly.*

FIGURE 18.5

The PDF Slideshow dialog box lets you choose which pictures to include in a single PDF file. You can include pictures stored in different file formats if you want. For even more fun, include some dirty pictures so anyone looking at your PDF slideshow will stay alert so they don't miss seeing any other naughty images you may have stored in the PDF file.

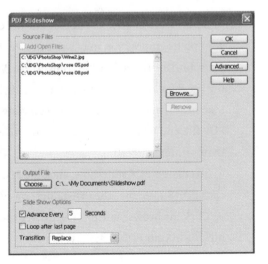

Click OK when you're done. Photoshop Elements creates your PDF slideshow file and displays a dialog box to let you know it's done. Click OK.

REMEMBER *Before anyone can view any pictures stored in a PDF slideshow file, they need a free copy of Adobe Acrobat Reader, which they can download from the Adobe Web site at http://www.adobe.com.*

How to Share Your Pictures with Other Programs

When you share your pictures with others, nobody cares what file format you use, just as long as they can see the picture clearly. Unfortunately, if you have a beautiful picture of a policeman beating the living daylights out of a minority, you won't be able to sell that picture to the news media unless you save that picture in a file format that other people's programs can recognize and open.

So to help you share your pictures with people who may be using different programs or even different computers, Photoshop Elements lets you convert files from one file format to another.

REMEMBER *Photoshop Elements can save files in over a dozen different file formats. For creating small files to transmit or post on the Internet, use the JPEG file format. For sharing files that others might want to edit later, save your files in the Photoshop PSD or TIFF file format. Most of the other file formats are designed to create files that older programs can recognize, such as the BMP and PCX file formats. For really obscure programs, Photoshop Elements can save files in strange file formats with names such as Pixar, Raw, Scitex, and Targa.*

Save Files Individually

If you only have one or two files that you need to convert, just open the picture you want to convert, click the File menu, and then click Save As. The Save As dialog box appears.

Click in the Filename text box and type a new name for your file if you want. Then click in the Format list box, choose a file format to use, such as TIFF, and click Save. Repeat this process for each picture you want to convert.

REMEMBER *To help you find files stored in different file formats easily, you may want to save your files in a separate folder (and give it a distinct name, such as PCX File Folder).*

Save Multiple Files Automatically

Saving files one at a time may be fine for a few files or for people suffering from obsessive compulsive behaviors who don't mind repeating the same tasks over and over again. But for the rest of us, Photoshop Elements offers a special batch conversion feature that can change dozens of files to a different file format with very little work or suffering on your part.

To convert multiple files automatically, first store all the pictures you want to convert in the same folder. Click the File menu and click Batch Conversion. The Batch dialog box appears, as shown in Figure 18.6.

Click the Source button. A dialog box pops up. Click the folder that contains the pictures you want to convert and click OK (Windows) or Choose (Macintosh).

Click the Convert File Type list box and choose the file type you want to convert all your files to, such as JPEG High Quality or TIFF.

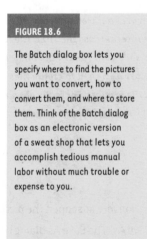

FIGURE 18.6

The Batch dialog box lets you specify where to find the pictures you want to convert, how to convert them, and where to store them. Think of the Batch dialog box as an electronic version of a sweat shop that lets you accomplish tedious manual labor without much trouble or expense to you.

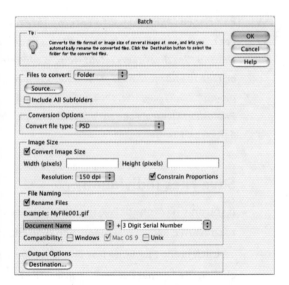

CAUTION *Photoshop Elements can only convert a batch of files to a single file type; for example, you can't tell Photoshop Elements to save some files as TIFF files and some as JPEG files.*

Click the Convert Image Size check box if you want to convert the size of your pictures. If you choose to change the image size, you must type a size (measured in pixels) in the Width and Height text boxes.

Click the Rename Files check box if you want Photoshop Elements to rename all your files automatically. If you choose to rename your files, you must type in the two list boxes in the File Naming category to specify how Photoshop Elements will give each file a unique name, such as adding a three-digit number to each file name.

Click the Destination button. A dialog box pops up so you can click the folder where you want to store your converted files. (You can always click the Make New Folder button to create a new folder at this time.) When you're done choosing a folder to store your converted files, click OK (Windows) or Choose (Macintosh).

When you're done defining how you want to convert your batch of files, click OK. Photoshop Elements converts your files and stores them in the format and folder you specified.

Where to Go from Here

By sharing your Photoshop Elements pictures as computer files, you can make multiple copies much faster than you could with even the fastest color printer in the world. Best of all, by not printing out your pictures, you save a tree (or a hemp plant) and save yourself from getting overcharged by printer manufacturers selling overpriced ink cartridges that cost nearly as much as the entire printer.

Whether you want to share your pictures by e-mail, through web pages, or via the old-fashioned way of copying files onto a storage device such as a CD, you can make sure that copies of your pictures will live virtually forever, much like the naked photographs of radio talk show host, Dr. Laura Schlessinger. Her naked photographs, taken when she was a much younger woman, will forever be circulating the Internet archives long after her name has been forgotten and turned into one of the harder answers to a trivia question on a game show such as *Jeopardy* for future generations to ponder over.

LESSON 19

What You'll Learn in This Lesson

- Getting used to layers

- Using grids and rulers

- Creating shadows

Tips and Tricks for Dealing with Photoshop Elements

(or How to Tolerate the Quirks and Annoyances of Photoshop Elements)

ONE POPULAR SCIENCE FICTION THEME INVOLVES the idea of multiple parallel universes that coexist simultaneously, where everything is identical except for one tiny change. In parallel-universe stories, characters often slip in and out of a different parallel universe and struggle to find their way back to their own plane of existence, usually with tragic (or sometimes comical) results.

Often less comical (and more tragic) results occur when ordinary people try to tackle the parallel universe of the computer industry, where instructions appear to be written in plain English but somehow never seem to make any sense. Computers can often make even the most battle-scarred computer veteran feel lost in a parallel universe, where everything appears logical except for the computer, the manual, and any messages that the program may desperately display on the screen.

So to help you survive the confusing computer manuals and equally obscure online help files that often substitute for an intuitive program that the manufacturer should have written in the first place, this lesson offers a quick refresher and overview of the different features of Photoshop Elements.

Despite any claims to the contrary by publishers, the best way to learn any program isn't from a book. The best way to learn a program is to dive right in, make plenty of mistakes, learn from your errors, and keep goofing around with the program every day until its more common commands become second nature and its more obscure commands become understandable if and when you may actually need them.

Of course, the best way to learn any program such as Photoshop Elements is to watch someone actually use it and ask that person plenty of questions. But until publishers can clone computer experts and put them in every home, most people will just have to settle with flipping through the pages of a book like this one when they need help in a hurry.

Get Used to Layers

Layers can isolate parts of a picture so you have the freedom to manipulate and alter different images without affecting the entire image. Unfortunately, layers often confuse beginners because they give the illusion that everything you see on your computer screen can be edited at any time. In reality what appears to be a single image may actually consist of separate layers, and it's this illusion (that everything consists of a single image) versus the reality (that a picture may actually consist of a handful of separate images) that can cause problems when trying to edit and modify a picture in Photoshop Elements.

Once you understand how layers work, you can take advantage of them to make editing your pictures faster or easier than before. Through creative use of layers, you can also create unique visual effects that would be impossible to do if you never used layers at all.

Select Images on Different Layers

Although selecting part of an image might seem straightforward, you might select part of an image and try to cut or copy it, only to run into a strange error message that appears in a dialog box that claims "no pixels are selected," as shown in Figure 19.1.

When you see this "no pixels are selected" error message, the first thing you want to do is smack your computer for being stupid—if you can see that you selected part of an image, why can't the computer see that, too?

The problem occurs because what you tried to select actually appears on a separate layer. So when you see this annoying "no pixels are selected" message, it means you didn't select anything that appears on the currently active layer.

To fix this problem, click the Window menu and click Layers to display the Layers palette, which highlights the currently active layer. Click the layer that contains the image you want to select and then choose the Cut or Copy command to finally select what Photoshop Elements should have selected in the first place.

Lock a Layer

Layers offer the convenience of storing images in separate locations so you can edit one image without the risk of messing up any other part of your picture. To further protect any images stored on separate layers, Photoshop Elements lets you lock a layer.

Locking a layer prevents anyone (including you) from modifying the images stored on that particular layer. If you want to modify an image on a locked layer, you can just unlock it and then modify it. Locking simply protects layers from accidental modifications.

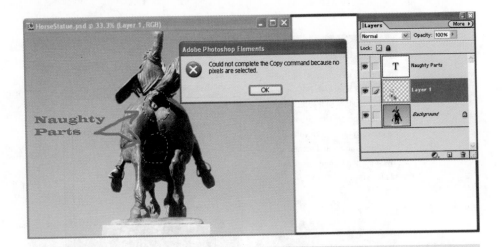

FIGURE 19.1

The "no pixels are selected" error message means you tried to select an image stored on another layer that isn't currently active. This picture shows that a sculptor took great care to make the statue of a horse anatomically correct from every possible viewing angle.

To lock a layer, click the Window menu and click Layers to display the Layers palette. Click the layer that you want to lock and click the Lock All icon on the Layers palette, as shown in Figure 19.2.

Photoshop Elements displays a padlock icon on the selected layer. To unlock a layer, just click that layer in the Layers palette and click the Lock All icon again.

Layer Images over One Another

Sometimes when you paste an image over another picture, the pasted image covers up part of the original picture, making the entire picture look unnatural and phony. To solve this problem, you need to go through four separate steps:

1. Paste the image over another picture. Note where the pasted image covers up part of the original picture.

2. Click the Window menu and click Layers to display the Layers palette. Clear the Layer Visibility check box of the layer that contains the pasted image. Photoshop Elements makes the pasted image temporarily invisible so you can see the part of the original picture that the pasted image covered up.

FIGURE 19.2

A padlock icon appears on every layer that is locked. This picture shows two locked layers of a bad B-movie poster that promotes a movie in which carnivorous squirrels run around attacking humans and turning them into Cajun stew.

Lock All icon

Locked layers

3. Use one of the selection tools, such as the Lasso tool, to select the part of the original picture that the pasted image covered up. Press CTRL-C (Windows) or CMD-C (Macintosh) to copy your selection and then press CTRL-V (Windows) or CMD-V (Macintosh) to paste your selection on a separate layer. At this point, you won't notice any difference in your picture.

4. Click the Window menu and click Layers to display the Layers palette. Click the Layer Visibility check box of the layer that contains the pasted image. Photoshop Elements now displays the pasted image, but without the pasted image covering up any part of the original picture, as shown in Figure 19.3.

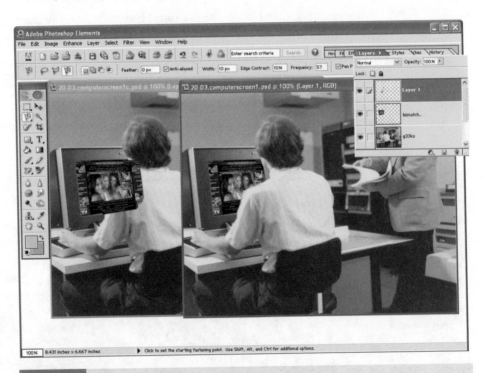

FIGURE 19.3

The picture on the left shows the bottom-right corner of the pornographic image covering up the programmer's left shoulder and cheek. In the picture on the right, part of the programmer's left shoulder and cheek have been copied and pasted directly over the pornographic image layer. Now the entire image looks natural among the two computer programmers fantasizing about a parallel universe where half-naked, sweaty centerfolds lust after computer programmers with bad posture, poor hygiene, and outdated dressing habits. (Photo courtesy of the U.S. Army)

Link Layers

Although layers can separate images from one another, you may find that two or more images should always appear in the same positions relative to one another. So to keep images together, Photoshop Elements lets you link multiple layers together. When you link layers, moving or altering the size or orientation of one image automatically changes any other linked images.

To link layers, click the Window menu and click Layers to display the Layers palette. Click a layer that contains an image that you want to link to other images. To link other layers to the currently active layer, click the Link check box, as shown in Figure 19.4.

Once you have linked images on separate layers together, you can click any layer that contains a linked image. With at least one of the linked layers highlighted, you can use the Move tool to move or rotate both images. If you click the Image menu, click Transform, and use any of the Transform commands, such as Perspective or Skew, Photoshop Elements alters all your linked images at the same time.

To unlink a layer, just click the Link check box again to clear the link icon.

Link check box

FIGURE 19.4

When a link icon appears in the Link check box, Photoshop Elements has linked the image on that particular layer to the currently active (highlighted) layer. In this picture, the two layers named President and Mars Face are linked together in an image that shows a NASA space probe searching for signs of intelligent life on Mars, because scientists have long since given up finding any signs of intelligent life in the White House.

(Photos courtesy of the Jet Propulsion Laboratory, National Aeronautics and Space Administration, and the White House.)

Group Layers

One way to create unique visual effects is to use grouped layers. When you group layers, the image on the bottom layer defines what parts of the images you can see in the other grouped layers. So if you group a layer containing an American flag on top of another layer containing an odd-shaped bottle, the odd-shaped bottle image defines what part of the American flag you can see, as shown in Figure 19.5.

To group layers, click the Window menu and click Layers to display the Layers palette. Click the layer directly above the layer that contains the image to define the boundaries of your other images.

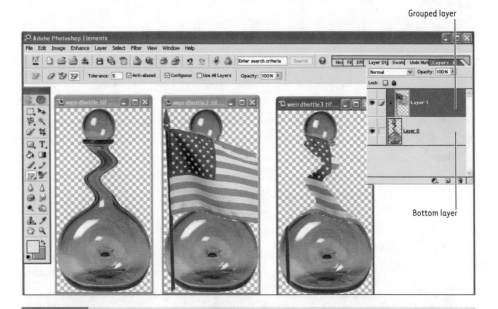

Grouped layer

Bottom layer

FIGURE 19.5

If the bottom layer of your group consists of an unusual shape, you'll only see the rest of your grouped images through the boundaries of that same unusual shape. The picture on the left shows the unusual shape of a bottle, the picture in the middle shows an American flag pasted over the bottle layer, and the picture on the right shows what happens when you group the American flag layer with the bottle layer, which creates a unique visual effect of a bottle with a patriotic neck, perfect for holding alcohol so people can get drunk on the Fourth of July, which is something that the Founding Fathers would surely approve of as an appropriate way to celebrate freedom.

REMEMBER *Without a transparent background, the image on the bottom layer of your group will simply define a rectangle for the other images in your group to appear within.*

Click the Layer menu and then click Group with Previous. Photoshop Elements underlines the bottom layer of your group and indents the name of the other layers of your group. If you want to group more layers, keep clicking each layer on top of any layers with an indented name.

REMEMBER *You can also link layers in a group to keep the images on the different layers perfectly aligned with one another.*

To remove a layer from a group, click the Window menu and click Layers to display the Layers palette. Then click the indented name of the layer you want to remove from the group, click the Layer menu, and then click Ungroup.

CAUTION *If you want to remove a layer from a group, move that group to the top of the Layers palette first before you choose the Ungroup command under the Layer menu. When you choose the Ungroup command, Photoshop Elements ungroups every layer from the top of the Layers palette down to the layer you want to ungroup, which could accidentally ungroup layers that you really want to keep grouped together.*

Merge Layers

When you're finally done aligning images on separate layers, you may want to merge them into a single layer to reduce the size of your file while also preventing you from accidentally moving the images and wrecking their perfect alignment with one another. To merge multiple layers, Photoshop Elements offers two commands: Merge Down and Merge Visible.

The Merge Down command simply merges the currently active layer with the layer directly below it. The Merge Visible command merges every visible layer (the layers with the eye icon displayed) into a single layer. So unlike the Merge Down command, which can only merge two layers, the Merge Visible command can merge two or more layers together.

To use the Merge Down command, click the Window menu and click Layers to display the Layers palette. Click the layer directly above the layer you want to merge with. Click the Layer menu and click Merge Down. Photoshop Elements magically smashes the two layers into a single layer.

To use the Merge Visible command, click the Window menu and click Layers to display the Layers palette. Clear the Layer Visibility check boxes (the ones that display the omnipotent eye icon) from every layer you do not want to merge. Then click the Layer menu and click Merge Visible. Photoshop Elements smashes all your visible layers into a single layer.

Use Grids and Rulers

When you're working with multiple images, you may find that aligning these images can be frustrating. So to help you align images right the first time, Photoshop Elements offers grids and rulers.

Grids display vertical and horizontal lines that crisscross an image. You can align your images up with these grid lines. Rulers appear on the top and left side of your picture so you can accurately measure exactly where to position an image, as shown in Figure 19.6.

FIGURE 19.6

Rulers and grids can help you align images to specific measurements. This picture shows a parallel universe where Earth has turned into a hellish inferno due to the carelessness and negligence of the human race. Despite having an infinite number of parallel universes to choose from, in none of them can you ever find an Earth cared for by intelligent human beings. (Photos courtesy of the National Aeronautics and Space Administration.)

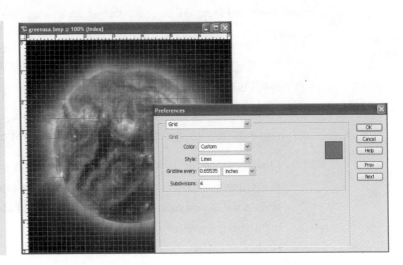

To turn on grids, click the View menu and then click Grid. Photoshop Elements displays grid lines across your picture. If you click the Edit menu, click Preferences, and then click Grid, a Preferences dialog box appears that lets you customize the color, spacing, and line appearance of your grid.

To display rulers, click the View menu and click Rulers. Photoshop Elements displays horizontal and vertical rulers. If you click the Edit menu, click Preferences, and then click Units & Rulers, a Preferences dialog box appears that lets you customize the measurement units of your rulers.

To turn off rulers or grids, click the View menu and click Grid or Rulers to remove the check mark from the View menu. Photoshop Elements removes the grid or ruler.

Make Shadows

One way that photography analysts spot fake or doctored photographs is to look at the shadows. If the shadow of a man falls to the right but another shadow of a nearby aircraft falls to the left, analysts can safely say that the photograph has been faked.

Because shadows can make your pictures look more realistic, you need to know how to add them to any image. In simple terms, creating a shadow involves copying an image, turning it black, positioning it on your picture, blurring it, and changing its opacity so it looks natural. Once you know the steps to creating a shadow, you need to learn how to do those same steps in Photoshop Elements:

1. Select the image you want to create a shadow for, using a selection tool such as the Magnetic Lasso tool or the Magic Wand.

2. Press CTRL-C (Windows) or CMD-C (Macintosh) and then press CTRL-V (Windows) or CMD-V (Macintosh) to copy and paste the selection of your image on a new layer.

3. Click the Window menu and click Layers to display the Layers palette. (For convenience, you may want to drag the Layers palette tab out of the Palette Well so the Layers palette appears in a separate window.) Photoshop Elements highlights the copy of your image (with its generic name, such as Layer 1) in the Layers palette.

4. Click the Layer menu and click Duplicate Layer. The Duplicate Layer dialog box appears. Click OK. Photoshop Elements displays three copies of your image in the Layers palette.

5. Click the top layer of your image in the Layers palette and click in the Layer Visibility check box to make this layer temporarily invisible.

6. Click the layer directly beneath this invisible layer in the Layers palette and select your image again with a selection tool such as the Magic Wand or the Magnetic Lasso tool.

7. Press D to turn the foreground color box to black and press ALT-BACKSPACE (Windows) or OPTION-BACKSPACE (Macintosh) to fill your selection with the foreground color of black.

8. Click the Move tool and drag the darkened image so that it appears to one side of your original image.

9. Click the Filter menu, click Blur, and click Gaussian Blur. The Gaussian Blur dialog box appears. Drag the Radius slider to soften the shadow image and click OK when you're done.

10. Click the Window menu and click Layers to display the Layers palette. Click the Opacity list box and drag the opacity level to a lower level, such as 55%. Photoshop Elements softens your shadow image some more.

11. In the Layers palette, click in the Layer Visibility check box of the layer you made temporarily invisible in step 5.

If everything worked out okay, you should see the shadow appearing underneath your original image. Your entire picture now consists of three separate layers, as shown in Figure 19.7:

- The original image
- The shadow of the image
- A copy of the original image that covers up most of the shadow image

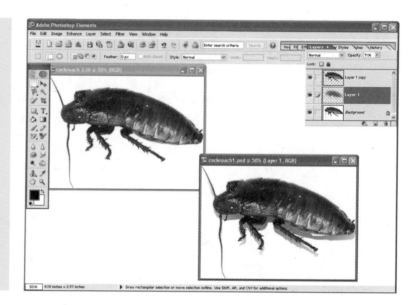

FIGURE 19.7

The picture on the left shows the original image. The picture on the right shows the final image with a shadow, which consists of three layers: the original image, the shadow, and part of the original image that the shadow covered up. In this case, you can see a cockroach without its shadow and then a cockroach with its shadow, which many people believe forecasts another six weeks of insect parts and droppings in the nation's hot dog supply.

Where to Go from Here

Learning any new skill, such as editing digital photographs with Photoshop Elements, requires nothing more than plenty of practice. The more you experiment with Photoshop Elements, the more you'll learn what works and what doesn't work.

Strictly speaking, there is no such thing as a mistake. Sometimes you may do something that creates a different result than you intended, but if you remember what you did wrong, you may be able to use those same steps to create the exact same results on a different picture, which may create a result that you want after all.

Although Photoshop Elements may appear to overwhelm you with so many different ways to manipulate an image, most Photoshop Elements commands give you four ways to change your pictures:

- Alter the physical shape or orientation
- Change colors, contrast, brightness, and so on
- Add, move, resize, or delete images
- Alter overall visual appearance

So the next time you come across an unfamiliar command, you can lump it into one of these four categories to help you remember what all the different Photoshop Elements commands do.

At this point, you can keep buying additional reference books to help you learn more about Photoshop Elements, but ultimately it's up to you to learn the program on your own. Good luck, have fun, and remember that the next time you're bored at work, you can load up Photoshop Elements and see how many different ways you can digitally modify the way your boss's face might look in a parallel universe. That should keep you amused for a while and also teach you more about Photoshop Elements at the same time.

Index